# *Financial Accounting*

## DeMYSTiFieD®

# DeMYSTiFieD® Series

Accounting Demystified
Advanced Statistics Demystified
Algebra Demystified
Alternative Energy Demystified
ASP.NET 2.0 Demystified
Biology Demystified
Biotechnology Demystified
Business Calculus Demystified
Business Math Demystified
Business Statistics Demystified
C++ Demystified
Calculus Demystified
Chemistry Demystified
Commodities Demystified
Corporate Finance Demystified, 2e
Data Structures Demystified
Databases Demystified, 2e
Differential Equations Demystified
Digital Electronics Demystified
Electricity Demystified
Electronics Demystified
Environmental Science Demystified
Everyday Math Demystified
Financial Accounting Demystified
Financial Planning Demystified
Financial Statements Demystified
Forensics Demystified
Genetics Demystified
Grant Writing Demystified
Hedge Funds Demystified
Human Resource Management Demystified
Intermediate Accounting Demystified
Investing Demystified, 2e
Java Demystified
JavaScript Demystified
Lean Six Sigma Demystified
Linear Algebra Demystified

Macroeconomics Demystified
Management Accounting Demystified
Marketing Demystified
Math Proofs Demystified
Math Word Problems Demystified
Mathematica Demystified
Matlab Demystified
Microbiology Demystified
Microeconomics Demystified
Nanotechnology Demystified
OOP Demystified
Operating Systems Demystified
Options Demystified
Organic Chemistry Demystified
Pharmacology Demystified
Physics Demystified
Physiology Demystified
Pre-Algebra Demystified
Precalculus Demystified
Probability Demystified
Project Management Demystified
Public Speaking and Presentations Demystified
Quality Management Demystified
Real Estate Math Demystified
Robotics Demystified
Sales Management Demystified
Six Sigma Demystified, 2e
SQL Demystified
Statistical Process Control Demystified
Statistics Demystified
Technical Analysis Demystified
Technical Math Demystified
Trigonometry Demystified
UML Demystified
Visual Basic 2005 Demystified
Visual C# 2005 Demystified
XML Demystified

The Demystified Series publishes over 125 titles in all areas of academic study. For a complete list of titles, please visit www.mhprofessional.com.

# Financial Accounting
## DeMYSTiFieD®

**Leonard Eugene Berry**

New York   Chicago   San Francisco   Lisbon   London   Madrid   Mexico City   Milan
New Delhi   San Juan   Seoul   Singapore   Sydney   Toronto

**The McGraw·Hill Companies**

1 2 3 4 5 6 7 8 9 10 DOC/DOC 1 9 8 7 6 5 4 3 2 1 0

ISBN 978-0-07-174102-6
MHID 0-07-174102-X

This publication is designed to provide accurate and authoritative information in regard to the subject matter covered. It is sold with the understanding that neither the author nor the publisher is engaged in rendering legal, accounting, securities trading, or other professional services. If legal advice or other expert assistance is required, the services of a competent professional person should be sought.

> —*From a Declaration of Principles Jointly Adopted by a Committee of the American Bar Association and a Committee of Publishers and Associations*

**Library of Congress Cataloging-in-Publication Data**

Berry, Leonard Eugene.
   Financial accounting demystified / by Leonard Eugene Berry.
     p. cm.
   Includes index.
   ISBN 978-0-07-174102-6 (alk. paper)
   1. Accounting. I. Title.
   HF5636.B47 2011
   657--dc22
                     2010029963

McGraw-Hill books are available at special quantity discounts to use as premiums and sales promotions or for use in corporate training programs. To contact a representative, please e-mail us at bulksales@mcgraw-hill.com.

This book is printed on acid-free paper.

*Dedicated to my wife Rebecca for her encouragement throughout the writing of this book and for her many suggestions while reviewing the manuscript.*

# About the Author

**Leonard Eugene Berry, Ph.D., CIA,** is Professor Emeritus and Director Emeritus in the School of Accountancy, Georgia State University in Atlanta. He is a retired CPA in the State of Georgia.

# Contents

# Acknowledgments

Many thanks to Professor Bert Richards, School of Accountancy, Georgia State University, for his significant effort in reviewing the manuscript and for checking all of the problems and solutions in this book. However, any errors that remain are my own.

Also, many thanks to Brian Foster, my editor at McGraw-Hill, for his timely support on this project.

# Introduction

*Financial Accounting DeMystified* is designed to be an important introductory source on the broad field of financial accounting, a field that provides the systems and procedures that produce the financial statements of a business. As such, this book should be useful for the following people:

- Students (undergraduate and MBA), as an excellent supplement to their text in a college course or as a review of the basics for those who have already completed a similar course. It would be particularly useful in an MBA course that uses the case study approach.

- Students (undergraduate and MBA), as a source of additional practice problems in preparing for a test. Also, individuals who are studying for a professional exam (such as the Certified Public Accountant (CPA) exam) may find the book useful as a source of additional practice problems.

- Investors, stockholders, and other decision makers who want to know the basics of financial accounting in order to better interpret financial statements and reports.

- Accountants who need a review of the fundamental concepts and procedures of financial accounting for an entry-level accounting position in business or a nonprofit organization.

- Individuals who are seeking college credit for financial accounting by examination.

Introductory Financial Accounting is normally covered in the sophomore year of a four-year college business program or in the second year of a two-year college program. The curriculum map which appears on the inside back cover shows how this introductory financial accounting book would fit into an undergraduate accounting curriculum.

In an MBA program, financial accounting is normally covered as a stand-alone course along with another stand-alone course in managerial accounting. In some programs these two courses may be combined. Many MBA programs use the case study approach in studying this subject. This book will be very useful as a supplement to case study textbooks on financial accounting.

Every attempt has been made to edit and check each problem and solution for correctness. However, with thousands of calculations, there could be a few errors. The author would appreciate an e-mail from anyone that identifies any such errors. Also, any suggestions for improvement of the textual material would be appreciated. Please send any errors or suggestions to accleb@yahoo.com. Please identify the page, line number(s), or the problem number involved.

## How to Use This Book

This book assumes that you have taken some business courses or have experience in business, but it does not require a background in accounting, although it would be helpful. It assumes that you have mathematical skill at the high school or higher level. Business mathematics and algebra would be most useful.

The format of this book is designed primarily for self-study and provides the major financial accounting concepts and procedures in a concise form. It contains an abundance of definitions, illustrations, quizzes, and a final exam. Each concept, term, or procedure is defined when it is first encountered. All terms in bold type are defined in the glossary at the end of the book. Each concept or procedure is then followed by examples, and each procedure is followed by a problem illustration with solutions, where applicable. Each chapter ends with a quiz, and the answers can be found at the back of the book. At the end of the book there is a comprehensive final examination, which covers the major concepts and procedures in the book.

If you have taken a course in financial accounting before and think you know the material in any specific chapter, answer all of the problems at the end of that chapter as a pretest. If you answer all questions—or most of them— correctly, then you could probably skip that chapter. However, a review would not hurt.

When studying a specific subject, you should spend as much time on a topic as is necessary to master it. Always answer the questions and problems after each chapter. The quizzes and exam can be taken and answered using the "open book" approach, but I suggest that you attempt to answer them *before* you look at the answers. If you get 80 to 90 percent correct, you can assume that you have successfully learned the material in that chapter. Of course, always spend more time reviewing the chapter material pertaining to the questions and problems that you missed. For the final exam, your goal should be to correctly answer at least 75 percent of the questions and problems.

Accounting is a subject that has a lot of procedures and details. It is best learned by repetitive practice. Working a lot of problems is essential. Go slowly. Completing a chapter per week would be a reasonable goal. Work all the illustrations in the text, making sure that you completely understand them. Then work the quizzes at the end of the chapter. You may want to search for additional financial accounting problems on the Internet and work them. There are plenty out there. Just type "financial accounting problems" in any search engine and see what you find.

Best wishes for a successful learning journey!

# Financial Accounting

## DeMYSTiFieD®

## chapter 1

# Financial Accounting: The Language of Business

## CHAPTER OBJECTIVES

*The purposes of this chapter are to*

- Define the *types* of businesses and discuss the importance of financial accounting information to these business enterprises and their external users

- Discuss the *form* of financial information provided to interested parties outside of the business

- Discuss the *underlying concepts* for preparing financial accounting and who determines these concepts

- Introduce the field of financial accounting

- Discuss the certification programs in the field of accounting

It has been said that accounting is the language of business. More specifically, financial accounting is the language used to communicate financial information about the performance and status of the business enterprise to parties outside the business. The major source of this information is from the financial accounting system, which produces the financial statements. These statements are critical pieces of information needed by interested parties to make decisions concerning that business. For example, banks need the statements to assess the business's ability to repay a loan. Investors need them to judge whether the business is a good investment opportunity. Current stockholders need them to evaluate how well the business is performing. Regulators need them to perform their legal responsibilities to society. And the list goes on.

But first, to understand financial accounting and how it performs its role in preparing the business's financial statements, an understanding of the types of businesses that create financial accounting information is needed.

# Types of Business Enterprises

A business enterprise exists to provide goods or service to consumers, incurs expenses, and accepts the risk for doing so. In return, the consumer usually provides a financial payment in the form of cash or a promise to pay cash. The resulting exchanges are called *financial transactions*. The financial accountant is responsible for processing these transactions. The following are the types of businesses enterprises:

- A **sole proprietorship** is a business owned by one person. It acquires assets and services, adds value and converts these assets into products or services, and sells the output to consumers. The sole proprietorship is not separate from its owner in terms of financial responsibility and liability. Thus, the owner is personally responsible for the business's debts and liabilities.

- A **partnership** is a business owned by two or more persons. Like the sole proprietorship, it acquires assets and services, adds value and converts these assets into products or services, and sells the output to consumers. As with the sole proprietorship, partners are personally responsible for the business's debts and liabilities. Partners normally draw up a legal document called a *partnership agreement* that specifies the partnership relationships, that is, how the profits will be divided, division of work, and other responsibilities.

- A **corporation** is a business entity that is financially and legally separated from its owners and is chartered by an individual state. Thus, its owners are not legally liable for the corporation's debts and liabilities. A corporation can be a profit or nonprofit enterprise. Ownership in a profit enterprise is divided into units called *common stock*.

Another way of classifying businesses is shown in Exhibit 1.1.

**EXHIBIT 1.1** Types of Business Operations

Business enterprises can also be classified as service, merchandising, and manufacturing organizations. As you will see later, the type of business enterprise will affect the content of and preparation of the financial statements. What follows is a basic summary of these three types of organizations.

*Service organizations* provide a service to the customer for a price or a fee. The most common types are law firms, consulting firms, accounting firms, engineering firms, and similar businesses. The major distinguishing feature of these organizations is that they do not have inventories for resale; however, they usually will have supplies of inventories for internal use. Their major assets are their human resources who provide the service to their clients.

*Merchandising organizations* purchase finished products or merchandise and resell them to customers. The most common types are retail companies and wholesalers. These companies do have inventories, which will require the accounting for these inventories on the balance sheet and computing Cost of Goods Sold on the income statement.

*Manufacturing organizations* purchase raw materials, labor, and overhead and convert them to a final product for resale. These organizations have the most complex accounting systems in that they have to account for several types of inventories: raw material, work in process, and finished goods. Accounting for manufacturing companies is not directly covered in this book, although most of the accounting concepts and principles covered in these pages do apply. You are advised to consult a book on cost accounting or managerial accounting for detailed accounting procedures.

*Financial organizations* are really service companies, but they are unique in that they deal primarily in services or intangible products related to money. The most common types of financial organizations are banks, savings and loans, and insurance companies.

## The Profession of Accounting in the United States

A basic familiarity with the professional people who are responsible for processing, reporting, and auditing financial information—the accountants—is now in order.

The profession of accounting is a broad field that encompasses several types of accountants. In the paragraphs that follow, several subspecialties of accountants are summarized. These are presented in terms of certification programs, but many accountants perform effectively without being certified. Accountants can be classified in different ways, but the following classifications are the most common ones.

- **Certified Public Accountant** (CPA). The CPA is a designation given to accountants who meet certain educational requirements, pass a rigorous qualifying examination, and possess qualifying public accounting experience requirements established by a state licensing authority (normally called a *State Board of Accountancy*). They are then licensed by this state authority to attest to the accuracy of organizational financial statements issued to external parties by a business or nonprofit entity. CPAs can be employed by a public accounting firm (which is the most common situation), operate their own practice, or work for a corporation or nonprofit or governmental organization. Also, many academic accountants are CPAs. CPAs may be proficient in state and federal tax accounting and provide tax services to their clients. Keep in mind that being a CPA is not required for every accounting function—only for those who attest to financial statements and are normally in public practice. Nevertheless, many accountants in all fields of accounting strive to be a CPA because of the qualifications, experience, and prestige that the designation carries.

- **Certified Management Accountant** (CMA). The CMA designation is awarded to accountants who have fulfilled the educational requirements, passed a rigorous exam, and met other requirements in management accounting established by the Institute of Management Accountants (IMA). The IMA issues a CMA certificate to those who qualify. Unlike the CPA, a state authority does not certify the CMA. CMAs are normally employed by a business to provide relevant and useful accounting information for internal managers.

- **Certified Internal Auditor** (CIA). The CIA designation is awarded to internal auditors who have met the educational requirements and passed a rigorous exam established by the Institute of Internal Auditors (IIA). CIAs are employed by businesses or governmental organizations; they are responsible for assuring the integrity of the accounting system, reviewing management and financial practices, and making recommendations for improvements.

- **Certified Fraud Examiner** (CFE). The CFE is a designation awarded by the Association of Certified Fraud Examiners (ACFE). This specialty in accounting is concerned with the detection, investigation, and prevention of fraud. The individuals practicing in this field are identified as forensic accountants or fraud auditors. Many of these accountants are employed by federal agencies, such as the Central Intelligence Agency, the Federal Bureau of Investigation, and the Drug Enforcement Agency.

- *Other Certification Programs.* The *Certified Government Auditing Professional (CGAP)* is a specialty designated for public sector internal auditing practitioners. The Institute of Internal Auditors administers this program. *The Certified Government Financial Manager (CGFM)* is a program for accountants and financial managers employed at the federal, state, and local government levels. The Association of Government Accountants (AGA) administers this program.

- *Noncertified Accountants.* There are many accountants who are employed by various organizations and are not certified by any of the certification programs mentioned previously. Most of these accountants aspire to be certified and undertake the preparatory education and work experience to complete a certification program. During their apprenticeship these individuals perform effectively and make an important contribution to the organization in which they are employed.

## Need for Financial Information by Businesses

The owners, managers, and external stakeholders of the business enterprises defined previously have a critical need for financial information—both managerial and financial.

*Owners and internal managers* need financial information to make decisions about the efficient allocation of resources (i.e., investment decisions), the planning of operations, the evaluation of operational performance, and a host of other decisions. The preparation of internal accounting information is performed by the *management accounting* function of the enterprise. Management accounting is not directly covered in this book. For further information, you can refer to a companion volume, *Management Accounting Demystified* by the author, which is also published by McGraw-Hill.

*External stakeholders* need financial information to assess the business for many different purposes. Discussed in the following paragraphs are the various external stakeholders and types of financial information needed.

These are the principal external stakeholders of the business enterprise:

- Shareholders and prospective investors
- Lenders
- Suppliers
- Customers
- Governmental and regulatory agencies

*Shareholders and prospective investors* need financial information to evaluate past performance of the business and to predict its future performance in order to decide whether to invest or continue investing in the business. They also need this information to evaluate the business's executives to determine whether they are effectively performing their role of adding value to the company.

*Lenders*, such as commercial banks, finance companies, pension funds, and insurance companies, need financial information from a business to assess the risk of making a loan to that business. The extent of risk and the financial well being of the business help the lender to determine the amount of a loan, the interest rate, security that is needed, and the terms of repayment. The business's financial statements are critical to the lender in making these decisions.

*Suppliers* usually sell to a business on credit. Depending on the type of business involved, the goods and services sold can range from expensive raw materials to consulting services that could result in substantial sums of accounts or notes receivable being incurred by the supplier. Like a bank or finance company, suppliers need financial statements to assess the business's ability to pay the amount of debt owed.

*Government and regulatory agencies* need financial statements for the purpose of performing the individual agency's oversight role established by law. For example, the Securities and Exchange Commission (SEC) is responsible for enforcing federal securities laws, truthfulness in corporate accounting and financial reporting, insider trading regulations, and a host of other oversight responsibilities. Obviously, accurate and timely financial information from the corporation is vital for the SEC to perform its job.

Several government agencies have responsibilities to regulate certain industries that enjoy a monopoly status. The most common example is the public utility company. Most states regulate the rates charged by these companies, and the relevant agencies require detailed financial information on revenues, expenses, and asset values in order to establish a reasonable rate of return on the assets owned by that business. This rate of return is then used to help establish the rate that the regulated company can charge its customers.

Although accounting principles and procedures for taxing authorities, such as the Internal Revenue Service (IRS), may significantly differ from those used by businesses to prepare financial statements, these taxing authorities still need financial statements from the corporation. Such information is useful for establishing tax policies and procedures for fair and equitable taxation of businesses.

# Form of Financial Information Provided to Outsiders

Financial accounting information prepared for external users is published in the form of financial statements, which are described in detail in Chapter 3 of this book. In brief, these statements are as follows:

- The **balance sheet,** or statement of financial position, is a statement that describes the financial situation of a business enterprise at a specific point in time, such as at the end of the month or year. It is stated in terms of assets, liabilities, and stockholders' equity.

- The **income statement,** or profit and loss statement, summarizes all of the revenues (sales) that a business has earned during a specific period of time (usually one year) less all of the expenses (resources) consumed in generating that revenue. The resulting figure is called *net income* and is an indication of the performance of the enterprise during the specified period of time (usually the fiscal year).

- The **statement of changes in stockholders' equity** shows the changes in stockholders' equity of the business entity during the same period of time as the income statement. Stockholders' equity is broadly comprised of contributed capital and retained earnings. Basically, the statement of changes in stockholders' equity is used to bridge the gap between the amount of stockholders' equity of a business at the beginning of the accounting period and the amount of equity at the end of the period. This statement takes into consideration such things as the increase in equity from issuance of stock and net income, and decreases in equity from dividends and a net loss.

- The **statement of cash flows** shows the amount of all cash flows coming into the business enterprise and the amount of cash flows that have gone out of that business enterprise during a specific period of time (usually the fiscal year). The statement is divided into operating activities, investing activities, and financing activities. This statement differs from the income statement, which is prepared using accrual accounting (to be explained later).

# The Rules for Preparing and Reporting Financial Accounting Information

## Generally Accepted Accounting Principles

Although the SEC has the authority by law to set rules for preparing financial statements to be issued to external parties, it has delegated this responsibility to a nongovernmental group. This group is the *Financial Accounting Standards Board (FASB)*, an independent body made up of businesspeople, financial executives, practicing accountants, and accounting academicians. It sets accounting standards that are commonly known as *generally accepted accounting principles (GAAP)* that govern the preparation of financial statements issued for use primarily outside the business entity. The FASB will be further discussed in Chapter 2.

GAAP is a set of concepts, principles, and procedures that have evolved over time by various professional bodies (prominent among these were the Accounting Principles Board—now defunct—which was established by the Institute of Certified Public Accountants in 1959). Since 1973, GAAP have been set by the FASB. However, several bodies, such as the American Institute of Certified Public Accountants (AICPA), the SEC, the American Accounting Association (AAA), and the Financial Executives Institute (FEI), may influence the FASB through formal input to its technical agenda and, in some cases, having members on the FASB. GAAP set by the FASB are not static; they continue to evolve and change as business conditions change.

Listing and detailing the specific Statement of Financial Accounting Standards is beyond the scope of this book. The approach in this book is to present the standards in the context of preparing the various elements of the balance sheet, income statement, and statement of cash flows. In this chapter and the next, broad concepts, assumptions, and principles that underlie these detailed standards will be presented.

First, underlying qualitative accounting concepts will be covered in the following paragraphs. Basic assumptions and principles for measuring and recognizing business transactions are covered in the Chapter 2.

# Making Financial Statements Useful: Underlying Objectives and Concepts

According to the Financial Accounting Standards Board the overriding objectives of the financial accounting system are to provide useful information for the following:

- Making investment and credit decisions
- Assessing future cash flows concerning the company's resources, claims to resources, and changes in them

The following basic qualitative concepts or characteristics follow from these objectives and guide the accountant in preparing financial statements to make them useful to users. The following concepts are taken from FASB Concepts Statement No. 2, "Qualitative Characteristics of Accounting Information" (as amended):

**Relevance**. Financial accounting information must be related to and significant to the decision being considered. As such, it must make a difference in a decision by helping users to form predictions about the outcomes of past, present, and future events or to confirm or correct prior expectations. In a nutshell, this information must be timely, have predictive value, and have feedback value. For example, a company is presently considering replacing a computer system. The cost of the system is not relevant. What is relevant is the future cost of a new system and the benefits compared thereto.

**Timeliness**. Providing of accounting information to decision makers before it loses its capacity to influence their decisions. For example, an investor who is considering the purchase of a stock would need current, timely information on the company via its financial statements in order to make an informed decision.

**Reliability**. Accounting information that is faithfully represented, capable of being verified, and reasonably free of error and bias. To be useful, financial information must be reliable as well as relevant. For example, a bank assessing whether to make loan to a company would expect the financial statements presented to be truthful, accurate, complete, and capable of being verified.

**Verifiability**. Two or more accountants get the same or very similar results (or a consensus) when using the same measurement methods. Verifiability is closely related to reliability.

**Understandability**. The quality of accounting information that enables users to perceive its significance in terms of how it is communicated and the use of clear and appropriate terminology. For example, an *informed* stockholder reading the financial statements should be able to understand the terminology, format, and other presentation without difficulty.

**Neutrality**. Accounting information is free from bias that is intended to attain a predetermined result or induce a particular mode of behavior; that is, accounting information cannot be selected to favor one set of interested parties over another. For example, a prospective investor in a company's stock should be assured that accounting methods and alternatives selected in preparing the financial statements were free of bias toward a predetermined result.

**Comparability**. The quality of accounting information that enables users to identify similarities in and differences between two sets of economic data. This requires accountants to measure and report accounting information in a similar manner among different business entities. For example, the financial statements for The Home Depot and Lowe's—two very similar companies—should be comparable.

**Consistency**. The same accounting policies and procedures must be used from period to period so that proper comparison and evaluation can be made of the business entity's progress over time. Business entities are allowed to change accounting methods, if they can show that the newly adopted accounting method is "preferable" to the old one. For example, if a business selects the first-in-first-out inventory method, it should use it consistently year-to-year unless circumstances clearly support the change to a different method.

**Materiality**. The magnitude of an omission or misstatement of accounting that, in light of surrounding circumstances, makes it probable that the judgment of a reasonable person relying on the information would have been changed or influenced by the omission. Simply said, it means that an item or transaction is material if it is large enough to influence an investor's decision. For example, a company purchases thirty waste paper baskets for its office users. Technically, this is a purchase of office equipment and could be recorded as an asset and depreciated. However, given their low value companies will likely write these off as expenses when purchased, since the cost of record keeping would outweigh any benefit of recording and depreciating.

**Conservatism**. When faced with two alternative measurements of valuation—both of which have reasonable support—the one that understates rather than overstates the business entity's net income or financial position must be selected. For example, a company that has been sued would report potential losses from such a suit in the statements or in its footnotes. However, it would not report potential gains from a lawsuit.

# QUIZ

1. (True or false?) The Financial Accounting Standards Board is responsible for certifying a CPA.

2. (True or false?) A partnership is a business entity in which the owners cannot be sued for debts incurred by the business.

3. (True or false?) The income statement reports on the financial performance of a business entity in terms of revenue earned and expenses incurred during a specific period of time.

4. (True or false?) The primary purpose of management accounting is to assist internal managers in their planning, controlling, and decision-making roles.

5. (True or false?) Generally accepted accounting principles were established by Congress in 1933 and are updated annually by the American Institute of Certified Public Accountants.

6. (True or false?) To be employed in a corporation's financial accounting function, an individual must legally be certified as a Certified Public Accountant.

7. For each of the following, check each item that is issued to external parties by the financial accounting function of a business enterprise:
   _____ A. Balance sheet
   _____ B. Approved annual budget
   _____ C. Cash flow statement
   _____ D. Income statement
   _____ E. Divisional cost report
   _____ F. Statement of changes in stockholders' equity

8. Which of the following is a primary user of financial statements?
   A. Customers
   B. Labor unions
   C. Investors and creditors
   D. Governmental agencies, e.g., the SEC or IRS
   E. All of the above
   F. None of the above

9. Financial accounting information is most effective when:
   A. The information aids internal management in controlling costs.
   B. The value of the information exceeds the costs of producing it.
   C. The information is produced by a computer-based accounting system.
   D. All of the information is based on estimates rather than historical costs.

10. **Which of the following financial statements is a snapshot of the financial position of the company at a specific date in time?**
    A. Statement of cash flows
    B. Income statement
    C. Statement of Changes in Financial Position
    D. Balance sheet

11. **Which of the following is a component of the quality of relevance?**
    A. Neutrality
    B. Verifiability
    C. Timeliness
    D. None of the above

12. **Which of the following organizations is *not* a source of generally accepted accounting principles?**
    A. The Financial Accounting Standards Board
    B. The Internal Revenue Service
    C. The Securities and Exchange Commission
    D. The American Institute of Certified Public Accountants
    E. The Financial Executives Institute

13. **Which of the following can *not* be sued for the business's debts?**
    A. The sole proprietorship
    B. A partnership
    C. A corporation
    D. Stockholders

14. **Which financial statement presents a summary of a business's assets, liabilities, and owners' equity?**
    A. Cash flow statement
    B. Spreadsheet
    C. Balance sheet
    D. Income statement

15. **Which of the following parties need financial information from a business to perform critical decisions?**
    A. Investors
    B. Investment bankers
    C. The Securities and Exchange Commission
    D. Pension funds
    E. All of the above

## chapter 2

# Basic Principles of Financial Accounting and Reporting

## CHAPTER OBJECTIVES

*The purposes of this chapter are to*

- Discuss how generally accepted accounting principles are developed
- Describe the basic assumptions underlying generally accepted accounting principles
- Describe the basic principles of accounting
- Describe measuring income and expenses using accrual accounting
- Introduce the accounting equation and its impact on the financial statements

## How Accounting Principles Are Established

The Securities and Exchange Commission (SEC) has the authority under the Securities Act of 1933 and the Securities Exchange Act of 1934 to establish reporting and disclosures requirements for corporations that issue financial statements. However, the SEC has elected to play its role in an oversight capacity and allow the accounting profession to set accounting principles. In the last chapter we defined generally accepted accounting principles (GAAP) for accounting and reporting as a body of principles that has emerged over time and has been accepted as authoritative. These principles were developed first under the leadership of the American Institute of Certified Public Accountants (AICPA), then through the Accounting Principles Board (APB), with input from other professional accounting and industrial organizations.

### What Is the Difference between Accounting Principles and Accounting Standards?

When the **Financial Accounting Standards Board** (FASB) was created in 1973 the common terminology was *accounting principles*. However, after the board's creation, the term *standards* crept into common usage. Yet old usage does not die easily, and the term *principles* is still preferred by many. For example, the auditor's opinion when attesting to financial statements uses the term *accounting principles*. We will use the term *principles* in this book and only use the term *standards* when referring to a standard issued by the FASB.

In 1973 all of the interested parties agreed that *one* independent organization would be more effective in establishing GAAP and the Financial Accounting Standards Board (FASB) was established with authority to issue accounting standards. The FASB essentially uses a political process in promulgating an accounting standard:

1. The first step is to add a topic to the FASB's technical agenda. The topic may originate from the FASB's own research staff, or the board may receive recommendations or suggestions from its stakeholders: the AICPA, the SEC, public accounting firms, and industry groups or financial organizations such as the Financial Executives Institute (FEI).

2. The second step is for the FASB research staff—whose responsibility is to analyze the issues involved and develop the accounting and economic effects of a potential standard—to develop a Discussion Memorandum or an Invitation to Comment. The Discussion Memorandum allows the staff to present their analysis in terms of the known facts from the accounting literature and various opinions by interested parties. An Invitation to Comment presents a potential solution to the issue being considered along

with various views by interested parties on the issue. The research staff then analyzes these inputs and uses them to consider a potential new standard.

3. The third step is for the FASB to issue an Exposure Draft of a proposed new standard. The purpose of this document is to present the proposed standard and ask for input by the public. This input may be in the form of written comments and/or through public hearings as directed by the FASB.

4. Finally, the revised standard is voted on and requires an affirmative vote of five of the seven board members. Dissenting members must present their reasons, which will be incorporated into the statement.

Over the years the FASB has developed a Conceptual Framework for Financial Reporting that sets forth interrelated objectives, concepts, and assumptions to be used as guides in establishing accounting standards. These guidelines have been promulgated to date in seven Statements of Financial Accounting Concepts, which can be accessed at the FASB Web site (www.fasb.org). In Chapter 1 we presented the seven qualities that financial accounting and reporting should possess, which were taken from Statement of Financial Accounting Concepts No 2. Building on these concepts, we will next present the basic assumptions that are the core to all seven of the concept statements. The FASB uses these assumptions in the creation of accounting standards. These underlying assumptions are often included in a list of generally accepted accounting principles.

# Basic Assumptions of Financial Accounting

An accounting principle can be thought of as a general rule that is postulated and *assumed* to be true. Its "truth" lies in its general acceptance by accountants over a long period of time and can be considered the foundation of accounting. Thus, when we state "accounting assumptions" that have been generally accepted, we are really stating the foundation of accounting principles. These assumptions are used not only by accountants as a guide to their recording and reporting of accounting data but also by the FASB in creating a new standard. Why? Because they are a part of the FASB's Conceptual Framework that the board uses in establishing accounting standards.

The following paragraphs identify and discuss the four major assumptions used in establishing accounting principles. They will be used to guide us throughout this book.

## Accounting Entity Assumption

An accounting entity sets the boundaries in which accounting records must be maintained and financial reporting must be completed. The accounting entity is normally a business or economic entity (corporation, partnership, or sole proprietorship). Governmental organizations and nonprofit groups can also be accounting entities.

The accounting entity is a distinct unit separate from its owners or shareholders. The accounting entity is different than a legal entity, particularly for partnerships and single proprietorships. While a corporation is a separate accounting entity and a separate legal entity from its owners, a partnership or sole proprietorship business is an accounting entity but is not a separate legal entity from its owners. The owners are personally responsible for the business's debts and liabilities.

Another aspect of an accounting entity is that all financial or economic transactions must be recorded and reported for that entity. This would include all transactions relating to divisions or subsidiary companies. For example, Home Depot has subsidiary companies in other countries. Home Depot should consolidate accounting transactions for these subsidiaries into one accounting/reporting entity and prepare consolidated financial statements.

## Monetary Unit Assumption

A business unit should only include quantifiable transactions. In the United States the dollar is assumed to be the most quantifiable common unit of measurement. This means when business units outside the United States are owned by a business entity, the currency for that business must be converted to the dollar. One problem with this assumption is that the monetary unit is assumed to be stable over time. Because of inflation, that stability does not occur. Nevertheless, GAAP holds that monetary transactions must be recorded at historical cost (see "Historical Cost Principle" in the next section).

## Going Concern Assumption

Unless there is information to the contrary, it is assumed that a business entity will operate indefinitely. This assumption is important for two reasons: (1) In measuring assets, it supports the recording of assets at their original costs. Otherwise, if the business were expected to fail, then these assets would be recorded at their liquidation value. (2) It allows certain estimates to be used.

For example, when depreciation is being recorded and it is assumed that the asset will be depreciated over its useful life, the going concern assumption allows for the asset to be depreciated over a long period of time.

## Time Period Assumption

Because of the going concern assumption, it is assumed that businesses will last for a long period of time. Yet interested parties need periodic information about finances and accounting to make decisions about the business. Thus, artificial time periods are established for reporting financial information to users. Normally, businesses report quarterly and annually. However, reports may be prepared monthly for specified users.

# Basic Accounting Principles for Measuring Financial Accounting Transactions

Now that the fundamental accounting concepts in Chapter 1 and the assumptions underlying accounting principles above have been covered, four broad accounting principles that guide accountants in measuring, recording, and reporting financial accounting transactions will be discussed.

## Historical Cost Principle

Assets and liabilities should be recorded at cost, which is the amount given or received in an exchange transaction. According to FASB Statement of Accounting Concepts No. 5, for assets this is the fair value of what is given in exchange (cash or a promise to pay cash) for the asset at its initial acquisition. For example, if Dell Computers purchased a new assembly line system for $10 million in exchange for a signed secured note, the asset would be valued at $10 million.

For liabilities, it is the current cash equivalent received in exchange for assuming the liability. For example, if Lexington Electronics borrowed $500,000 from a lending institution and signed an interest-bearing promissory note, the liability would be valued at $500,000.

As stated under the monetary unit assumption, asset values, for example, tend to appreciate over time. However, with few exceptions, under the historical cost principle the asset values are not restated.

## Full Disclosure Principle

A fundamental purpose of financial reporting is to provide full disclosure information necessary for users of the financial statements to make informed decisions. If there is information other than that provided on the financial statements themselves, then this information should be reported. Such information could be pending lawsuits, pension plan details, executive stock options, and any other information that would have a material effect on the future of the business. This information is usually reported in footnotes within the financial statements.

## Realization Principle

Revenue is recognized when the product is delivered or the service is completed, without regard to the timing of cash flow. (Accrual accounting will be discussed later in this chapter.) Revenue recognition should meet three tests: (1) the earnings process is virtually complete, (2) there is reasonable certainty as to the collectability of the asset to be received, and (3) the exchange value can be determined. Generally, these tests are met at the point of sale. This usually occurs when the goods or services sold to a buyer (the customer) are delivered, which means the title of the merchandise is transferred.

There are some important exceptions to the point-of-sale criteria. One example is *construction projects*, such as the building of a bridge or erection of a large building, that take a long period of time (usually several years) to complete and for which payments are made by the owner of the project during the construction process. Revenue is recognized as percentages of the contract are completed. Another example is the *end of the production process*, when the price of the item is known and there is a ready market. The mining of silver and gold fit these criteria.

## Matching Principle

Expenses are recognized in the same period as the related revenue. This is based on the assumption that there is a cause-and-effect relationship between revenues and the expenses expended in generating the revenues. Thus, operationally, this means that revenues are recognized first using the realization principle and then the related expenses are recognized using the matching principle.

This principle seems straightforward, but it can be difficult to implement. For example, sales and expenses (cost of goods sold) by a retail establishment would show a strong cause-and-effect relationship and would be relatively easy to determine. However, other expenses don't have a direct cause-and-effect relationship with revenues. For example, the amount of a building to write off against revenue during a period in the form of depreciation is very difficult to determine. Normally, this requires a systematic allocation process, which will be discussed later in this book.

A summary of accounting concepts, assumptions, and principles is shown in Exhibit 2.1.

---

**EXHIBIT 2.1** Summary of Accounting Concepts, Assumptions, and Principles

### Objectives of Accounting and Reporting

- To provide useful information for making investment and credit decisions.
- To provide useful information for assessing future cash flows concerning the company's resources, claims to resources, and changes in them.

| Basic Concepts (From Chapter 1) | Description |
|---|---|
| 1. Relevance | Financial accounting information must be related to and significant for the decision being considered. As such, it must make a difference in a decision by helping users to form predictions about the outcomes of past, present, and future events or to confirm or correct prior expectations. |
| 2. Timeliness | Providing of accounting information to decision makers before it loses its capacity to influence their decisions. |
| 3. Reliability | Accounting information that is faithfully represented, capable of being verified, and reasonably free of error and bias. |
| 4. Verifiability | Two or more accountants get the same or very similar results (or a consensus) when using the same measurement methods. Verifiability is closely related to reliability. |
| 5. Understandability | The quality of accounting information that enables users to perceive its significance in terms of how it is communicated and the use of clear and appropriate terminology. |
| 6. Neutrality | Accounting information is free from bias that is intended to attain a predetermined result or induce a particular mode of behavior; i.e., accounting information cannot be selected to favor one set of interested parties over another. |
| 7. Comparability | The quality of accounting information that enables users to identify similarities in and differences between two sets of economic data. This requires accountants to measure and report accounting information in a similar manner among different business entities. |

*(Continued)*

| EXHIBIT 2.1   *(continued)* Summary of Accounting Concepts, Assumptions, and Principles | |
|---|---|
| 8. Consistency | The same accounting policies and procedures must be used from period to period so that proper comparison and evaluation can be made of the business entity's progress over time. |
| **Basic Assumptions** | **Description** |
| 1. Accounting entity | The accounting entity sets the boundaries for which accounting records must be maintained and financial reporting must be completed. |
| 2. Monetary unit | A business unit should only include quantifiable transactions. In the United States, the unit of measurement for accounting is the dollar. |
| 3. Going concern | Unless there is information to the contrary, it is assumed that a business entity will operate indefinitely. |
| 4. Time period | Because of the going concern assumption it is assumed that businesses will last for a long period of time. |
| **Broad Principles** | **Description** |
| 1. Historical cost | Assets and liabilities should be recorded at cost, which is the amount given or received in an exchange transaction. |
| 2. Full disclosure | Full disclosure of all relevant information is necessary for users of the financial statements to make informed decisions. |
| 3. Realization | Revenue is recognized when the product is delivered or the service is completed, without regard to the timing of cash flow. |
| 4. Matching | Expenses are recognized in the same period as the related revenue based on the assumption that there is a cause-and-effect relationship between revenues and the expenses expended in generating the revenues. |

# Measuring Income and Expenses Using Accrual Accounting

The **accrual basis of accounting** means that revenues are recognized when they are *earned* using the realization principle and expenses are recognized in the period when they are *incurred* using the matching principle regardless of when the cash is received or paid. This contrasts with the *cash basis of accounting,* which means that revenues are recognized when cash is received and expenses are recognized when cash is expended. In most situations accrual accounting is superior to the cash basis of accounting. That is so because it provides a better matching of revenues and expenses and gives a more realistic picture of how well the company has done during a period of time.

Under accrual accounting the accountant must deal with two different types of situations: deferrals and accruals.

1. A *deferral* occurs when cash is received before it is earned or cash is paid before an expense has been incurred. For example, a magazine company normally receives subscription payments in advance of earning the revenue. This is recorded as an increase in Cash (an asset) and an increase in Subscriptions Received in Advance (a liability), and the latter is written off when the revenue is earned.

   Another example is when a company pays for property insurance in advance of incurring the expense. This is recorded as an increase in Prepaid Insurance and a decrease in Cash. The prepayment is written off when the expense is actually incurred, in this case usually at the end of the period.

2. An *accrual* occurs when cash is received after the revenue is earned or cash is paid after the expense is incurred. Most accruals occur at the end of an accounting period. For example, an accounting firm provides a service to a client and completion of the services crosses into the next accounting period, and the client does not pay until the next accounting period. At the end of the present accounting period, the firm records an increase in Accounts Receivable (an asset account) and an increase in Fees Earned (a revenue account) for the amount of services earned this period.

   Another example, a company pays employees biweekly but the end of the payroll period occurs between pay dates. In order to match payroll expenses that have occurred since the last pay date with the revenue earned, the company must accrue the amount of payroll expense as of the end of the period. The payroll expense account would be increased for this amount, and Wages Payable (a liability account) would be increased.

As stated previously, accruals are often triggered and recorded at the end of an accounting period as well as adjustments to accruals or deferrals that previously have been recorded. Recall that the time period assumption requires that financial statements be issued at the end of various periods, such as a year or quarter. This requires the setting of a cutoff date for preparation of the statements, which is the last day of the period involved. In order to recognize all revenues earned and all expenses incurred, the accountant must make *adjusting entries* to the accounting records before the statements are prepared. Some common adjustments are the recording of depreciation, accruing wages that have occurred since the last payroll but haven't been paid, accruing revenue that has been earned but not recorded, adjusting deferred revenue accounts for revenues earned, and adjusting deferred expense accounts for expenses incurred. Adjusting entries will be covered in more detail in Chapter 4.

## Dual Entity Concept

In Chapter 3 we examine the financial statements in more detail. To fully understand the elements of the financial statements and their relationships, familiarity with the dual entity concept and the accounting equation is necessary.

The **dual entity concept** states that an accounting transaction affects (increases or decreases) at least two accounts on the balance sheet (e.g., asset, liability, or stockholders' equity elements). For example, a company purchases a piece of equipment on credit and signs a note promising to pay in the future. Two accounts are affected: an increase in the Equipment account (an asset) and an increase in Notes Payable (liability). In accounting, this dual aspect is the basis for the double-entry bookkeeping system, which was developed in the fourteenth century in Italy (a more contemporary term is the accounting information system). Similar to the dual entity concept, double-entry book-keeping systems require at least two entries to be made in the accounts. This concept can best be understood by using the so-called accounting equation.

## The Accounting Equation

The **accounting equation** is based on the fact that assets are acquired by using either borrowed money (liabilities) or contributed capital (stockholders' equity). Thus, the following algebraic equation holds:

$$\text{Assets} = \text{Liabilities} + \text{Stockholders' Equity}$$

While the dual entity concept requires at least two entries to be made in the accounts, the accounting equation requires that the equation itself must always balance after these entries are made.

This equation and its application to the accounting system can best be understood with a practical example: Builder's Supply Company was established on July 1, 2010. Consider the following transactions that took place during the remainder of the year:

1. One thousand (1,000) shares of the Builder's Supply Company were sold at $100 per share.

2. Three computers were acquired for $3,000.

3. A lease was signed on the retail building, and the first month's rent was paid at $5,000.

4. Merchandising items were acquired for $10,000 on credit.

5. During the first week of operation, $2,000 worth of merchandise was sold to customers for cash. The cost of the inventory sold was $1,600.

6. A telephone bill of $200 was paid.

7. The company purchased $300 worth of office supplies for cash that were used up during the month.

Each of these transactions is posted in Exhibit 2.2 and is discussed immediately after the table.

**EXHIBIT 2.2** Summary of Transactions
+ = Increase; – = Decrease

| | Assets | | = | Liabilities + Stockholders' Equity | | |
|---|---|---|---|---|---|---|
| Cash | Inventory | Office Equipment | | Accounts Payable | Common Stock | Revenues |
| 1. +$100,000 | | | = | | +$100,000 | |
| 2. –$3,000 | | +$3,000 | = | | | |
| 3. –$5,000 | | | = | | | –$5,000 |
| 4. | + $10,000 | | = | +$10,000 | | |
| 5. (a) +$2,000 | (b) –$1,600 | | = | | | (a) +$2,000 (b) –$1,600 |
| 6. –$200 | | | = | | | –$200 |
| 7. –$300 | | | = | | | –$300 |
| Total $93,500 | + $8,400 | +$3,000 | = | +$10,000 | +$100,000 | –$5,100 |
| | $104,900 | | = | | $104,900 | |

*Transaction # 1:* Assets (Cash) are increased by $100,000 ($100 × 1,000 shares), and Stockholders' Equity (Common Stock) is increased by $100,000. Note that the equation is in balance: $100,000 = $100,000.

*Transaction # 2:* Assets (Office Equipment) are increased by $3,000, and Assets (Cash) are decreased by $3,000. Although both entries are on the left side of the equation, they balance out. Therefore, the equation is still in balance: $100,000 = $100,000.

*Transaction # 3:* Assets (Cash) are decreased by $5,000, and Stockholders' Equity (increase in expenses) is decreased by $5,000. The equation is still in balance: $95,000 = $95,000.

*Transaction # 4:* Assets (Inventory) are increased by $10,000, and Liabilities (Accounts Payable) are increased by $10,000. The equation is still in balance: $105,000 = $105,000.

*Transaction # 5:* This transaction has two parts: (a) Assets (Cash) are increased by $2,000, and Stockholders' Equity (Revenues) is increased by $2,000; (b) Expenses (cost of goods sold) is increased by $1,600 (expenses increased, which are deducted from Stockholders' Equity) and Assets (Inventory) are decreased by $1,600. Note that, although expenses have increased, they are offset against revenues. Thus, Stockholders' Equity is decreased by the amount of these expenses. The equation is still in balance: $105,400 = $105,400.

*Transaction # 6:* Stockholders' Equity (expenses increased but are deducted from Stockholders' Equity) is decreased by $200, and Assets (Cash) are decreased by $200. The accounting equation is $105,200 = $105,200.

*Transaction # 7:* Since the supplies have been used up relatively quickly, they are charged off as expenses. Stockholders' Equity (expenses are increased) is decreased by $300, and Assets (Cash) is decreased by $300. The accounting equation becomes $104,900 = $104,900.

Thus, after all transactions have been posted the accounting equation

$$Assets = Liabilities + Stockholders'\ Equity$$

reads:

$$\$104,900 = \$10,000 + \$100,000 + (-\$5,100)$$

or

$$\$104,900 = \$104,900$$

Although, the company has had a loss for the period, the accounting equation is in balance. In the jargon of accountants—the books are balanced.

## QUIZ

1. (True or false?) An accounting standard issued by the FASB is automatically accepted as a generally accepted accounting principle.

2. (True or false?) The Conceptual Framework for Financial Reporting is a foundation for the creation of Generally Accepted Auditing Standards.

3. (True or false?) The going concern assumption states that an organization will continue in business indefinitely.

4. (True or false?) The cost principle states that an item is valued at cost and is constantly updated as the cost changes.

5. (True or false?) The accounting equation is always stated as: Assets = Liabilities + Stockholders' Equity.

6. A computer store orders 10 computers from a wholesaler in March, receives them in April, and pays for them in May. Which of the following statement is correct using the realization principle?
   A. The wholesaler recognizes the sales revenue in April.
   B. The computer store recognizes the computers as cost of goods sold in May.
   C. The computer store enters the computers into the books as an asset in March.
   D. None of the above is correct.

7. A music store purchases 300 DVDs from a wholesaler and records them as an Asset (inventory) in the accounting records in July. Which of the following is true concerning the matching principle?
   A. The 300 DVDs should be expensed when they are received.
   B. The 300 DVDs should be expensed as cost of goods sold when they are sold and the cash is received.
   C. The 300 DVDs should be expensed as cost of goods sold when the revenue is recognized.
   D. None of the above.

8. A retail establishment that only reported the number of each appliance in its inventory would violate which accounting assumption?
   A. Period assumption
   B. Going concern assumption
   C. Accounting entity assumption
   D. Monetary unit assumption

9. **Which of the following events is best for recognizing revenue?**
   A. When costs are recovered
   B. Receipt of cash
   C. Point of sale
   D. End of the production process

10. **An insurance agency receives premiums in advance and records an increase in cash and an increase in premiums received in advance. This would be an example of an accounting:**
    A. Deferral
    B. Accrual
    C. Gain
    D. None of the above

11. **Show the effects on total assets (increase = I; decrease = D; no effect = NE) for the following:**
    _____ A. The company issues stock for cash.
    _____ B. The company pays an accounts payable with cash.
    _____ C. The company writes a check for insurance in advance.
    _____ D. The company purchases a piece of equipment on credit.

12. **For each item, indicate which major balance sheet category it would fall under (A = Assets), (L = Liabilities), (SE = Stockholders' Equity):**
    _____ A. Office Equipment
    _____ B. Land
    _____ C. Accounts Payable
    _____ D. Common Stock
    _____ E. Bonds Payable
    _____ F. Retained Earnings

13. **Using the accounting equation, enter the missing amount in the following:**

    $$\text{ASSETS} = \text{LIABILITIES} + \text{STOCKHOLDERS' EQUITY}$$

    A. $10,000 = $6,000 + _____
    B. $50,000 = _____ + $40,000
    C. _____ = $8,000 + $12,000

14. **A business includes a footnote to fully explain the company's pension plan. This would be based on the:**
    A. Realization principle.
    B. Full disclosure principle.
    C. Conservatism concept.
    D. Need to satisfy the company union.

15. **The period assumption means:**
    A. The company will remain in business for an indefinite period of time
    B. That revenue should be matched with the related expenses in the same period that they occur
    C. The life of the company can be divided into artificial time periods for reporting purposes
    D. None of the above

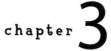

## chapter 3

# The Balance Sheet and Income Statement— A Closer Look

## CHAPTER OBJECTIVES

*The purposes of this chapter are to*

- Present and define the major elements of the balance sheet
- Present and define the major elements of the statement of changes in stockholders' equity
- Present and define the major elements of the income statement

## The Balance Sheet

As stated in Chapter 1, the **balance sheet** lists the financial condition of the business at a specific point in time (usually at the end of an accounting period). As such, it contains three major categories:

1. All assets owned by the business
2. All liabilities incurred to finance these assets

3. All contributed capital and retained earnings, representing the amount of financing provided by stockholders and earnings retained in the firm

The balance sheet gets its name from the fact that the two sides (Assets vs. Liabilities and Stockholders' Equity) must balance each other out. Thus, it is based on the accounting equation that we discussed in the previous chapter:

$$\text{Assets} = \text{Liabilities} + \text{Stockholders' Equity}$$

The balance sheet elements are often presented either side by side or vertically, where the assets are presented on top with the liabilities and stockholders' equity on the bottom. A recent balance sheet for NIKE, Inc. is presented in Exhibit 3.1. The elements of the balance sheet will now be defined and discussed. Note that NIKE elects to net some items on the balance sheet and, in some cases, provides more information in a footnote. The accounting procedures pertaining to each of the elements on the balance sheet will be discussed in subsequent chapters.

### Balance Sheet vs. the Statement of Financial Condition

What is the statement of financial condition? The more contemporary title for the balance sheet is the *statement of financial condition*, and it is the one preferred by the FASB. Yet the balance sheet has been in existence from the beginning of business in the United States and is still widely used. Both the balance sheet and the statement of financial position portray the financial condition of the company. Thus, the two titles mean the same thing and are interchangeable. The term *balance sheet* will be used in this book.

# Assets

Assets are economic resources owned by a business that are intended to be used up in the future and usually could be converted into cash. They could be tangible (e.g., buildings) or intangible (e.g., goodwill). Assets are divided into two major categories: current assets and long-term assets.

## Current Assets

Assets that are expected to be sold or used up within the next year or operating cycle are *current assets*. (Usually, the operating cycle is the average time period between buying inventory and receiving cash proceeds from its eventual sale.) Current assets are comprised of very liquid assets (e.g., cash and cash equivalents), assets for sale (e.g., inventory), and productive assets (e.g., plant

**EXHIBIT 3.1**   NIKE, Inc. Balance Sheet May 31, 2007

| Assets | (In Millions) |
|---|---|
| Current Assets | |
| Cash and Cash Equivalents | $1,856.7 |
| Short–Term Investments | 990.3 |
| Net Receivables | 2,494.7 |
| Inventories | 2,121.9 |
| Deferred Income Taxes | 219.7 |
| Prepaid Expenses | 393.2 |
| **Total Current Assets** | **$8,076.5** |
| Property, Plant, and Equipment | $3,619.1 |
| Less: Accumulated Depreciation | $1,940.8 |
| Plant, Property, and Equipment, Net | 1,678.3 |
| Goodwill | 130.8 |
| Intangible Assets | 409.9 |
| Deferred Income Taxes and Other Assets | 392.8 |
| **Total Assets** | **$10,688.3** |
| **Liabilities** | |
| Current Liabilities | |
| Current Portion of Long–Term Debt | $30.5 |
| Accounts Payable | 1,040.3 |
| Notes Payable | 100.8 |
| Accrued Liabilities | 1,303.4 |
| Income Taxes Payable | 109.0 |
| **Total Current Liabilities** | **$2,584.0** |
| Long–Term Debt | 409.9 |
| Deferred Income Taxes and Other Liabilities | 668.7 |
| Redeemable Preferred Stock | 0.3 |
| **Total Long–Term Debt** | **$1,078.9** |
| **Stockholders' Equity** | **$7,025.4** |
| **Total Liabilities and Stockholders' Equity** | **$10,688.3** |

and equipment). They are listed in the current assets section of the balance sheet in order of liquidity with the most liquid being listed first (liquidity means the ease with which they can be converted into cash).

   *Cash and Cash Equivalents.* These are the most liquid of current assets. **Cash** comprises currency, coins, checks, and cash in savings accounts. **Cash equivalents** are those instruments that mature within 90 days at acquisition, such as Treasury bills and commercial paper. **Marketable securities** may be defined as cash equivalents but are usually listed separately. In Exhibit 3.1 NIKE bundles marketable securities into Short-Term Investments, which shows a balance of $990.3 million.

---

### What Are Marketable Securities?

**Marketable securities** are short-term investments from extra cash that can be converted back to cash at a readily marketable price.

---

   *Accounts Receivable.* Receivables result from a business selling products or services to customers on credit. Seller's terms dictate the period, but most receivables are due within 30 days; therefore, they are liquid assets. Businesses understand that they will be unable to collect all of the receivables from customers. Therefore, as a cost of doing business, the company normally will estimate an allowance for uncollectible accounts and charge that expense off in the current period. The accumulated balance in the uncollectible account is deducted from the Accounts Receivable balance on the balance sheet. In Exhibit 3.1 NIKE has elected to show receivables net of allowances. The following is an illustration of how receivables might appear on a balance sheet, if the allowances were included:

| | |
|---|---|
| Accounts Receivable | $1,000,000 |
| Less Allowance for Uncollectible Accounts | $25,000 |
| Net Accounts Receivable | $975,000 |

   *Inventories.* The content of Inventories on the balance sheet depends on the type of business that company is in. If it is the merchandising (retail or wholesale) business, there is normally only one merchandising inventory account. However, if it is a manufacturing company, it will include a Raw Materials account, a Work in Process account, and a Finished Goods account. As stated in Chapter 1, this book does not directly address accounting for manufacturing organizations.[1]

Inventories are recorded at cost but may be stated at a different value—for example, lower of cost or market. These methods are covered later in this book. Inventories are shown for NIKE on Exhibit 3.1 as $2,121.9 million.

*Prepaid Items.* Prepaid items are deferrals, which were briefly discussed in Chapter 2. A prepaid item is recorded as an asset because it represents an expenditure whose benefit to the company will be received at some time during the next year or operating cycle. It cannot be turned into cash, but it is a current asset because the company will not have to expend cash for the item in the near future. For example, a company may have paid for advertising in advance. This would be a current asset, as the benefit from the advertising will be received in the near future. In Exhibit 3.1 Deferred Income Taxes and Prepaid Expense are shown as $219.7 and $393.2 million respectively.

## Long-Term Assets

Fixed assets that that are not intended for resale and are held for longer than one year or an operating cycle are long-term assets. They include Plant, Property, and Equipment, Intangibles, and other assets. Some companies may include long-term investments, such as bonds or stocks in other companies, as part of this category. However, they can also be shown as a separate section between current assets and long-term assets.

*Land.* This balance represents the cost of land that is used by the company for operational activities. It normally is the site where buildings and other structures are situated and used to conduct the normal business of the company. Land is not used up; therefore, it is not depreciated.

*Plant and Equipment.* Long-lived assets that are used by the company in the production of its income are plant and equipment. Plant refers to the buildings and related structures that house the company's production or business activities. They are recorded at cost along with any improvements made during their life. Depending on the type of business in which the company is involved, equipment includes such items as production

---

[1]A companion book, *Management Accounting Demystified* by the author and published by McGraw-Hill is recommended for manufacturing accounting.

machinery, office equipment, and retail equipment. Equipment items are recorded at cost, including delivery and installation costs.

Buildings and equipment are depreciable assets and are depreciated over their useful life. The accountant selects a depreciation method (these methods are discussed in Chapter 9) and computes an annual depreciation charge for each item. The expense is charged against income on the income statement. The related entry is an increase to the Accumulated Depreciation account. The latter is deducted from the cost of the asset on the balance sheet, resulting in what is called the *net book value* of the asset. In Exhibit 3.1 NIKE itemized Property, Plant, and Equipment less Accumulated Depreciation at $1,678.3 million. However, many companies show Plant, Property, and Equipment net of depreciation as one line item.

## More Information about Book Value

What is book value? *Book value* normally refers to the carrying value of an asset on the books (accounting records). Using the cost principle, this means the cost of the asset at acquisition along with any improvements. *Net book value* refers to the carrying value of an asset less accumulated depreciation.

*Leases.* Some companies lease property instead of purchasing it. There are two types of leases: operational and capital. Operational leases are normally for an asset whose term is substantially less than the useful life of the asset; the lessor is responsible for the repair and maintenance of the asset. The lease payments are charged in the period in which they occur. Capital leases, on the other hand, are a purchase of the asset, regardless of the form of contractual agreement. Typically, this purchase occurs when the life of the lease is essentially the same as the useful life of the asset. Capital leases are recorded in the accounting records and are shown in the Plant, Property, and Equipment section of the balance sheet and amortized over the life on the lease. Exhibit 3.1 reveals that NIKE does not have capital leases.

*Natural Resources.* Natural resources are timber, mineral deposits, oil fields, and things that are different from depreciable assets in that they are physically extracted during company operations and are replaceable only through natural processes. The original cost of the asset is recorded on the balance sheet; as the resource is depleted, the amount of depletion is charged as an expense on the income statement, and the related entry is deducted from the cost of the natural resource on the balance sheet.

*Intangible Assets.* Nonmonetary and nonphysical assets that are recorded at cost and are expected to benefit the business in the future are intangible assets. Some examples are copyrights, patents, trademarks, franchises, and goodwill. With the exception of goodwill and trademarks, most intangibles are amortized over their legal life or useful life and shown on the balance sheet net of amortization. Although goodwill and trademarks are not amortized, they should be reviewed annually for any impairment; any amount that is worthless (i.e., the fair market value is less than the carrying value) should be written off. Note that in Exhibit 3.1 NIKE lists Intangible Assets at $409.9 million and Goodwill at $130.8.

---

### What Is the Difference between Amortization and Depreciation?

**Amortization** is the process of prorating the value of an asset (usually an intangible) and charging it to expense over its legal or useful life. **Depreciation** is the spreading of the cost of a fixed asset against income over its useful life due to wear and tear from use and passage of time.

---

*Other Assets.* Every company may have miscellaneous assets that cannot be shown in any of the above categories. These are normally noncurrent prepaid items and noncurrent deferrals. For example, in Exhibit 3.1 NIKE lists Deferred Income Taxes. Deferred income taxes result from the difference between tax expense for book (GAAP) purposes and annual taxes paid to the Internal Revenue Service based on the tax law. The accounting for deferred taxes is a more advanced accounting topic and is not included in this book.

# Liabilities

Liabilities are legal debts or obligations to lenders, suppliers, employees, and the like, that the company undertakes during the course of business. In order to settle the debt or obligation it is expected that the business must transfer assets (money or goods) or provide services to other entities in the future. Liabilities are classified as either current liabilities or long-term liabilities.

## Current Liabilities

Current liabilities are obligations of the business that are to be settled in cash within the next year or operating cycle, whichever period is longer. They include the following:

*Payables.* These include Accounts Payable, Taxes Payable, Wages Payable, and Notes Payable. Although Notes Payable are normally found under

Long-Term Liabilities, the company may sign a short-term note, for example, to purchase inventory. In Exhibit 3.1 NIKE lists balances for Accounts Payable, Notes Payable, Accrued Liabilities, and Income Taxes Payable. Accrued liabilities are other expenses that NIKE incurred but have not been paid in cash, for example, interest and salaries. It also lists the Current Portion of Long-Term Debt, which is the amount of interest due on a long-term debt that is due in the next year but has not been paid.

There are a host of unique short-term payables that could be included under Current Liabilities. A few of these are included below:

- Interest Payable
- Warranties Payable
- Insurance Payable
- Advertising Payable
- Litigation Payable
- Rebates Payable
- Royalties Payable

## Long-Term Liabilities

Long-term liabilities are obligations that are due beyond a year or an operating cycle and require the payment of cash, goods, or services to settle. Since the obligations are for the long term, there usually is a financing arrangement that requires a periodic payment of principal and interest. Typical long-term liabilities are notes payable, bonds payable, and mortgage loans.

*Notes Payable* is a promissory debt agreement with a financial institution or an individual that is due in excess of one year or one operating cycle. The most common promissory note is a mortgage note secured by a claim to real property. Exhibit 3.1 shows that NIKE has elected to bundle its notes payable and bonds payable debt into a one-line entry: Long-Term Debt.

*Bonds Payable* is a long-term debt security obligation issued by the company (usually a corporation) to lenders. The lenders, or investors, may sell these bonds to other investors prior to their maturity. Bonds are issued at $1,000 par per bond and require repayment of principal and interest on a semiannual basis. Thus, bonds sold and due in 10 years would have 20 interest periods. As will be discussed later, the recording of bonds by the accountant is somewhat complex. When the bond is sold, two types of interest are involved: a stated rate and a market rate. The *stated rate* is the rate of interest shown on the bond when it is issued and is the rate used to pay the holder the semiannual interest payment. The *market rate* is the rate in effect on the open market at the time the bond is sold. Obviously, the company must accept the market rate when the bonds are sold. Thus, three things can happen when bonds are sold:

1. The stated rate could equal the market rate. In this case the Bonds Payable account is increased by the face amount of the bonds. For example, say that $100,000 worth of bonds was sold at a stated market rate of 6 percent. The Bonds Payable account would be increased by $100,000 (the face value of the hundred bonds). Interest would be paid at the end of each six months in the amount of $3,000 ($100,000 × 6% × 6/12).

2. If the stated rate of interest is greater than the market rate, the company will want more money from the sale to cover the difference, because the stated interest will have to be paid over the life of the bond. To handle this, the bond is sold at a premium, which, in effect, is interest received in advance. The premium would be recorded as such and must be amortized over the life of the bond against interest expense. As an example, assume that a company sells $100,000 face amount of bonds at 105 (meaning the market rate is less then the stated rate), due in 10 years, at a stated rate of 6 percent. The following is what the entries on the books would show:

   a. Cash would increase by $105,000 ($100,000 × 1.05).

   b. Bonds Payable would increase by $100,000.

   c. Premium on Bonds Payable (a liability account) would increase by $5,000.

   d. Each six months the interest would be paid and the premium would be amortized. The cash payment for interest would be $3,000 (6% × 6/12 × $100,000). Using the simple, straight-line method, the premium would decrease (amortize) by $250 ($5,000/20 semiannual periods), and interest expense would decrease by $250. Thus, the effective amount of interest would be $2,750 ($3,000 − $250).

   e. At the end of the first year after two interest payments, the balance sheet would show the following:

| | |
|---|---|
| Bonds Payable | $100,000 |
| Add: Premium on Bonds Payable | 4,500 |
| Bonds Payable | $104,500 |

3. If the stated rate of interest is less than the market rate, the company will sell the bonds at a discount, receiving less cash than the face value. The difference is a discount, which is recorded as such and, like a premium, is amortized over the life of the bonds against interest expense. Assume in the previous example that the $100,000 face value of bonds were sold at 93 (meaning the market rate is greater than the stated rate), due in 10 years, at a stated rate of 6 percent. The following is how the entries on the books would show:

   a. Cash would increase by $930,000 ($100,000 × .93)

   b. Bonds Payable would increase by $100,000.

   c. Discount on Bonds Payable would increase by $7,000 (which, in effect, is a prepaid interest account).

   d. Each six months the interest would be paid and the discount would be amortized: Using the straight-line method, the cash payment for interest would be $3,000 (6% × 6/12 × $100,000). The discount would decrease (amortize) by $350 ($7,000/20 interest periods) and interest would increase by $350. Thus, the effective amount of interest would be $3,350 ($3,000 + $350).

   e. At the end of the first year after two periods of interest payments, the balance sheet would show the following:

| Bonds Payable | $100,000 |
|---|---|
| Less: Discount on Bonds Payable | 6,300 |
| Bonds Payable | $93,700 |

**Other Long-Term Liabilities**   There can be numerous other types of long-term liabilities, depending on the company and the type of industry in which the company does business. The most common one is deferred taxes, which, as discussed previously, results from differences in computing net income under generally accepted accounting principles and the federal or state income tax laws. In this case it is a deferred liability, whereas under Other Assets it was a prepaid expense. The details on how this is computed are complex and are reserved for intermediate accounting texts.

Another example of Other Long-Term Liability is warranty liabilities. Many companies sell products to customers with a guarantee or warranty to fix any deficiencies in the performance of these products. An estimate is made each year of the expenses that will be required to repair or replace these deficiencies. An expense account is charged, and the Warranty Obligations account is increased. Exhibit 3.1 shows that NIKE has bundled Deferred Income Taxes and Other Liabilities together. NIKE also shows redeemable preferred stock outstanding. Redeemable preferred stock is also known as **callable preferred stock**. It is a type of stock that can be called on or after a specific date by NIKE. The stock is called at a specified price and once it is returned to the NIKE, the stock is retired.

# Stockholders' Equity

Stockholders' equity represents the capital received from investors (owners) in return for shares of stock (common or preferred) and earnings retained in the business. Stock that has been sold is often referred to as *paid-in capital*. Thus, stockholders' equity contains two major categories: contributed (paid-in) capital and retained earnings. It should be pointed out that stockholders' equity is really the residual capital in the business. That is, using the accounting equation, if you deduct total liabilities from total assets, the remaining amount is the residual ownership in the business. Both common and preferred stock may be issued at par value.

### Common Stock

Common stock represents the basic ownership in the corporation. As such common-stock holders have several rights:

- The right to vote on such important corporate matters as the election of the boards of directors, mergers, and stock awarded to employees
- The right to share in any dividends declared by the company to its common-stock holders
- A preemptive right, which is to be given the option to buy a proportional amount of any additional shares that are issued by the company
- The right to receive periodic financial statements about the performance of the corporation
- The right to share in the liquidation of the company, but only after creditors, preferred-stock holders, and other priority claims have been satisfied.

### Preferred Stock

Nonvoting preferred-stock holders are not true owners of the company; nevertheless, their stock has certain preferences over common stock:

- A preference as to dividends, which are usually paid each period; the amount of dividend is usually stated as a percentage of the preferred stock's par value
- A preferred position in the event of liquidation after a creditor has been paid
- A maturity date, at which the company will buy back the stock

Preferred stock may have a callable or redeemable feature that allows the corporation to buy back the preferred stock at its option. Also, the preferred stock may have a provision that allows the holder to convert it to common stock or another security of the corporation at specified exchange rate.

### Retained Earnings

Retained earnings is that portion of net income that is retained by the corporation rather than being paid out to common-stock holders in the form of dividends. The company may elect to restrict a part or all of retained earnings. This is often done as part of a bond covenant to protect the bondholders. If retained earnings are restricted, the amount should be separated from unrestricted retained earnings.

### Treasury Stock

Treasury stock occurs when the company repurchases its own stock and elects not to retire it. It is normally shown after retained earnings on the balance sheet and is deducted from contributed capital. Treasury stock is often purchased and used to issue stock to employees for stock options as part of a compensation plan.

# Statement of Changes in Stockholders' Equity

The **statement of changes in stockholders' equity** is issued to reconcile the beginning and ending balances of the Stockholders' Equity account. This statement may also be called a *statement of changes in capital stock and retained earnings* or another title. There are two major elements to the statement: contributed capital (paid-in capital) and retained earnings. As an illustration, Exhibit 3.2

**EXHIBIT 3.2** NIKE, Inc. Statement of Changes in Stockholders' Equity for the Year Ended May 31, 2007

|  | (In Millions) |
|---|---|
| **Contributed Capital, May 31, 2006** | **$1,450.1** |
| Add: Stock issuances during the year | 512.7 |
| **Total Contributed Capital, May 31, 2007** | **$1,962.8** |
| **Retained Earnings, May 31, 2006** | **$4,713.4** |
| Add: Net Income for the year | 1,491.5 |
| Subtract: Dividends | (1,319.7) |
| **Total Retained Earnings, May 31, 2007** | **$4,885.2** |
| **Other Equity, May 31, 2006** | **$121.7** |
| Add: Additions during year | 55.7 |
| **Total Other Equity, May 31, 2007** | **$177.4** |
| **Total Stockholders' Equity, May 31, 2007** | **$7,025.4** |

portrays the statement issued by NIKE. Note, however, that the format may vary from company to company.

# Income Statement

An **income statement** measures the economic performance of a business over a period of time, usually a quarter or a year. In doing so, it summarizes all revenues, expenses, gains, and losses and ends up with net income for the period. Users of the financial statements will look to the income statement to evaluate the performance of the business and, specifically, the performance of senior management. Users will also be interested in this statement to evaluate the ability of the company to pay dividends on stock and interest on any bonds payable.

The FASB Statement of Financial Accounting Standard (SFAS) No. 130 requires a company to report using the comprehensive concept of income. It requires two major categories: net income and other comprehensive income. SFAS 130 does not require a specific format for the financial statement in which comprehensive income is reported. However, it does require the display of net income as a component of comprehensive income in that statement and that the statement be displayed with the same prominence as other financial statements. Exhibit 3.3 illustrates an income statement using the comprehensive income concept.

## Net Revenues

Revenues (sales) are revenue received from the sale of goods and services from the company's normal operations. Any sales discounts, returns, and allowances are netted against gross revenues.

## Cost of Goods Sold

For a merchandising (retailing) company, the **cost of goods sold** represents the amount of inventory sold to customers during the period. For a manufacturing company it represents the cost of goods manufactured that have been sold during the period. The latter would include cost of raw materials, labor, and overhead consumed in the manufacturing process to manufacture the finish product.

## Selling and Administrative Expenses

- *Selling expenses.* These are all expenses incurred by the company in generating sales, such as sales commissions, advertising, and promotions.
- *Administrative expenses.* These are all general expenses to operate the company, such as executive salaries, office salaries, supplies, depreciation, bad debt expense, and insurance that are not related to the sales function.

## Discontinued Operations

Discontinued operations refers to gains or losses resulting from the selling, abandoning, or otherwise disposing of part of a company's operations. For example, Home Depot sold its home construction division, which required the separate reporting of the sale on the income statement.

## Extraordinary Items

These items refer to a gain or loss from an event that is unusual in nature and infrequent in occurrence. For example, Wal-Mart suffered flooding in several stores in Louisiana during Hurricane Katrina. These losses would be written off on the income statement as an extraordinary item.

**The Difference between a Revenue and a Gain and between an Expense and a Loss**

*Revenue* and *expenses* result from the selling of the company's product or services, whereas, a *gain* or *loss* results from some peripheral activity, such as the one-time selling of a piece of equipment. A gain will add to the income statement's bottom line, and a loss will be subtracted from its bottom line.

# Earnings Per Share

In addition to the items just mentioned, a company must report earnings per share and diluted earnings per share. Basically, *earnings per share (EPS)* is a metric computed by dividing the net income by the number of common stock

| | EXHIBIT 3.3 Illustration of a Comprehensive Income Statement | |
|---|---|---|
| + | Net revenues | $XXXX |
| − | Cost of goods sold | XXXX |
| = | Gross margin | XXXX |
| − | Selling and administrative expenses | XXXX |
| = | Income from operations | XXXX |
| + | Other revenue and gains | XXXX |
| − | Other expenses and losses | XXXX |
| = | Income from continuing operations before income taxes | XXXX |
| − | Income tax expense | XXXX |
| = | Income from continuing operations | XXXX |
| +/− | Discontinued operations (net of tax) | XXXX |
| +/− | Extraordinary items (net of tax) | XXXX |
| = | Net income | XXXX |
| +/− | Other comprehensive income/expense items (net of tax) | XXXX |
| = | Comprehensive income | XXXX |
| | Earnings per share: | |
| | Undiluted | XXXX |
| | Diluted | XXXX |

shares outstanding. The earnings per share is usually broken down further into earnings from continuing operations, discontinued operations, income/loss from extraordinary items, and cumulative effects of accounting changes and adjustments. *Diluted earnings per share* is a metric that takes earnings per share a step further. It assumes that any outstanding convertible securities can be converted to common stock, thereby diluting the value of the EPS. This potential dilution is computed into the diluted earnings per share. Such outstanding securities could be convertible preferred shares, convertible debentures, stock options, and warrants.

# QUIZ

1. (True or False?) The balance sheet is a summary of the changes in assets, liabilities, and stockholders' equity during a period of time.

2. (True or False?) Marketable securities are those short-term investments from extra cash that can be converted back to cash at a readily marketable price.

3. (True or false?) Net book value refers to the market value of an asset less accumulated depreciation.

4. (True or false?) The income statement reports the amount of revenues and gains less any expenses or losses for a company during a period of time.

5. (True or false?) The diluted earnings per share is included as an element on the balance sheet.

6. List the statement in which each of the following would be included by entering BS for balance sheet, IS for income statement, or N for neither:
   _____ A. Inventory
   _____ B. Sales
   _____ C. Cost of goods sold
   _____ D. Marketable securities
   _____ E. Dividends
   _____ F. Gain on sale of property
   _____ G. Prepaid interest
   _____ H. Stockholders' investment (contributed capital) in company

7. Which of the following is *not* a characteristic of the balance sheet?
   A. The assets are usually listed in order of their liquidity.
   B. The balance sheet provides information that is useful for evaluating the profitability of the business during a period of time.
   C. The major elements of the balance sheet are assets, liabilities, and stockholders' equity.
   D. Retained earnings are one of the two elements in the Stockholders' Equity section.

8. Which of the following is not usually classified as a current asset on the balance sheet?
   A. Inventories
   B. Marketable securities
   C. Prepaid insurance
   D. Patents

9. **Which of the following would most likely be included under Current Liabilities on the balance sheet?**
   A. Current portion of interest on bonds payable
   B. Pension obligations
   C. Lease obligations
   D. Notes payable maturing in three years.

10. **Assets that a company expects to convert to cash within one year are called:**
   A. Intangible assets
   B. Pension assets
   C. Long-term notes
   D. Current assets

11. **Under which heading would patents and goodwill be classified on the balance sheet?**
   A. Property, Plant, and Equipment
   B. Long-Term Investments
   C. Intangible Assets
   D. Stockholders' Equity

12. **Which of the following would be classified under Stockholders' Equity on the balance sheet?**
   A. Investment in bonds
   B. Accumulated depreciation
   C. Common stock
   D. Intangibles

13. **On the income statement a positive gross margin results from:**
   A. Selling and administrative expenses that are less than sales.
   B. Cost of goods sold that is less than sales.
   C. Cost of goods sold that is less than net income.
   D. Cost of goods sold that is greater than selling and administrative expenses.

14. **In the income statement Net Sales means:**
   A. Sales discounts and returns and allowances have been deducted from gross sales.
   B. Purchase discounts have been deducted from gross sales.
   C. Freight on items sold has been deducted from sales.
   D. Bad-debt expense has been deducted from gross sales.

15. **Which of the following would not be included in a comprehensive income statement?**
   A. Gains
   B. Gross margin
   C. Extraordinary items
   D. Accumulated depreciation
   E. Cost of goods sold

## chapter 4

# The Accounting Process: Analyzing and Recording Business Transactions

## CHAPTER OBJECTIVES

*The purposes of this chapter are to*

- Explain the double-entry accounting system
- Introduce the structure of the accounting system
- Explain how to analyze business transactions
- Explain how to enter transactions into the journals and ledgers

In today's modern world all larger businesses employ computer technology to process business transactions and to prepare financial statements. There is no human being with green eyeshades laboriously recording transactions into the system with pen and ink and manually processing all of the data to complete preparation of the financial statements. Once a human being enters a transaction into the system, the accounting software takes over and the computer does all of the work. However, in order for the accountant to properly interact with the computer—that is, tell it what to do—he or she must understand how the computer program processes the transactions and prepares the statement. To do so, the accountant must manually work though the accounting process, step by step, to gain a full understanding of what happens inside the computer. That is the purpose of this and the next chapter. If you are not interested in the mechanics of accounting, you could perhaps skip this chapter; however, if you were to do so, you would have difficulty later in understanding and making necessary journal entries. Therefore, it is strongly suggested that you *do* read this chapter.

# The Double-Entry Accounting System

The double-entry accounting system is based on the **dual entity concept** discussed in Chapter 2, which states that a business transaction must be recorded in at least two different accounts of the financial accounting system. A double entry is really an internal control to assure that the two or more affected accounts are always changed as required by the transaction and that the accounts are always in balance. But how does this work? Up to this point, when a transaction occurred, we simply stated how much each of the affected accounts was increased or decreased. However, the procedure is a little more complex than this. Actually, the double-entry accounting system uses debits and credits to effect changes in the accounts. Thus, an understanding of debits and credits work is essential, as we will be using them throughout the remainder of this book. But first, a basic familiarity with the components of the accounting system is in order: the general ledger, T-accounts, and the general journal.

## The General Ledger

The **general ledger** is a collection of accounts that form the major accounting records of a business that uses the double-entry accounting system. It is sometimes referred to as a *chart of accounts*, as each account is numbered in the sequence in which it occurs on the financial statements. Assets are listed in order of liquidity, and liabilities are listed in order of when they are due to be liquidated (the nearest to be liquidated is listed first). There is an account for each record of assets, liabilities, and stockholders' equity. All balance sheet accounts are permanent accounts, because they are *not* closed out at the end of an accounting period. All revenue, expenses, and dividend accounts are *temporary* accounts, because they are closed to retained earnings at the end of the period.

An account in the general ledger is traditionally known as a *T-account* because it has a space for a debit on its left side and space for a credit on its right side. In other words, in a double-entry system, *debit* simply means the left side of an account and *credit* means the right side of the account:

**Accounts Receivable**

| Debit | Credit |
|-------|--------|

While the account is often referred to and shaped like a *T*, it frequently has different formats. For example, an alternative format of accounts receivable would look like the one in Exhibit 4.1.

This format has the advantage of containing a lot of information and allows for a running balance.

**EXHIBIT 4.1**  Alternate Account Format in the General Ledger

**Accounts Receivable**

| Date | Ref. | Debit | Credit | Balance |
|------|------|-------|--------|---------|
|      |      |       |        |         |

Next, let's examine how debits and credits affect the accounts in the general ledger.

## Rules of Debits and Credits

The rules of debits and credits are based on the accounting equation (Assets = Liabilities + Stockholders' Equity). Based on the double-entry book-keeping system, the left side of the account must equal the right side of each account. Further, the total of all the accounts on the left side of the accounting equation must equal the total of all the accounts on the right side. To record changes to an account based on a business transaction, one must debit or credit that account. If the account is on the left side of the accounting equation (i.e., it is an asset account), all debits *increase* that account and all credits *decrease* the account. If the account is on the right side of the accounting equation (i.e., it is a liability or stockholders' equity account), all debits *decrease* that account and all credits *increase* that account.

What about revenue, expense, and dividend accounts? These accounts are called *temporary accounts* in that they are used during the period to collect revenues, expenses, or dividends and are closed out at the end of the period to retained earnings. (This topic will be discussed in more detail in Chapter 5.) These temporary accounts can be thought of as subsidiary accounts to retained earnings. That is, revenue accounts act like retained earnings for the rules of debits and credits: an increase to a revenue account requires a credit, and a decrease requires a debit. Likewise, because expenses offset revenues, an increase to an expense account or a dividend account requires a debit, and a decrease requires a credit.

The rules of debits and credits are summarized in Exhibit 4.2.

**EXHIBIT 4.2**   Summary of the Rules of Debits and Credits

- Asset accounts are increased by debits and decreased by credits.
- Liability accounts are increased by credits and decreased by debits.
- Equity accounts are increased by credits and decreased by debits.
- Revenue accounts are increased by credits and decreased by debits.
- Expense accounts are increased by debits and decreased by credits.
- Dividend accounts are increased by debits and decreased by credits

The following are two transactions to illustrate the rules of debits and credits and how they are entered into the accounts.

**Transaction 1.**  A new company sells $200,000 of common stock and deposits the proceeds into the bank. The transaction requires a debit (increase) in Cash of $200,000 and a credit (increase) in Common Stock of $200,000. The transactions would be posted to the account as shown below:

| Cash | | Common Stock | |
|---|---|---|---|
| 200,000 | | | 200,000 |

Note that the accounting equation is in balance:

$$\text{Assets} = \text{Liabilities} + \text{Stockholders' Equity}$$

$$\$200,000 = \$0 + \$200,000$$

**Transaction 2.**  The same company purchases $10,000 worth of equipment and pays cash. The transaction requires a debit (increase) in the equipment account and a credit (decrease) in the cash account. The transaction would be posted to the accounts as shown below with the resulting balance.

| Cash | | Equipment | | Common Stock | |
|---|---|---|---|---|---|
| 200,000 | | 10,000 | | | 200,000 |
| Bal. 190,000 | 10,000 | | | | |

Note that the accounting equation is still in balance:

$$\text{Assets} = \text{Liabilities} + \text{Stockholders' Equity}$$

$$(\$190,000 + 10,000) = \$0 + \$200,000$$

A summary of the account relationships in the general ledger is shown in Exhibit 4.3.

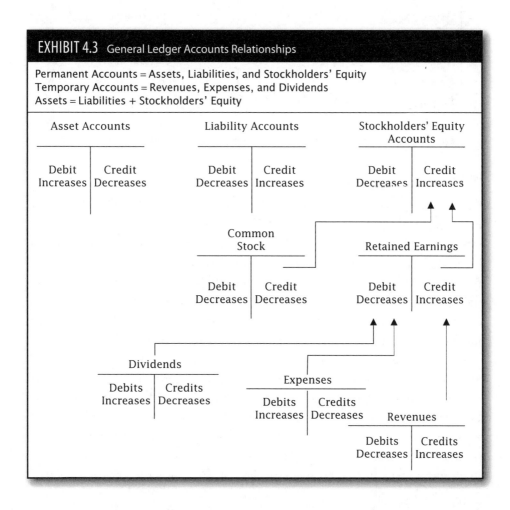

**EXHIBIT 4.3**  General Ledger Accounts Relationships

Permanent Accounts = Assets, Liabilities, and Stockholders' Equity
Temporary Accounts = Revenues, Expenses, and Dividends
Assets = Liabilities + Stockholders' Equity

## Normal Account Balances

Another feature of each account is what is called a *normal balance*. Using the accounting equation (Assets = Liabilities + Stockholders' Equity), the normal balance of each account is shown in Exhibit 4.4. The normal balances in Exhibit 4.4 are stated as such because the double entity concept requires that the carrying balances in all accounts on one side of the accounting equation must equal or balance the balances in all accounts on the other side of the accounting equation. That is, if the total of all Asset debit balances is $100,000, then the total of all of the Liability plus the Stockholders' Equity account credit balances on the right side of the equation must be $100,000.

| EXHIBIT 4.4  Normal Balances of Asset, Liability, and Stockholders' Accounts ||
| --- | --- |
| **Type of Account** | **Normal Balance** |
| Asset | Debit balance |
| Liability | Credit balance |
| Stockholders' Equity | Credit balance |
| Revenue | Credit balance |
| Expense | Debit balance |
| Dividend | Debit balance |

## The General Journal

The **general journal** is often referred to as the *book of original entry into the accounting system*; that is, it is the first point where all business transactions are entered into the accounting records. The term "general" is used because it is not a specialized journal, such as a sales journal. All transactions that are not entered into special journals are entered into the general journal. In the previous example of the rules of debits and credits, we entered transactions directly into each account, because doing so provided a clear illustration of how debits and credits operate. In actuality, however, all transactions first are entered into a journal.

Why is a journal needed in addition to an account? A journal is needed because it enters transactions into the system in chronological order and the journal allows for an explanation of the transaction just below the entry. The former is a significant advantage. If an accountant were looking for a particular transaction, he or she would have difficulty finding it among all the transactions in the many accounts maintained by a large company. He or she would find it much more easily in the journal, especially if the date were known. A typical format of a general journal is illustrated in Exhibit 4.5. Illustrative entries are included in Exhibit 4.6.

The Date column in Exhibit 4.5 reflects the date of the business transaction. The names of the accounts that are debited and credited are shown in the

**EXHIBIT 4.5** The General Journal

| Date | Account Title | Acct. No. | Debit | Credit |
|------|---------------|-----------|-------|--------|

Account Title column. All debit entries for a particular transaction are recorded first in the Debit column, then the credit entries for that transaction follows immediately after the debit entries. In other words, the account(s) that is credited is always listed after the last debit entry, in case of multiple debit entries, and indented. (See transaction number two in the illustration below.) The account number is the number of the account as specified in the chart of accounts. The dollar sign is never used in journals, accounts, trial balances, and worksheets.

### More Information about Journals and Accounts: Journalizing vs. Posting

In accounting terminology when a business transaction is entered into a journal, it is *journalized*. When the entry is transferred to an individual account, it is *posted*. Remember that in a computerized environment the computer does all of this after the data is entered.

### An Illustration of Analyzing and Journalizing Transactions

Assume the following transactions:

1. On January 2, 2xxx, a new company was started, and $100,000 of common stock was sold to the public for cash.

2. On January 12, 2xxx, office furniture was purchased for $10,000, and computers for $1,000 were purchased on account.

3. On January 15, 2xxx, the company had $5,000 revenue on account.

t4. On January 16, 2xxx, the company paid one year's rent in advance, for $21,000.

**Required**: Journalize the above transactions into the general journal.

| EXHIBIT 4.6  The General Journal | | | | |
|---|---|---|---|---|
| **Date** | **Account Title** | **Acct. No.** | **Debit** | **Credit** |
| Jan. 2, 2xxx | Cash | 1 | 100,000 | |
| | Common Stock | 30 | | 100,000 |
| | Sold 1,000 shares of stock | | | |
| Jan. 12, 2xxx | Office Furniture | 6 | 10,000 | |
| | Computer Equipment | 7 | 1,000 | |
| | Accounts Payable | 20 | | 11,000 |
| | Purchased office furniture and computers | | | |
| Jan. 15, 2xxx | Accounts Receivable | 2 | 5,000 | |
| | Sales Revenue | 40 | | 5,000 |
| | Recorded sales revenue | | | |
| Jan. 16, 2xxx | Prepaid Rent | 3 | 21,000 | |
| | Cash | 1 | | 21,000 |
| | Prepaid rent one year in advance | | | |

Exhibit 4.6 shows how the transactions are entered into the journal. The following is an explanation of the analysis of each entry:

1. The Cash account is debited because a debit increases an asset account. The Common Stock account is credited, since a credit increases a stockholders' equity account.

2. The Office Furniture and Computer Equipment accounts are debited because a debit increases an asset account. The Accounts Payable account is credited since a credit increases a liability account. Note that the two debit entries are listed first.

3. The Accounts Receivable account is debited because a debit increases an asset account. Sales Revenue (a temporary account) is credited since a credit increases a stockholders' equity account. (Note that a revenue account acts like a subsidiary account of the stockholders' equity section during the accounting year but is closed out before the balance sheet is prepared.)

4. The Prepaid Rent account is an asset account because the rent was paid in advance and has not been used up. Thus, being an asset account, it is

debited to increase its balance. The Cash account is credited because a credit decreases an asset account.

The next step is to post the transactions into the relevant accounts. The alternative account format is used for this purpose. The postings are made in Exhibits 4.7a through 4.7h. It is assumed that the journalizing of the transactions was on page 1.

### EXHIBIT 4.7a

| Cash | | | | Account No. 1 |
|------|------|---------|--------|---------|
| Date | Ref. | Debit | Credit | Balance |
| Jan. 2 | P. 1 | 100,000 | | 100,000 |
| Jan. 16 | P. 1 | | 21,000 | 79,000 |

### EXHIBIT 4.7b

| Accounts Receivable | | | | Account No. 2 |
|---------------------|------|-------|--------|---------|
| Date | Ref. | Debit | Credit | Balance |
| Jan. 15 | P. 1 | | 5,000 | 5,000 |

### EXHIBIT 4.7c

| Prepaid Rent | | | | Account No. 3 |
|--------------|------|-------|--------|---------|
| Date | Ref. | Debit | Credit | Balance |
| Jan. 16 | P. 1 | | 21,000 | 21,000 |

### EXHIBIT 4.7d

| Office Furniture | | | | Account No. 6 |
|------------------|------|--------|--------|---------|
| Date | Ref. | Debit | Credit | Balance |
| Jan. 12 | P. 1 | 10,000 | | 10,000 |

### EXHIBIT 4.7e

| Computer Equipment | | | | Account No. 7 |
|--------------------|------|-------|--------|---------|
| Date | Ref. | Debit | Credit | Balance |
| Jan. 12 | P. 1 | 1,000 | | 1,000 |

### EXHIBIT 4.7f

| Accounts Payable | | | | Account No. 20 |
|------------------|------|-------|--------|---------|
| Date | Ref. | Debit | Credit | Balance |
| Jan. 12 | P. 1 | | 11,000 | 11,000 |

### EXHIBIT 4.7g

| Common Stock | | | | Account No. 30 |
|--------------|------|-------|---------|---------|
| Date | Ref. | Debit | Credit | Balance |
| Jan. 2 | P. 1 | | 100,000 | 100,000 |

### EXHIBIT 4.7h

| Sales Revenue | | | | Account No. 40 |
|---------------|------|-------|--------|---------|
| Date | Ref. | Debit | Credit | Balance |
| Jan. 15 | P. 1 | | 5,000 | 5,000 |

The next step would be to take a trial balance. This will be covered in Chapter 5.

## QUIZ

1. (True or false?) A trial balance that balances means that the total of all debit account balances equals the total of all credit account balances.

2. (True or false?) The point of original entry into the accounting system is the general ledger.

3. (True or false?) A law firm receives an advance fee from a client. The firm's accountant would debit Cash and credit Earned Fees.

4. (True or false?) According to the rules of debits and credits, expense accounts are debited to increase the account balances.

5. (True or false?) The normal balance in the Accumulated Depreciation account would be a debit balance.

6. A prepaid expense is an expense that has been:
   A. Paid and incurred
   B. Incurred before it has been paid
   C. Paid before it has been incurred
   D. None of the above

7. Accounts that normally have credit balances are:
   A. Assets, Liabilities, and Shareholders' Equity
   B. Liabilities, Shareholders' Equity, and Revenues
   C. Liabilities, Shareholders' Equity, and Dividends
   D. Accumulated Depreciation, Liabilities, and Dividends

8. Which of the following statements is true?
   A. The journal is part of the general ledger.
   B. The specialized journals are part of the chart of accounts.
   C. Each account in the general journal has a page number.
   D. All transactions journalized in the general journal are then posted to an account in the general ledger.

9. Which of the following accounts normally has a debit balance?
   A. Dividends
   B. Assets
   C. Expense
   D. All of the above

10. **A retail store sells $100,000 of merchandise during a month on account that cost $60,000. Which of the following entries would the accountant make?**
    A. Debit Cost of Goods $60,000, and credit Inventory $60,000.
    B. Debit Accounts Receivable $100,000, and credit Inventory $100,000.
    C. Debit Accounts Receivable $100,000, credit Inventory $60,000, and credit Revenue $40,000.
    D. None of the above

11. **An advertising firm paid cash for a one-year building lease in advance. The correct journal entries would be:**
    A. Debit Prepaid Leases, and credit Cash.
    B. Debit Lease Expense, and credit Cash.
    C. Debit Prepaid Leases, and credit Accounts Payable.
    D. Debit Building, and credit Cash.

12. **The board of directors declared a dividend and paid it immediately to all stockholders. The correct entries would be:**
    A. Debit Dividend Expenses, and credit Cash.
    B. Debit Dividends, and credit Cash.
    C. Debit Dividends, and credit Dividends Payable.
    D. None of the above

13. **Which of the following statements is correct?**
    A. All accounts in the general ledger are numbered.
    B. When transactions are posted to an account, the journal page number is included.
    C. The general journal is often called the *book of original entry*.
    D. All of the above

14. **After a transaction is analyzed, the next likely step is:**
    A. Posting to an account in the general ledger
    B. Enter it into a worksheet
    C. Journalizing into the general journal
    D. None of the above

15. **An Internet company receives a cash payment for future ads to be included on its Web site. The correct journal entries would be:**
    A. Debit Cash, and credit Ad Revenue.
    B. Debit Cash, and credit Retained Earnings.
    C. Debit Cash, and credit Ad Revenue Received in Advance.
    D. Debit Accounts Receivable, and credit Ad Revenue Received in Advance.

# The Accounting Process: Preparation of the Worksheet, Adjusting and Closing Entries

*The purposes of this chapter are to*

- Define the accounting cycle
- Explain how to prepare the worksheet
- Explain how to take a trial balance
- Explain how to make adjusting entries
- Explain how to make closing entries

- Illustrate the accounting cycle
- Describe specialized journals

# The Accounting Cycle

In the last chapter, we examined the components of the accounting system, the rules of debits and credits that drives the system, and the ways transactions are entered into the general journal and posted to the general ledger. The latter steps are actually part of what is called the **accounting cycle.** The accounting cycle is a series of steps that the accountant goes through from the point that a business transaction occurs until the financial statements are prepared. A summary of these steps are listed below:

- **Step 1.** Identify a business transaction, which is found on a source document, such as an invoice. All transactions entered into the accounting system must have a supporting source document.
- **Step 2.** Analyze the transaction; that is, determine what amounts are to be journalized, which accounts are affected, and whether the accounts are to be debited or credited.
- **Step 3.** Journalize the transaction by recording it into the appropriate journal as a debit and credit.
- **Step 4.** Post the journal entries to the appropriate accounts in the general ledger.
- **Step 5.** Prepare a trail balance and a worksheet at the end of a period in which statements are to be prepared. Verify that the sum of debits equals the sum of credits.
- **Step 6.** Make adjusting entries to all appropriate accrual and deferred accounts onto the worksheet. These entries are then journalized and posted to the accounts.
- **Step 7.** Prepare and make closing entries to all temporary revenue and expenses accounts.
- **Step 8 (Optional).** Prepare an adjusted trial balance after the closing entries are made to determine if all debits and credits balance.
- **Step 9.** Prepare the financial statements.

Steps 1 through 4 were covered in the last chapter. We now turn to step 5, the preparation of a trial balance and the worksheet.

# The Trial Balance and the Worksheet

As the business progresses during a fiscal year, hundreds and perhaps even thousands of transactions may occur that are entered into the accounting system. At the end of the accounting period (usually at year-end), it is time to "close out the books." Several procedures take place at this time. First, the accountant prepares a worksheet, which includes a trial balance of all the accounts in the accounting system. A **trial balance** is simply a listing of the current balances of all accounts in the general ledger. A major purpose of the trial balance is to check that the total of all debits equals the total of all credits.

The trial balance is entered directly on the worksheet. The **worksheet** (see Exhibit 5.1) is a tool used by accountants to assemble all of the accounts (the trial balances) in the general ledger in one place in order to make any adjustments to the accounts prior to preparation of the financial statements. It starts with the unadjusted trial balance taken from the general ledger being placed in columns two and three (see Exhibit 5.1). Any required adjustments to entries for the appropriate accounts are entered into the next two columns.

**EXHIBIT 5.1** The XYZ Company Worksheet for the Year Ended December 31, 2xxx

| Account | Unadjusted Trial Balance | | Adjustments | | Income Statement | | Balance Sheet | |
|---|---|---|---|---|---|---|---|---|
| | Dr. | Cr. | Dr. | Cr. | Dr. | Cr. | Dr. | Cr. |
| | | | | | | | | |

## What Are Adjusting Entries?

**Adjusting entries** are made at the end of the accounting period in order to allocate revenue and expenses to the proper accounting period using the revenue recognition and matching principles (see Chapter 2). As mentioned, most companies use the accrual basis of accounting, which means that all revenue is recognized when it is earned regardless of when the cash is received. This is based on the realization principle. Likewise, all expenses are recognized when they are incurred in generating the revenue earned. This is based on the matching principle. This gives rise to accruals and deferrals that were discussed in Chapter 2. At the end of the accounting period, the accruals and deferrals must be adjusted as needed and entered on the worksheet.

Finally, the adjusted balances are transferred to the appropriate columns on the income statement or balance sheet. Some accountants may insert an additional set of columns after the adjustments columns and include the adjusted trial balances to check that debits equal credits prior to entering the balances into the appropriate financial statement column. The totals in the income statement and balance sheet accounts are the preliminary financial statements.

The **worksheet** is an informal document that is not considered a permanent part of the accounting records but nevertheless is a very useful tool for preparing the financial statements. All adjustments in the adjustments columns must be journalized to become part of the accounting records. As stated earlier, a computer program will prepare the worksheet internally and the accountant then decides which accounts require adjustments and makes the input entries. Then the computer program prepares the financial statements.

### What Are Closing Entries?

*Closing entries* are journal entries necessary to close out the temporary Revenue, Expense, and Dividend accounts to Retained Earnings, which is a permanent account.

The final step is to close out all of the temporary revenue and expenses accounts to an account labeled Income Summary, and this account is then closed out to Retained Earnings. All of these entries must be journalized. At this point some companies may prepare a post-closing trial balance.

## An Extended Illustration of the Accounting Cycle

The Glitzy Magazine Company was established on January 1, 2xxx. The following are transactions that occurred during the first month of its operation. At the end of the month, management directed that financial statements be prepared so that they could assess how well the company had performed in its first month of operation.

### Transactions

1. On January 2, Glitzy sold 10,000 shares of common stock at a par value of $100 each.

2. On January 3, a building was rented at $5,000 per month and two month's rent was paid in advance.

3. On January 4, printing presses were purchased for $100,000, and a five-year note was signed for the balance. The terms of the note were 6 percent per annum, to be paid at the end of each year along with $20,000 on the principal. The equipment is to be depreciated evenly over 10 years, with an estimated $5,000 remaining value at the end of 10 years.

4. On January 5, office furniture was purchased for $30,000, and cash was paid. The office furniture is to be depreciated evenly over 10 years, with a $2,000 salvage value at the end of 10 years.

5. On January 7, the company purchased $1,000 in office supplies on account. It was assumed that they would be used up within one month; therefore, they were immediately written off as an expense.

6. On January 10, the company purchased property insurance on all equipment for $5,000 remaining value per year, paid in advance.

7. On January 14, the company purchased $10,000 worth of paper on account, to be used in printing the magazines. The paper was used up in January.

8. On January 15, the company paid its first payroll of $19,000. The company pays $19,000 for salaries twice each month. The payroll is made on the fifteenth of the month and on the first day of the following month.

9. On January 15, the company received $50,000 in one-year subscriptions, paid in advance by subscribers.

10. On January 25, the company received $30,000 in advertising revenue for its first issue, to take place on February 15.

**Required.** Following the steps in the accounting cycle, prepare the financial statements required by management.

## Solution

- **Steps 1 to 3.** The transactions are analyzed and recorded in the journal (see Exhibit 5.2). They are recorded in sequence by date.

- **Step 4.** The journal entries are posted in journal sequence into the following ledger accounts. All transactions were on page 1 of the general journal (see Exhibits 5.3a through 5.3m). The accounts are in account sequence.

**EXHIBIT 5.2**   The Glitzy Magazine Company General Journal

| Date | Account Title | Account No. | Debit | Credit |
|------|---------------|-------------|-------|--------|
| Jan. 2, 2xxx | Cash | 10 | 1,000,000 | |
| | Common Stock | 60 | | 1,000,000 |
| | (10,000 shares of common sold at $100 par value.) | | | |
| Jan. 3 | Prepaid Rent | 30 | 10,000 | |
| | Cash | 10 | | 10,000 |
| | (Two months of rent were paid in advance.) | | | |
| Jan. 4 | Printing Equipment | 40 | 100,000 | |
| | Notes Payable | 51 | | 100,000 |
| | (Printing presses purchased using 5-year note.) | | | |
| Jan. 5 | Office Furniture | 41 | 30,000 | |
| | Cash | 10 | | 30,000 |
| | (Office furniture was purchased for cash.) | | | |
| Jan. 7 | Office Supplies Expense | 80 | 1,000 | |
| | Accounts Payable | 50 | | 1,000 |
| | (Office supplies purchased on account.) | | | |
| Jan. 10 | Prepaid Property Insurance | 31 | 5,000 | |
| | Cash | 10 | | 5,000 |
| | (Purchased insurance on printing and office equipment, paid in advance.) | | | |
| Jan. 14 | Paper Expense | 81 | 10,000 | |
| | Accounts Payable | 50 | | 10,000 |
| | (Printing paper purchased and used on account.) | | | |
| Jan. 15 | Salaries Expense | 82 | 19,000 | |
| | Cash | 10 | | 19,000 |
| | (Payroll was made for mid-month.) | | | |
| Jan. 15 | Cash | 10 | 50,000 | |
| | Unearned Subscriptions Revenue | 70 | | 50,000 |
| Jan. 25 | Cash | 10 | 30,000 | |
| | Unearned Advertising Revenue | 71 | | 30,000 |

## EXHIBIT 5.3a

| Cash | | | | Account No. 10 |
|---|---|---|---|---|
| Date | Ref. | Debit | Credit | Balance |
| Jan. 2 | P. 1 | 1,000,000 | | 1,000,000 |
| Jan. 3 | P. 1 | | 10,000 | 990,000 |
| Jan. 5 | P. 1 | | 30,000 | 960,000 |
| Jan. 10 | P. 1 | | 5,000 | 955,000 |
| Jan. 15 | P. 1 | | 19,000 | 936,000 |
| Jan. 15 | P. 1 | 50,000 | | 986,000 |
| Jan. 25 | P. 1 | 30,000 | | 1,016,000 |

## EXHIBIT 5.3b

| Prepaid Rent | | | | Account No. 30 |
|---|---|---|---|---|
| Date | Ref. | Debit | Credit | Balance |
| Jan. 3 | P. 1 | 10,000 | | 10,000 |

## EXHIBIT 5.3c

| Prepaid Property Insurance | | | | Account No. 31 |
|---|---|---|---|---|
| Date | Ref. | Debit | Credit | Balance |
| Jan. 10 | P. 1 | 5,000 | | 5,000 |

## EXHIBIT 5.3d

| Printing Equipment | | | | Account No. 40 |
|---|---|---|---|---|
| Date | Ref. | Debit | Credit | Balance |
| Jan. 4 | P. 1 | 100,000 | | 100,000 |

## EXHIBIT 5.3e

| Office Furniture | | | | Account No. 41 |
|---|---|---|---|---|
| Date | Ref. | Debit | Credit | Balance |
| Jan. 5 | P. 1 | 30,000 | | 30,000 |

## EXHIBIT 5.3f

| Accounts Payable | | | | Account No. 50 |
|---|---|---|---|---|
| Date | Ref. | Debit | Credit | Balance |
| Jan. 7 | P. 1 | | 1,000 | 1,000 |
| Jan. 14 | P. 1 | | 10,000 | 11,000 |

## EXHIBIT 5.3g

| Notes Payable | | | | Account No. 51 |
|---|---|---|---|---|
| Date | Ref. | Debit | Credit | Balance |
| Jan. 4 | P. 1 | | 100,000 | 100,000 |

## EXHIBIT 5.3h

| Common Stock | | | | Account No. 60 |
|---|---|---|---|---|
| Date | Ref. | Debit | Credit | Balance |
| Jan. 2 | P. 1 | | 1,000,000 | 1,000,000 |

**EXHIBIT 5.3i**

| Unearned Subscriptions Revenue | | | Account No. 70 | |
|---|---|---|---|---|
| Date | Ref. | Debit | Credit | Balance |
| Jan. 15 | P. 1 | | 50,000 | 50,000 |

**EXHIBIT 5.3j**

| Unearned Advertising Revenue | | | Account No. 71 | |
|---|---|---|---|---|
| Date | Ref. | Debit | Credit | Balance |
| Jan. 25 | P. 1 | | 30,000 | 30,000 |

**EXHIBIT 5.3k**

| Office Supplied Expense | | | Account No. 80 | |
|---|---|---|---|---|
| Date | Ref. | Debit | Credit | Balance |
| Jan. 7 | P. 1 | 1,000 | | 1,000 |

**EXHIBIT 5.3l**

| Paper Expense | | | Account No. 81 | |
|---|---|---|---|---|
| Date | Ref. | Debit | Credit | Balance |
| Jan. 14 | P. 1 | 10,000 | | 10,000 |

**EXHIBIT 5.3m**

| Salaries Expense | | | Account No. 82 | |
|---|---|---|---|---|
| Date | Ref. | Debit | Credit | Balance |
| Jan. 54 | P. 1 | 19,000 | | 19,000 |

- **Step 5.** Prepare the worksheet (Exhibit 5.4). (See step 6 for explanations of adjustments.)
- **Step 6.** Journalize adjusting entries:

| a. | Jan. 31 | Rent Expense | 5,000 | |
|---|---|---|---|---|
| | | Prepaid Rent | | 5,000 |

One month's rent was recognized: $\left( \dfrac{10,000}{2} \right) = 5,000.$

**EXHIBIT 5.4** The Glitzy Magazine Company Worksheet for the Month Ended January 31, 2xxx

| Account | Trial Balance | | Adjustments | | Income Statement | | Balance Sheet | |
|---|---|---|---|---|---|---|---|---|
| | Dr. | Cr. | Dr. | Cr. | Dr. | Cr. | Dr. | Cr. |
| Cash | 1,016,000 | | | | | | 1,016,000 | |
| Prepaid Rent | 10,000 | | | (a) 5,000 | | | 5,000 | |
| Prepaid Property Ins. | 5,000 | | | (b) 274 | | | 4,726 | |
| Printing Equipment | 100,000 | | | | | | 100,000 | |
| Accumulated Depreciation—Printing Equipment | | | | (c) 792 | | | | (g) 792 |
| Office Furniture | 30,000 | | | | | | 30,000 | |
| Accumulated Depreciation—Office Furniture | | | | (d) 233 | | | | (g) 233 |
| Accounts Payable | | 11,000 | | | | | | 11,000 |
| Wages Payable | | | | (e) 19,000 | | | | 19,000 |
| Notes Payable | | 100,000 | | | | | | 100,000 |
| Common Stock | | 1,000,000 | | | | | | 1,000,000 |

(Continued)

**EXHIBIT 5.4** *(continued)* The Glitzy Magazine Company Worksheet for the Month Ended January 31, 2xxx

| Account | Trial Balance Dr. | Trial Balance Cr. | Adjustments Dr. | Adjustments Cr. | Income Statement Dr. | Income Statement Cr. | Balance Sheet Dr. | Balance Sheet Cr. |
|---|---|---|---|---|---|---|---|---|
| Unearned Subscriptions Revenue | | 50,000 | | | | | | 50,000 |
| Unearned Advertising Revenue | | 30,000 | | | | | | 30,000 |
| Office Supplies Expense | 1,000 | | | | 1,000 | | | |
| Paper Expense | 10,000 | | | | 10,000 | | | |
| Salaries Expense | 19,000 | | (e) 19,000 | | 38,000 | | | |
| Rent Expense | | | (a) 5,000 | | 5,000 | | | |
| Insurance Expense | | | (b) 274 | | 274 | | | |
| Depreciation Expense | | | (c) 792 (d) 233 | | 1,025 | | | |
| Interest Expense | | | (f) 100 | | 100 | | | |
| Net Loss | | | | | | 55,399 | 55,399 | |
| Totals | 1,191,000 | 1,191,000 | 25,299 | 25,299 | 55,399 | 55,399 | 1,211,125 | 1,211,125 |

| b. | Jan. 31 | Insurance Expense | 274 | |
| | | Prepaid Insurance | | 274 |

Twenty days of insurance was recognized: $\dfrac{20}{365} \times 5{,}000 = 274$.

| c. | Jan. 31 | Depreciation Expense | 792 | |
| | | Accumulated Depreciation— Printing Equip. | | 792 |

Assume one month's depreciation of printing equipment:

$$\left(\frac{100{,}000 - 5{,}000}{10}\right) = 9{,}500 \text{ for one year's depreciation.}$$

(Original cost less salvage value divided by 10 years = $9,500) 1/12 × 9,500 = 792 one month's depreciation.

| d. | Jan. 31 | Depreciation Expense | 233 | |
| | | Accumulated Depreciation— Office Furn. | | 233 |

Assume one month's depreciation of office furniture:

$$\left(\frac{30{,}000 - 2{,}000}{10}\right) = \$2{,}800 \text{ for one year's depreciation.}$$

(Original cost less salvage divided by 10 years = $2,800) (1/12 × 2,800 = 233 one month's depreciation.)

| e. | Jan. 31 | Salaries Expense | 19,000 | |
| | | Salaries Payable | | 19,000 |

Second half of January salaries are recognized.

| f. | Jan. 31 | Interest Expense | 100 | |
| | | Interest Payable | | 100 |

$$\text{Interest Accrued for one month: } 100,000 \times .06 \times \frac{1}{60} = \$100$$

g. Note that no revenue was recognized since both subscription and advertising will not be recognized until February, when the first issue is mailed to subscribers.

h. Note that the accumulated depreciation is a credit balance account and is called an *asset offset* or *contra-asset* account. It will be deducted from the original cost of the asset on the balance sheet to give a net book value of the asset.

i. Assume that all of the above journal entries were posted to the relevant accounts.

- **Step 7.** Prepare closing entries.

Making closing entries requires the temporary revenue and expenses accounts to be closed to an account called *Income Summary* (which is another temporary account). To close the expense accounts (a debit balance account), simply credit each account by the amount of the final balance and debit the Income Summary account. To close revenue accounts (a credit balance account), do the opposite. After all of the revenue and expense accounts have been closed to the Income Summary account, the Income Summary account is closed to Retained Earnings. The result of the process is that all of the temporary accounts have a zero balance. Net income (in the previous example, a net loss) has been closed to Retained Earnings.

In our example, assume that the balances in the temporary accounts are the amounts shown in the Income Statement columns of the worksheet. The following are the closing entries for Glitzy Magazine Company at the end of January 31, 2xxx. (In actuality, the books would not be closed until the end of the year. However, we are closing the books for illustration purposes.)

| | | | | |
|---|---|---|---|---|
| a. | Jan. 31 | Income Summary Expense | 1,000 | |
| | | Office Supplies Expense | | 1,000 |

| | | | | |
|---|---|---|---|---|
| b. | Jan. 31 | Income Summary | 10,000 | |
| | | Paper Expenses | | 10,000 |

c.

| Jan. 31 | Income Summary | 38,000 | |
|---|---|---|---|
| | Salaries Expenses | | 38,000 |

d.

| Jan. 31 | Income Summary | 5,000 | |
|---|---|---|---|
| | Rent Expense | | 5,000 |

e.

| Jan. 31 | Income Summary | 274 | |
|---|---|---|---|
| | Insurance Expense | | 274 |

f.

| Jan. 31 | Income Summary | 1,025 | |
|---|---|---|---|
| | Depreciation Expense | | 1,025 |

g.

| Jan. 31 | Income Summary | 100 | |
|---|---|---|---|
| | Interest Expense | | 100 |

At this point the balance in the Income Summary account would be as shown in Exhibit 5.5. (It is assumed that the previous credit entries were made to the appropriate expense accounts and the related debit entries were made to the account shown in Exhibit 5.5.)

## EXHIBIT 5.5

| Income Summary Account | | | | Account No. 90 |
|---|---|---|---|---|
| Date | Ref. | Debit | Credit | Balance |
| Jan. 31 | P. 2 | 1,000 | | 1,000 |
| Jan. 31 | P. 2 | 10,000 | | 11,000 |
| Jan. 31 | P. 2 | 38,000 | | 49,000 |
| Jan. 31 | P. 2 | 5,000 | | 54,000 |
| Jan. 31 | P. 2 | 274 | | 54,274 |
| Jan. 31 | P. 2 | 1,025 | | 55,299 |
| Jan. 31 | P. 2 | 100 | | 55,399 |

At this point, the Income Summary account would be closed to Retained Earnings with the following entry.

| Jan. 31 | Retained Earnings | 55,399 | |
|---------|-------------------|--------|--------|
| | Income Summary | | 55,399 |

Note that the Retained Earnings account will have a $55,399 debit balance because of the loss, since no revenue could be recognized at this point in time. A debit balance in what is normally a credit balance account may seem unusual. However, since this is a start-up company, it is not uncommon for such a company to have a negative (debit) balance in Retained Earnings for several years until the company reaches profitability.

- **Step 8.** Prepare a post-closing trial balance.

    Some companies will complete this step, others will not, as the worksheet in effect has the post-closing trial balances. The one exception is the Retained Earnings account, which can be determined after the Income Summary is closed. For purposes of this illustration this step is skipped.

- **Step 9.** Prepare the financial statements.

    The income statement for Glitzy Magazine Company is shown in Exhibit 5.6.

**EXHIBIT 5.6** Glitzy Magazine Company Income Statement for the Period January 1–31, 2xxx

| | | |
|---|---|---|
| Subscription Revenue | | $0.00 |
| Advertising Revenue | | 0.00 |
| Total Revenue | | $0.00 |
| Less: Expenses | | |
| Office Supplies | $1,000 | |
| Magazine Paper | 10,000 | |
| Salaries | 38,000 | |
| Rent | 5,000 | |
| Insurance | 274 | |
| Interest | 100 | |
| Depreciation of Equipment | 1,025 | |
| Total Expenses | | 55,399 |
| Net Loss | | ($55,399) |

The balance sheet for Glitzy Magazine is shown in Exhibit 5.7.

| EXHIBIT 5.7   Glitzy Magazine Company Balance Sheet January 31, 2xxx | |
| --- | --- |
| **Assets** | |
| Current Assets | |
| Cash | $1,016,000 |
| Prepaid Rent | 5,000 |
| Prepaid Property Insurance | 4,726 |
| Total Current Assets | $1,025,726 |
| Property, Plant, and Equipment | 130,000 |
| Less: Accumulated Depreciation | 1,025 |
| Plant Property and Equipment, Net | $128,975 |
| Total Assets | $1,154,701 |
| **Liabilities** | |
| Current Liabilities | |
| Accounts Payable | $11,000 |
| Wages Payable | 19,000 |
| Interest Payable | 100 |
| Notes Payable | 100,000 |
| Unearned Subscriptions Revenue | 50,000 |
| Unearned Advertising Revenue | 30,000 |
| Total Current Liabilities | $210,100 |
| **Stockholders' Equity** | |
| Common Stock | $1,000,000 |
| Retained Earnings | (55,399) |
| Total Stockholders' Equity | $944,601 |
| Total Liabilities and Stockholders' Equity | $1,154,701 |

# Specialized Journals

Up to this point it has been assumed that all transactions are journalized into the general journal. However, in larger companies where there are thousands of transactions such an approach would be very inefficient. For example, think about a vendor that sells products to three hundred customers. If there were only one sale per month to each of these customers, the number of individual transactions journalized in the general journal and posted to the accounts receivable account would be voluminous. To streamline the accounting process, all companies use specialized (special) journals to record repetitive transactions. The most common of these journals are sales journals, purchases journals, cash receipts journals, and cash disbursement journals. All other transactions that do not fit in or relate to these special journals are recorded in the general journal.

In addition to specialized journals, businesses use subsidiary accounts that are tied to an overall control account in the general ledger. For example, each business would want a record of, and track the history of, individual customer sales. Therefore, companies will have—in addition to the Accounts Receivable Control account—a subsidiary account for each customer. The total of all subsidiary customer accounts must equal the Accounts Receivable Control account total. Other control subsidiary account relationships exist in the accounting system.

To summarize the journal and ledger accounts relationships: transactions are first recorded into a specialized or the general journal; then they are posted to a ledger account (usually a control account) periodically, and finally, if appropriate, they are posted to a subsidiary account daily. With modern computer technology, all of these recordings can be done on a daily basis or even on a real-time basis.

The four major journals are discussed in the following sections.

## Sales Journal

The simplest form of a sales journal would look like that in Exhibit 5.8.

**EXHIBIT 5.8**  Sales Journal

| Date | Invoice Number | Customer Name | Ref. | Amount A/R Dr. Sales Cr. |
|---|---|---|---|---|
|  |  |  |  |  |
|  |  |  |  |  |

The totals of the last column would be debited to the Accounts Receivable Control account periodically with each transaction being posted to the individual customer subsidiary account daily. The total of the last column would also be posted to the sales account periodically.

In larger companies, more information would be entered into the sales journal. Exhibit 5.9 is an example of what electronics retail businesses might want recorded.

| EXHIBIT 5.9   Sales Journal | | | | | | | |
|---|---|---|---|---|---|---|---|
| Date | Invoice Number | Customer Name | Ref. | Dr. A/R | Cr. Computer Sales | Cr. TV Sales | Cr. Electronic Sales |
| | | | | | | | |
| | | | | | | | |

The individual customer transactions would be posted to the subsidiary customer accounts daily. The total of the Accounts Receivable column and the Sales columns would be posted periodically but at least by the end of an accounting period. Further, a company would break out the number of sales columns necessary to provide sales information needed. Finally, the totals of all of the credit columns must equal the total of the Accounts Receivable debit.

## Purchases Journal

All credit purchases are recorded in the purchases journal. Cash purchases would be recorded in the cash disbursements journal below. Exhibit 5.10 is an example of a purchases journal.

| EXHIBIT 5.10   Purchases Journal | | | | | | | |
|---|---|---|---|---|---|---|---|
| Date | Invoice Number | Vendor Name | Ref. | Dr. Inventory Purchases | Dr. Supplies | Dr. Equipment | Cr. Accounts Payable |
| | | | | | | | |
| | | | | | | | |

In addition to the Accounts Payable Control account, a company would have a subsidiary ledger of each individual vendor's account to record all transactions daily. Each subsidiary ledger would have the date, invoice number, terms of the purchase, and a running balance. Purchases on the subsidiary ledger would be done daily.

Totals of each debit account column and the totals of the Accounts Payable column would be posted periodically but at least by the end of the accounting period.

## Cash Receipts Journal

Only cash receipts would be recorded in the cash receipts journal. Exhibit 5.11 is an example of a cash receipts journal.

**EXHIBIT 5.11** Cash Receipts Journal

| Date | Customer Name | Ref. | Dr. Cash Received | Dr. Sales Discounts | Cr. A/R | Cr. Sales |
|------|---------------|------|-------------------|---------------------|---------|-----------|
|      |               |      |                   |                     |         |           |
|      |               |      |                   |                     |         |           |

The totals of each column would be posted to the respective general ledger accounts periodically. In addition, each customer's subsidiary account related to the Accounts Receivable Control account would be posted to daily. Additional columns could be added to the cash receipts journal as needed.

## Cash Disbursements Journal

Cash payments would be recorded in the cash disbursements journal, including cash purchases. Exhibit 5.12 is an example of a cash disbursements journal.

**EXHIBIT 5.12** Cash Disbursements Journal

| Date | Check Number | Ref | Dr. Account Name | Dr. Accounts Payable | Cr. Purchases Discount | Cr. Cash |
|------|--------------|-----|------------------|----------------------|------------------------|----------|
|      |              |     |                  |                      |                        |          |
|      |              |     |                  |                      |                        |          |

Each transaction would have a check number recorded in the second column. Individual accounts that had cash purchases would be listed in column four (e.g., Supplies and Insurance). Credit purchases would be recorded in the purchases journal, discussed previously. The total of the Accounts Payable, Purchases Discounts, and Cash accounts would be recorded in the ledger accounts periodically. In addition, individual vendor accounts in the accounts payable subsidiary ledger would be posted daily.

## QUIZ

1. (True or false?) Accountants prepare an unadjusted trial balance at the end of an accounting period, which is useful in preparing financial statements.

2. (True or false?) Dollar signs are entered in the journal when transactions are journalized.

3. (True or false?) The first step in the accounting cycle is to record a transaction in the general ledger.

4. (True or false?) A trial balance is simply a listing of the current balances of all accounts in the general ledger.

5. (True or false?) A deferred income account would never require an adjustment at the end of the accounting period.

6. The purpose of the closing process in the accounting cycle is to:
   A. Close out the permanent account balances
   B. Record the necessary end of the accounting year adjusting entries
   C. Close the revenue and expense accounts to the Income Summary account
   D. None of the above

Use the following information for questions 7 through 9: The board of directors declares a dividend on December 1, which is payable on February 1. The company closes its books on December 31.

7. What would be the entries on December 1, assuming that the company uses a dividend account?
   A. A debit to Retained Earnings and a credit to Dividends Payable
   B. A debit to Dividends and a credit to Dividends Payable
   C. A debit to Dividends and a credit to Accounts Payable
   D. None of the above

8. On December 31 what would be the closing entry?
   A. A debit to Retained Earnings and a credit to Dividends
   B. A debit to Dividends Payable and a credit to Dividends
   C. A debit to Income Summary and a credit to Dividends
   D. None of the above

9. **On February 1 what would be the entry when the dividends are paid?**
   A. A debit to Dividends Payable and a credit to Dividends
   B. A debit to Retained Earnings and a credit to Cash
   C. A debit to Retained Earnings and a credit to Dividends
   D. A debit to Dividends Payable and a credit to cash

10. **On September 1, a company signed a one-year note for $10,000 at a 6 percent interest rate. What would be the adjusting entry on December 31, the end of the accounting period?**
    A. A debit to Interest Expense for $200 and a credit to Interest Payable for the same amount
    B. A debit to Interest Payable for $200 and a credit to Cash for the same amount
    C. A debit to Interest Expense for $600 and a credit to Cash for the same amount
    D. None of the above

11. **On December 1 a building management company received $40,000 of rent in advance for a large building. The term of the rental contract is one year. What would be the entry on December 1?**
    A. Debit Cash for $40,000, and credit Rent Payable for the same amount.
    B. Debit Unearned Rental Income for $40,000, and credit Rent Payable for the same amount.
    C. Debit Cash for $40,000, and credit Unearned Rental Income for the same amount.
    D. None of the above

12. **On its post-adjusted trial balance, assume that a company had a balance of $10,000 in Notes Receivable. What closing entry would be made?**
    A. Debit to Income Summary for $10,000, and credit Notes Receivable for the same amount.
    B. There is no closing entry, since Notes Receivable is a permanent account.
    C. Debit Retained Earnings for $10,000, and credit Notes Receivable for the same amount.
    D. None of the above

13. **Which of the following accounts would most likely *not* require an adjusting entry at the end of the accounting period?**
    A. Prepaid Rent
    B. Accounts Payable
    C. Unearned Rental Income
    D. Subscriptions Received in Advance

14. **The Accumulated Depreciation account is:**
    A. An asset account
    B. An expense account
    C. A stockholders' equity account
    D. An asset-offset (contra) account

15. **At the end of the accounting period the Income Summary account had a credit balance of $105,000. The entry to close this account would be:**

   A. Debit Income Summary for $105,000, and credit Retained Earnings for the same amount
   B. Debit Income Summary for $105,000, and credit Net Income for the same amount
   C. Debit Income Summary for $105,000, and credit Dividends Payable
   D. None of the above

## chapter 6

# Managing and Accounting for Cash and Investments

## CHAPTER OBJECTIVES

*The purposes of this chapter are to*

- Discuss the composition of cash and cash equivalents
- Explain the valuation and reporting of cash and cash equivalents
- Present internal controls for cash and cash equivalents
- Discuss the managing of cash balances
- Explain accounting procedures for cash and cash equivalents
- Explain accounting for petty cash
- Explain the accounting for and disclosure of investments, both long-term and short-term

# Composition of Cash and Cash Equivalents

Cash and cash equivalents are the most liquid assets found on a company's balance sheet. **Cash** is the most liquid asset and is generally defined as those unrestricted items that are acceptable to a bank for deposit. Specifically, cash includes such items as these:

- Cash on deposit with a bank
- Coin and currency
- Checks
- Money orders
- Bank credit card sales
- Traveler's checks

Companies usually find themselves with excess cash; the holding of that cash represents an investment. As such, the company will invest this excess in very short-term securities in order to earn interest. These holdings are called *cash equivalents*. **Cash equivalents** are generally defined as liquid assets that are readily convertible into cash and will mature in a relatively short period of time not to exceed 90 days from the date of acquisition. Cash equivalents should have a low risk of loss of value. They include such items as these:

- Money market deposits
- Government bonds or Treasury bills that mature within three months
- Commercial paper
- Any interest-bearing financial security that matures within three months

### What Is the Difference between Cash Equivalents and Short-Term Investments

Cash equivalents are investments in securities maturing within 90 days. Short-term investments are generally investments in securities maturing in excess of 90 days but within one year.

Cash and cash equivalents specifically exclude any funds on hand or on deposit that have restrictions, such as compensating balances (funds held as collateral on a loan and sinking funds held to pay bond debts). Also excluded from cash are postage stamps (they are a prepaid expense) and postdated checks (they are receivables).

# Valuing and Reporting of Cash and Cash Equivalents

Since cash equivalents can be converted to cash immediately, they are reported at the face value of the instruments involved. Both cash and cash equivalents are normally bundled and reported as one figure on the Current Asset section of the balance sheet. Further, the individual types of cash equivalents are not broken out but may be explained in a footnote, if material. As an example of reporting cash and cash equivalents, NIKE, Inc. had $2.2 billion in cash and cash equivalents as of August 31, 2009.

# Managing Cash

While cash management may be performed by the treasurer function, the accountant has an important role of providing information for the treasurer's use. Good cash management simply means having cash available when the company needs it and ensuring that excess cash is invested to maximize the asset's return to the company. Doing so requires the accountant to provide cash budgets, accurately account for cash and cash equivalents, and report cash flows to relevant company managers in a timely manner. It also requires the accountant to establish adequate controls to protect cash and prevent fraud and theft. The latter is discussed in the next section.

To summarize, here are the steps in good cash management:

1. *Prepare a cash budget to evaluate cash needs.* Preparation of cash budgets will be covered in Chapter 12. Cash budgets should be used to determine the right level of cash to have on hand. Excess cash should be invested temporarily in short-term investment. From these investments, securities are then sold as needed to maintain the right level of cash.

2. *Manage and maximize cash flow to assure that the right balance of cash is on hand when needed.* The involved relationships are summarized in Exhibit 6.1.

   To maximize cash flow, the company must use methods that assure that billing and collections of receivables as well as the payment of payables are operating as efficiently as possible. Some possibilities are to require deposits

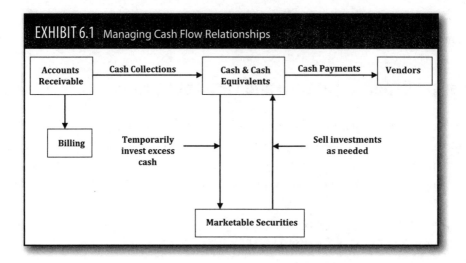

**EXHIBIT 6.1** Managing Cash Flow Relationships

upfront, bill promptly, and follow up on overdue invoices in a timely manner. On the payment side—in order to hold onto cash as long as possible—wait as long as allowed to pay down payables. However, do not incur costly late charges that might hurt the company's relationship with vendors.

3. *Establish systems and internal controls to assure that cash is used effectively and efficiently and safeguarded from theft and fraud.* The next section will address this step in more detail.

# Cash Internal Controls

Because cash is a very sensitive asset, it is critical for a company to have a written set of internal controls over this asset and to have procedures to assure that they are followed. A summary of a good set of cash internal controls follows.

## Separation of Duties

Basically, one person or activity should *not* have control over all cash functions. This arrangement is necessary so that errors and irregularities can be detected and fraud deterred. Separation of duties is of paramount importance. Good internal controls should separate the following functions:

- The authorization of a transaction
- The signing of checks

- The recording of transactions
- The custody of assets (especially cash)

## Cash Receipts

- Cash sales should begin at the point of sale (e.g., at a point-of-sale terminal). All cash sales should be documented (e.g., with sales tickets or register tapes).
- Cash receipts at the end of a shift or end of day should be counted and compared to register tapes.
- Cash over/under should be recorded and forwarded to the accounting function where an entry should be made in the Cash Over-Under account.
- Checks received through the mail should be listed as they are received. The listing should be forwarded to the accounting function in a timely manner.
- All cash receipts should be deposited at the end of the day.

## Cash Disbursements

- All disbursements should be made by check (excluding petty cash payments), and checks should be prenumbered and accounted for.
- All disbursements should be supported by proper documentation (e.g., an invoice) prior to payment.
- Only authorized persons should approve and make disbursements.
- The person approving the disbursement should not be the same person signing the check.
- Spoiled checks (i.e., misprinted, mutilated, or otherwise in error) should be voided and recorded as such.

## Bank Reconciliation

A key cash internal control is the performance of monthly bank reconciliations. This function would involve the following:

- The person or function performing the bank reconciliation should not be the same person or function involved in receiving cash or making cash disbursements (i.e., approving the payment or writing the checks).

- The bank should mail the bank statement that contains cleared checks directly to the person or function responsible for performing the bank reconciliation.

# Procedures for Preparation of the Bank Reconciliation

Basically, the bank reconciliation compares the ending balance on the bank statement to the ending balance shown in the cash account in the general ledger on the same date as the bank statement. In a business of any size these two balances will rarely agree. Differences occur because of deposits in transit, checks that were written by the company but not received by the bank for payment (called *outstanding checks*), interest paid by the bank but not recorded by the company, collections of notes receivable made by the bank for the company, bank service charges, and checks deposited by the company but returned to the bank for nonpayment (NSF, or *not sufficient funds*) but not recorded by the company.

To account for these differences, a bank reconciliation is needed. An example is shown in Exhibit 6.2.

| EXHIBIT 6.2  XYZ Corporation Bank Reconciliation | | | |
|---|---|---|---|
| **Ending Balance per the Bank Statement December 31, 2xxx** | | **Ending Balance per the Company General Ledger December 31, 2xxx** | |
| Cash balance per bank | $xxxx | Cash balance per company | $xxxx |
| **Add:** | | **Add:** | |
| Deposits in transit | xxxx | Interest paid by bank | xxxx |
| | | Collections made by bank | xxxx |
| **Subtract:** | | **Subtract:** | |
| Outstanding checks | (xxxx) | Service bank charges | xxxx |
| | | Returned checks (NSF) | xxxx |
| **Add/subtract:** | | **Add/subtract:** | |
| Bank errors | xxxx | Errors on the books | xxxx |
| True cash balance | $xxxx | True cash balance | $xxxx |

Any errors found during the bank reconciliation will usually require an adjustment to the general ledger Cash account to bring the balance into agreement with the bank balance. To illustrate the bank reconciliation, let's use an example. Assume the following data.

The Berry Industries maintains a bank account with First National Bank and received a bank statement as of November 30, 2xxx. The bank statement showed an ending balance of $13,960. The accountant reviewed the Cash account in the general ledger and found that the Cash ending balance at November 30 was $3,668. The accountant further reviewed the bank statement and transactions in the Book Cash account and found the following items:

1. The bank account was charged $320 on November 20 for printed checks.

2. The bank account was increased by $32 on November 30 for interest earned during November.

3. The bank collected a note receivable for Berry Industries on November 29 in the amount of $4,000 and deposited it into the Berry account. At the same time, the bank withdrew $160 from the bank account as a collection fee.

4. The bank account was charged $140 on November 30 for maintaining the checking account.

5. The bank account was charged $400 on November 15 for a check that was returned for insufficient funds. The bank charged the account $40 for processing the returned check.

6. During November, Berry Industries wrote checks totaling $200,000, of which $12,084 had not cleared the bank and were, therefore, outstanding. In addition, checks totaling $800 written in October had not cleared the bank.

7. The company collected accounts receivable in the amount of $5,800 on November 30 and posted that amount to the books on November 30. The collections of $5,800 were deposited in the bank on December 1.

8. In reviewing the Cash account for November, the accountant found that the Cash account showed cash sales of $580. However, the bank statement showed the amount deposited was actually $616. After a further review the accountant found that the $616 amount was correct.

**Required**: Using the above information:

1. Prepare the bank reconciliation for Berry Industries.

2. Make any journal entries required after completing the bank reconciliation.

The complete bank reconciliation is shown in Exhibit 6.3.

| **EXHIBIT 6.3**  Berry Industries Bank Reconciliation | | | |
|---|---|---|---|
| **Ending Balance per the Bank Statement November 30, 2xxx** | | **Ending Balance per the Company Cash Account in the General Ledger November 30, 2xxx** | |
| Cash balance per bank | $13,960 | Cash balance per company | $3,368 |
| **Add:** | | **Add:** | |
| Deposits in transit | 5,800 | Interest paid by bank | 32 |
| | | Collections made by bank | 4,000 |
| **Subtract:** | | **Subtract:** | |
| Outstanding checks for Nov. | (12,084) | Bank service charges | (140) |
| Outstanding checks for Oct. | (800) | Bank collection fee | (160) |
| | | Printed checks | (320) |
| | | Returned checks (NSF) | (440) |
| **Add/subtract:** | | **Add:** | |
| Bank errors | 0 | Errors on the books | 36 |
| True cash balance | $6,876 | True cash balance | $6,876 |

Listed below are the explanations of the actions taken on each item given for Berry Industries.

- **Item 1.** The bank service charge must be deducted from the book balance on the bank reconciliation and requires a journal entry to the Cash account:

| November 30, 2xxx | Bank Service Charge Expense | 140 | |
|---|---|---|---|
| | Cash | | 140 |

- **Item 2.** The interest added to the bank account must be added to the books on the bank reconciliation statement and requires a journal entry to the Cash account:

| November 30, 2xxx | Cash | 32 | |
|---|---|---|---|
| | Interest Earned | | 32 |

- **Item 3.** The bank's collection of the notes receivable requires it to be added to the book balance on the bank reconciliation and requires a journal entry to the Cash account. At the same time, the bank service charge for collecting the account receivable must be deducted from the book balance on the bank reconciliation, and it also requires a journal entry. (Note: The service charge should not be netted against the notes receivable collected.):

| November 30, 2xxx | Cash | 3,840 | |
| | Bank Service Charge | 160 | |
| | Notes Receivable | | 4,000 |

- **Item 4.** The monthly bank service charge must be deducted from the book balance on the bank reconciliation and requires a journal entry to the book Cash account:

| November 30, 2xxx | Bank Service Charge | 140 | |
| | Cash | | 140 |

- **Item 5.** The check returned for NSF and the processing fee must be deducted from the book balance on the bank reconciliation and requires the check to be added to the books by a journal entry as an account receivable, assuming that it can be collected. If it cannot be collected, the company would start collection proceedings or charge the check off as an expense. The bank returned fee should be added to Accounts Receivable and collected from the customer. However, if it cannot be collected, it would be charged as an expense also.

| November 30, 2xxx | Accounts Receivable | 440 | |
| | Cash | | 440 |

- **Item 6.** The checks written during November and October that are outstanding must be deducted from the bank balance on the bank reconciliation. They do not require an entry to the books, as such entries have already been made during the month.

- **Item 7.** These deposits in transit of $5,800 must be added to the Bank Statement column on the bank reconciliation, as they did not reach the bank until December 1. No entry is required to the books.

- **Item 8.** The difference between the bank deposits of $616 in sales and the book entry for the same item of $580 is $36. This amount must be added to the books in the bank reconciliation. An entry is required to adjust the books for the difference:

| November 30, 2xxx | Cash | 36 | |
|---|---|---|---|
| | Sales | | 36 |

# Petty Cash

As stated earlier, all disbursements should be made by check, except for minor expenditures for which the writing of a check would be impractical. These types of small expenditures include such things as delivery charges, postage due on deliveries, emergency fuel purchases, small purchases of office supplies, and taxi fare. The company will use a petty cash fund (also called an *imprest fund*) for these types of disbursements. Although a petty cash fund can be relatively small, in larger companies it can run into thousands of dollars. Since the fund involves the holding of cash, it can be susceptible to theft or fraud. Therefore, a responsible person outside of the activity should audit the fund and its record-keeping periodically.

## Petty Cash Accounting and Reporting Procedures

At the time the fund is established, appropriate policies and procedures should be established for operating the fund. These would apply to the size of the fund, the type of expenditures that can be made from the fund, and the maximum amount that can be paid for a disbursement. In large petty cash funds, prenumbered vouchers should be created when expenditures are made with an appropriate receipt attached. In smaller petty cash funds the receipt will suffice. A custodian should be appointed to administer the fund; that person is held responsible for the cash on hand. The custodian should create a petty cash log of expenditures from the fund to include the date, explanation, voucher number, and the type of expenditures. The log may contain a running balance.

To establish the fund, a check should be written to the petty cash fund from the regular cash account. For example, Berry Industries establishes a petty cash fund of $5,000 on January 1, 2xxx. The entry would be:

| January 1, 2xxx | Petty Cash Fund | 5,000 | |
|---|---|---|---|
| | Cash | | 5,000 |

As expenditures are made, the custodian will maintain vouchers and/or receipts along with the cash remaining in the fund. At some point (either when the fund runs low on cash or it is at the end of the accounting period), the fund will require reimbursement. The custodian will attach the vouchers or receipts to a reimbursement form and submit it for reimbursement. The custodian must maintain a copy of the reimbursement form and receipts. The accountant function will receive a copy of the paid reimbursement and will make a journal entry to record the expenses. For example, Berry Industries had the following vouchers submitted for reimbursement on October 10, 2xxx:

- Delivery charges          $400
- Postage stamps           $200
- Fuel purchases            $500
- Miscellaneous expenses    $200

The entry for reimbursement would be:

| October 10, 2xxx | Delivery Expenses | 400 | |
| | Office Supplies Expenses | 200 | |
| | Fuel Expenses | 500 | |
| | Miscellaneous Expenses | 200 | |
| | Cash | | 1,300 |

For reporting purposes on the balance sheet, the petty cash fund is not normally reported separately unless it is a significant amount. It is combined with the cash and cash equivalents balance and reported as such.

## Investment in Securities

Short-term investments of excess cash are part of a portfolio of investments by a company that can be converted to cash within the next year. Long-term investments are made to earn income or to exert significant influence on another company. A company's portfolio of investments (both long term and short term) are categorized as follows, and the categories are usually based on the intent of management in making the investment.[1]

- **Held-to-maturity securities.** *Debt* securities (*not* equity securities) that the company has the positive intent and ability to hold to maturity. These

[1]Financial Accounting Standard No. 115: *Accounting for Certain Investments in Debt and Equity Securities*, May 1993.

securities are generally purchased for the purpose of earning interest or selling for a profit in the future. They are reported at cost less any impairment (e.g., amortized cost) plus any accrued interest. Finally, these securities are usually classified as noncurrent assets (e.g., bonds) but can be classified as a current asset (e.g., Treasury bills or corporate notes maturing within one year). A comprehensive illustration is presented in the next section.

- **Trading securities.** These are *debt and equity* securities that are bought using excess cash and held principally for the purpose of selling them in the near term (usually within days or weeks). At the end of the reporting period, trading securities are reported at fair market value based on the mark-to-market principle. **Mark-to-market** means the recording of a value of securities, portfolios, or accounts to reflect the *current* market value rather than the *book* value. An adjustment will need to be made to the Trading Securities account for the unrealized gain or loss in market value. The unrealized gains and losses would be *included* in the earnings during the current period. The offsetting debit or credit to the Unrealized Gain/Loss journal entry can be made directly to an investments account, or an adjustment account (called *Allowance to Adjust Trading Securities to Market Value*) can be created and added to or subtracted from the investment account on the balance sheet. Trading securities are reported as current assets on the balance sheet at their fair value. A comprehensive illustration is presented later in this chapter.

- **Available-for-sale securities.** *Debt and equity* securities that are *not* classified as either held-to-maturity securities or trading securities and are reported on the balance sheet at fair value. They are held for an indefinite period of time with no intention of selling before maturity. Thus, most of these types of securities will be classified as noncurrent on the balance sheet, unless the company decides to sell them within one year.

  Similar to trading securities, changes in market value of available-for-sale securities over time result in an unrealized gain or loss. An *unrealized gain or loss* means that a security has a gain or loss in market value but the security has not yet been sold.[2] Unrealized gains and losses from available-for-sale securities are excluded from earnings on the current income statement. They are reported as a separate component of stockholders' equity

---

[2]See Financial Accounting Standard No. 157: *Fair Value Measurements*, September 2006, for the standard on determining fair value.

as Other Comprehensive Income and entered below the Retained Earnings line on the balance sheet. A comprehensive illustration is presented later in this chapter.

- *Investment in equity securities for influence or control.* Companies may make a long-term investment in equities of another company with the intent of influencing the corporate policy of that company or to take control of that company. The question is, how much control is necessary and how do you define it? The FASB established guidelines for this purpose; they are as follows:

  - Holdings of less than 20 percent are deemed to have little influence over the investee. These holdings are accounted for using fair value similar to available-for-sale securities (i.e., net unrealized gains or losses are computed and are reported as a separate component of stockholders' equity on the balance sheet).

  - Holdings between 20 percent and 50 percent are deemed to have significance over the operating and financial policies of the investee. They are accounted for using the so-called equity method. The *equity method* means that the investor records the initial investment at cost and the investor reports its proportional share of the investee's income on its income statement each period. For example, if the investee reported $100,000 in net income and the investor owned 30 percent of the investee's common stock, it would report $30,000 in income on its income statement.

  - Holdings of more than 50 percent are deemed to have a controlling interest in the investee. The financial statements of the investee must be consolidated with those of the owner-investor in this situation. Consolidated financial statement accounting is not covered in this book but is covered in advanced accounting books.

## Accounting Illustration for Held-to-Maturity Securities

### Short-Term Investments in Held-to-Maturity Securities

Assume that on December 1, 2xxx, XYZ Company purchases $20,000 of Treasury bills that expire in 90 days. XYZ's fiscal year ends on December 31. Assume that at the end of December the T-bills had accrued interest of $200. At this date, there would be no impairment in the value of the T-bills, as these are very liquid assets. (Note: If the company had invested in bonds as a held-to-maturity investment and if a premium or discount were involved, the premium or discount would have to be amortized as shown for long-term investments in the next section.)

The entries at December 1 and December 31 for the above illustration are as follows:

| December 1 | Short-Term Investments | 20,000 | |
|---|---|---|---|
| | Cash | | 20,000 |

| December 31 | Short-Term Investments | 200 | |
|---|---|---|---|
| | Interest Revenue | | 200 |

On the December 31 balance sheet, the Current Asset section would include the fair value of the short-term security as follows:

| Short-Term Investments | $20,000 |
|---|---|

## Long-Term Investments in Held-to-Maturity Securities

*Purchase of Bonds at a Premium:* Assume that on July 1, 2xxx, XYZ Company buys $100,000 in 6 percent, 10-year bonds at 107 and the company plans to hold the bonds to maturity. The "107" number represents a premium on the bonds. (Remember that the purchaser must pay a premium when the contract rate on the bond is greater than the going market rate.) Assume also that interest on these bonds is paid semiannually on June 30 and December 31. Since the bonds had been purchased at a premium, the premium must be amortized over the life of the bonds, because at the time of redemption the company would receive only $100,000, not $107,000. The amortization of the premium will, in effect, reduce the amount of interest income reported, since it is a return of the initial investment.

The purchase of the bond would be recorded as follows:

| July 1, 2xxx | Investment in Bonds | 107,000* | |
|---|---|---|---|
| | Cash | | 107,000 |

*Instead of adding the premium of $7,000 to the investment account, some companies may establish a separate premium account for accounting purposes and add it to the investment on the balance sheet. The result will be the same.

The interest payment and amortization of the premium at December 31 would be recorded as follows:

| December 31, 2xxx | Cash | 3,000 | |
|---|---|---|---|
| | Interest Income | | 2,650 |
| | Investment in Bonds | | 350 |

(Interest payment: $100,000 × .06 × 6/12 months = $3,000; amortization of premium: $7,000 × 6/120 months = $350 using the straight-line method.)

The Investment in Bonds would be shown in the Noncurrent Assets section of the balance sheet as follows:

| Investment in Bonds | $106,650 |
|---|---|

*Purchase of Bonds at a Discount:* Assume the same facts as in the previous illustration, except that the bonds had a contract interest rate of 7 percent and bonds are purchased at a discount for 98. This means that the contract rate of interest was less than the market rate and the investor will only purchase the bonds when they are less than their face value, thus making up the differential. A discount amortization will, in effect, increase the amount of interest income reported by the company.

The following is how the purchase of the bonds is recorded:

| July 1, 2xxx | Investment in Bonds | 98,000 | |
|---|---|---|---|
| | Cash | | 98,000 |

A record of the cash interest payment and amortizization of the discount at December 31 would look like this:

| December 31, 2xxx | Cash | 3,500 | |
|---|---|---|---|
| | Investment in Bonds | 100 | |
| | Interest Revenue | | 3,600 |

The Investment in Bonds would be shown in the Noncurrent Assets section of the balance sheet as follows:

| Investment in Bonds | $100,100 |
|---|---|

## Accounting Illustration for Trading Securities

Since management intends to hold **trading securities** for a very short time, they are always short-term investments and are shown in the Current Assets section of the balance sheet. Assume that XYZ Company purchases $50,000 of Deacon Industries' common stock on December 1, 2xxx and intends to hold the shares for six months and sell them for a gain then use the proceeds in operations. Assume that at the end of the company's fiscal year on December 31, the stock has increased in value to $53,000. Make journal entries at both dates.

The purchase of stock would be recorded as follows:

| December 1, 2xxx | Trading Securities | 50,000 | |
| | Cash | | 50,000 |

At December 31, 2xxx, the company would need to adjust the investment account using fair market value:

| December 31, 2xxx | Trading Securities | 3,000 | |
| | Unrealized Gain on Trading Securities | | 3,000 |

The Trading Securities balance of $53,000 ($50,000 + 3,000) would be reported in the Current Assets section of the balance sheet, and the Unrealized Gain on Trading Securities would be reported in the income statement. If the securities had suffered a loss, the loss amount would have been reported on the income statement.

Alternatively, the company could have established an account, Allowance to Adjust Trading Securities to Market Value, and debited this account instead of the Trading Securities account. The allowance account would be added to Trading Securities in the Current Assets section of the balance sheet. The purpose of this separation is to provide more information by showing the cost of the investments on one line and any adjustments to the cost for changes in market value on a separate line.

## Illustration of Accounting for Available-for-Sale Securities

**Available-for-sale securities** are debt or equity securities held for the purpose of earning a return that will be used for operating purposes in the future. As such, they act very much like trading securities and, therefore, are accounted for exactly like trading securities, *with one exception*. This exception is how the changes in value are handled. With trading securities the unrealized gain or loss is reported on the income statement as shown previously. With available-for-sale securities the unrealized gain or loss is reported in the Stockholders' section of the balance sheet under the name of Unrealized Gain/Loss—Other Comprehensive Income.

## Accounting for Investments in Equity Securities Purchased for Significant Influence

As stated previously, a company may hold securities for the purpose of influencing the policy or exerting control of another company. This situation applies where the percentage of holding is greater than 20 percent. For example, assume that XYZ Company purchased 30 percent of Johnson Company's common stock for $900,000 on January 1, 2xxx. The entry at time of purchase would be:

| January 1, 2xxx | Investments | 900,000 | |
|---|---|---|---|
| | Cash | | 900,000 |

At the end of Johnson's fiscal year June 30, 2xxx, it reported net income of $100,000. XYZ would make the following entry in its books:

| June 30, 2xxx | Investment | 30,000 | |
|---|---|---|---|
| | Investment Income | | 30,000 |
| | (To record share of Johnson Company's net income: $100,000 × 30% = $30,000) | | |

The investment account is shown on the balance sheet under Noncurrent Assets, and the investment income is reported on the income statement.

As stated previously, the accounting procedure applies to a company that owns 20 percent to 50 percent of another company. If the company owns more than 50 percent of another company, then the two company's financial statements must be consolidated. This complex procedure is not covered in this book but is reserved for advanced accounting books.

A summary of the account and reporting procedures for investments are shown in Exhibit 6.4.

**EXHIBIT 6.4** Summary of Accounting and Reporting Procedures for Investments

| Type | Valuation | Classification on the Balance Sheet | Treatment of Unrealized Gains/Losses |
|------|-----------|-------------------------------------|--------------------------------------|
| Held-to-maturity (debt securities) | Amortized cost (including accrued interest) | Usually noncurrent | Not recognized |
| Trading (debt or equity securities) | Fair value | Current asset | Report on the income statement |
| Available-for-sale (debt or equity securities) | Fair value | Current or noncurrent | Report on the balance sheet |
| Investments for influence | Equity method (20-50% control) | Noncurrent | N/A |
| Investments for control | Consolidate financial statements | Noncurrent | N/A |

# QUIZ

1. The following items were in possession of the company's cash receipts function on February 28. Which of the items is not included in the Cash account on the balance sheet for February 28?
   A. Coins and currency
   B. A customer's traveler's check endorsed to the company
   C. A customer's check dated February 28
   D. A customer's check dated March 1

2. A reimbursement form and receipts are submitted to replenish a $1,000 petty cash fund. The form contains receipts for $950, but there is only $20 in cash left in the fund. Which of the following is correct?
   A. Cash should be credited for $950.
   B. Petty Cash should be debited for $950.
   C. Cash Over/Short account should be debited for $30.
   D. Petty Cash should be credited for $30.

3. When the responsible person performs a bank reconciliation, he or she would handle deposits in transit by:
   A. Deducting it from the bank balance
   B. Adding to the book balance
   C. Adding it to the bank balance
   D. Adding it to both the bank and book balance

4. In performing the bank reconciliation, which of the following items will require a journal entry by the depositing company?
   A. A bank error
   B. The bank's collection of an accounts receivable
   C. Outstanding checks
   D. Deposits in transit

5. (True or False?) A petty cash fund is a cash fund used to pay small amounts in excess of $100.

6. When the petty cash custodian makes a payment from the petty cash fund, he or she should immediately make which of the following journal entr(ies)?
   A. Debit each affected expense account
   B. Credit the cash account
   C. Credit the petty cash account
   D. No entry is required at the time of a petty cash payment

7. **Which of the following is *not* a major step in managing cash in a business?**
   A. Establishing good relations with a bank
   B. Preparation of a cash budget
   C. Maximizing cash flow
   D. Establishing a system of internal controls for cash

8. **When a bank reconciliation is performed, the total of outstanding checks would be:**
   A. Deducted from the book balance
   B. Added to the bank balance
   C. Deducted from the bank balance
   D. None of the above

9. **With available-for-sale securities, which of the following is true?**
   A. They are, in effect, all securities not classified as trading or held-to-maturity.
   B. They are not expected to be actively traded.
   C. They can be debt or equity securities.
   D. All of the above
   E. None of the above

10. **XYZ Co. purchased $200,000 of held-to-maturity bonds at 98. This will result in XYZ making the recording as:**
    A. Debit Investment in Bonds $196,000, and credit Cash for $196,000.
    B. Debit Investment in Bonds for $200,000, credit Cash for $196,000, and credit Bond Revenue for $4,000
    C. Debit Investment in Bonds for $196,000, debit Prepaid Interest for $4,000, and credit Cash for $200,000.
    D. None of the above

The following information pertains to problems 11 through 13: XYZ Co. purchases $100,000 of stock on June 1 with the intent of selling it in 90 days for use in operations.

11. **What would the journal entry be on June 1?**
    A. A debit to Held-to-Maturity Securities for $100,000, and a credit to Cash.
    B. A debit to Trading Securities for $100,000, and a credit to Cash.
    C. A debit to Available-for-Sale Securities for $100,000, and a credit to Cash.
    D. None of the above

12. **Irrespective of your answer in question 11, assume that the stock purchase was for Trading Securities. Also, assume that the company's books were closed on June 30 and the stock had increased in value by $3,000. What would be the journal entry on June 30?**

   A. Debit Trading Securities for $3,000, and credit Dividend Revenue for $3,000.
   B. Debit Unrealized Gain on Investments for $3,000, and credit Trading Securities for $3,000.
   C. Debit Trading Securities for $3,000, and credit Unrealized Gain on Investments for $3,000.
   D. None of the above

13. **Assuming that the securities were Trading Securities and $3,000 of interest had accrued at June 30, how would the investments be shown on the balance sheet on June 30?**

   A. Trading Securities $103,000
   B. Trading Securities $97,000
   C. Trading Securities $100,000 and interest was shown on the Stockholders' Equity section.
   D. None of the above

14. **JJ Company purchased 25 percent of CC Company's stock. At the end of the month, CC reported income of $100,000. What journal entry would JJ make at the end of the month?**

   A. A debit to Investments for $25,000, and a credit to Investments Income for $25,000
   B. A debit to Investments for $25,000, and a credit to Gains on Investment of $25,000
   C. No entry would be made, since CC had not paid the proportionate share of income to JJ
   D. None of the above

15. **Refer to question 14. During the year JJ purchased an additional 35 percent of CC's common stock, which gave it 60 percent of CC's stock and effective control of the company. On June 30 of next year, CC had income of $110,000. What journal entry would JJ make on its books?**

   A. A debit to Investments for $66,000, and a credit to Investment Income for $66,000
   B. No entry would be made, but the financial statements of the two companies would be consolidated.
   C. A debit to Available-for-Sale Securities for $66,000, and a credit to Retained Earnings for $66,000
   D. No entry would be made, since CC did not pay JJ for its share of the income

## chapter 7

# Accounting for Sales and Receivables

## CHAPTER OBJECTIVES

*The purposes of this chapter are to*

- Explain the recording of credit sales
- Explain the accounting for sales returns and allowances
- Explain the accounting for warranties
- Define receivables
- Explain the estimating and accounting for uncollectible receivables
- Explain the write-off of an account and subsequent recovery of a receivable
- Explain the accounting for notes receivables

## Recording Sales and Sales Returns and Allowances

A seller of merchandise will generally have three types of sales: sales for cash, sales on account, or sales by credit card. All sales require a supporting (source) document before sales entries can be made into the accounting system. Usually, the source document will be a sales invoice or a cash register receipt. Of course, in many businesses these transactions along with their source documents are processed electronically without hard documents being created. All transactions and source documents can be retrieved from the system as needed.

Using the revenue recognition principle, all sales are recorded when the title passes to the purchaser. For the cash customer, the title will pass when he or she takes possession of the goods, usually at a cash register. If the goods are shipped, the title will pass when the merchandise or products are shipped to the customer.

Often a business will provide a reduction in price in order to sell merchandise that has a defect or is lower in quality, or simply to entice customers to purchase the product. This practice is called *sales allowances*. Sales allowances are separated from the sales and recorded in a separate account called Sales Returns and Allowances. The latter is called a contra (or contra-revenue) account. The normal balance for a contra-revenue account is a debit balance, and the balance is deducted from Gross Sales (a credit balance account) on the income statement. For example, suppose on August 1, 2xxx, a company sold $10,000 worth of merchandise for cash and gave $500 in allowances to the customer. The entry would be:

| August 1, 2xxx | Cash | 9,500 | |
| | Sales Returns and Allowances | 500 | |
| | Sales | | 10,000 |

In addition to sales allowances, businesses will have goods returned because of damage or defect, or for other reasons. When the items are received, a credit memorandum is prepared, if the items were sold on account. If the items were sold for cash, a cash refund form is prepared when the money is refunded. Either the credit memorandum or the cash refund form becomes the source document for an accounting entry. All sales returns are debited to the Sales Returns and Allowances account, and the offsetting credit will be made to Accounts Receivable or Cash, depending on how the items were sold. Companies that have significant amounts of returns or allowances may create two separate accounts for each.

### Why Is a Contra (Contra-Revenue) Account Used for Sales Returns and Allowances?

Management must manage the level of sales returns and allowances to keep them at an acceptable level. Keeping them in a separate account and not netting them against sales provides a practical way to keep track of them for this purpose.

# Accounting for Sales Warranties

Providing warranties on products or services is a wise marketing tool to entice customers. In some companies this expense can be very significant. The problem facing the accountant is that the warranty may be exercised in an accounting period later than the sale. If the expense were recorded in an accounting period later than when the sale was made, the principle of matching revenues with their related expenses would be violated. To overcome this problem, the accountant must estimate the warranty expenses at the time of sale or at the end of the accounting period for those products or services sold during the current period. The estimate is recorded as a debit to Warranty Expense and a credit to Estimated Warranty Liability. For example, assume that on January 15, 2xxx, Rotopillar Tractors sold a tractor to a customer for $50,000 and the accountant estimates a warranty cost of $1,500. The entry would be:

| January 15, 2xxx | Warranty Expense | 1,500 | |
| | Estimated Warranty Liability | | 1,500 |

When a product is returned for repair, the cost of repair would not be expensed. Instead the accountant would debit the cost to the Estimated Warranty Liability account and credit Cash or Accounts Payable.

# Selling Products and Merchandise on Credit

To attract customers, most businesses will sell their goods or services on credit—either as an accounts receivable, a notes receivable, or through the use of credit cards. Vendors who sell goods to a business normally will allow payment of the goods sometime after they are delivered. This gives rise to an accounts receivable or, in some cases, a notes receivable. Accounts receivable are usually collected from up to two months from the date of sale. Thus, they are considered a current asset on the balance sheet. Notes receivable will be discussed later in this chapter. Merchandising businesses, such as retail stores, will usually sell for cash or accept credit cards.

Whether sales are made on account or through use of credit cards, there is a cost to extending credit to customers. If the business sells on account, the customer's creditworthiness must be investigated and collections of the receivables must be monitored. Of course, all customers will not pay the amount on their accounts, which gives rise to a bad debt expense. While credit cards help solve some of these problems, they come with a fee or service charge being deducted by the credit card company. For example, assume that on December 20, 2xxx, XYZ Company sold $5,000 of goods on credit cards. Also, assume the bank card company charges 2 percent on all credit card sales. The business may have an arrangement with the bank card company for same-day funding electronically into their bank account. In this case the entry would be

| December 20, 2xxx | Cash | 4,900 | |
| | Bank Card Service Charge | 100 | |
| | Sales | | 5,000 |
| | ($5,000 × 2% = $100) | | |

In some cases, there may be a delayed collection from the bank card company. When that occurs, the sale is initially recorded as a credit sale. In the previous illustration, assume that the business did not collect from the bank card company until January 5, 2xxx. Two entries would be

| December 20, 2xxx | Accounts Receivable | 5,000 | |
| | Sales | | 5,000 |
| January 5, 2xxx | Cash | 4,900 | |
| | Bank Card Service Charge | 100 | |
| | Accounts Receivable | | 5,000 |

## Accounting for Uncollectible Receivables

As mentioned, a business accepts the fact that some customers will not pay the balance on their accounts. At some point, a determination must be made that a late account is uncollectible and is to be written off as a bad debt. This is based on the fact that generally accepted accounting principles (GAAP) require the business to report only receivables on which it expects to receive payment (i.e., net realizable value). Therefore, a provision must be made in the accounting system to reflect the recognition of uncollectible accounts. There are two ways of handling this provision: the **direct write-off method** or the **allowance method**.

## Direct Write-Off Method

The simpler of the two methods is the **direct write-off method**. That is so because the uncollectible accounts are written off and the expense recognized in the period in which the receivable becomes worthless. Assume that Office Providers sold office supplies to the John Smith Company on February 1, 2xxx, for $2,000 and properly recorded the sale, and that on August 1, 2xxx it was determined by Office Suppliers that this account was uncollectible, since John Smith went bankrupt. The entry would be

| August 1, 2xxx | Uncollectible Accounts Expense | 1,000 | |
| | Accounts Receivable | | 1,000 |

Although the direct write-off method may be simple, it may not be correct and not GAAP. The only time that it would be acceptable is where the amount of uncollectible accounts expense is considered immaterial. Remember that the concept of materiality means that an item or transaction is material if it is large enough to influence the judgment of an informed investor's decision. The direct write-off method may also be incorrect because it violates the matching principle. That is, the write-off of the receivable may be in a different reporting period than when the sale was made. Thus, the uncollectible expense would not be matched with the sale in the same period that the sale was made. To correct these problems, accountants have developed the allowance method, which is covered in the next section.

## Allowance Method

The **allowance method** is a process for determining the amount of uncollectible accounts by making an estimate of uncollectible accounts at the end of each accounting period. That is done to match the uncollectible accounts expense with the related sales that occurred that period. The problem faced by accountants is that it is extremely difficult to determine which specific accounts in the portfolio of accounts receivable will actually be uncollectible. In addition, it would be costly to evaluate each of the thousands of accounts receivable in a large company in order to make this determination. Therefore, the process requires a method to estimate the amount of total uncollectible accounts. Once the amount is determined, the Uncollectible Accounts Expense account is debited and an account called Allowance for Uncollectible Accounts (*not* the

Accounts Receivable account) is credited. The latter is a contra-asset account and is offset against Accounts Receivable on the balance sheet.

There are two methods used for estimating the amount of uncollectible accounts expense: the percentage-of-sales method and the method for aging of accounts receivable. The former method is discussed next.

## The Percentage-of-Sales Method

The *percentage-of-sales method* focuses on the income statement by evaluating the total sales for the period and estimating how much of these sales will be uncollectible, regardless of when the individual accounts will become uncollectible. If the company has both cash and credit sales, this method applies only to credit sales. Carefully evaluating the past history of uncollectible accounts and looking at future economic conditions that may affect the collection of receivables and help the accountant to determine the percentage of sales.

As an example, assume that at June 30, 2xxx, XYZ Company had $45,000 in sales during the period and $40,000 were in credit sales. Also, assume that the accountant has determined that, overall, 5 percent of these credit sales will be uncollectible. Thus, the estimate of uncollectible accounts expense would be $2,000 = ($40,000 \times .05)$. The journal entry for the expense would be

| June 30, 2xxx | Uncollectible Accounts Expense | 2,000 | |
|---|---|---|---|
| | Allowance for Uncollectible Accounts | | 2,000 |

Assume that the balance of accounts receivable at June 30 was $60,000. The balance sheet would show the following net realizable value of Accounts Receivable:

| Accounts Receivable | $60,000 |
|---|---|
| Less: Allowance for Uncollectible Accounts | 2,000 |
| | $58,000 |

## Writing Off of an Uncollectible Account Using the Percentage-of-Sales Method

Suppose on September 1, 2xxx, XYZ decided that an individual account with a balance of $1,500 was uncollectible. The following entry would be made to write off this account:

| September 1, 2xxx | Allowance for Uncollectible Accounts | 1,500 | |
|---|---|---|---|
| | Accounts Receivable | | 1,500 |

### The Accounts Receivable Aging Method

A weakness of the percentage-of-sales method is that it does not take into consideration the length of time that accounts have been outstanding. That is, accounts that have been outstanding for, say, 90 days have a higher probability of being uncollectible than those that have been outstanding for 30 days. The **accounts receivable aging method** attempts to overcome this weakness. It does so by, first, setting up an aging schedule and, then, by making an estimate of how much of each age's balance will not be collectible. For example, take the June 30 balance of $60,000 accounts receivable of XYZ Company. Assume the schedule in Exhibit 7.1 for this balance.

**EXHIBIT 7.1** XYZ Company Accounts Receivable Aging Schedule

| Age of Account | End of Accounting Period Balance of Accounts Receivable | Estimated Uncollectible Percentage | Amount Needed in Allowance Account at End of Period |
|---|---|---|---|
| 1–30 Days | $20,000 | 1 | $200 |
| 31–60 Days | 30,000 | 4 | 1,200 |
| 61–90 Days | 8,000 | 8 | 640 |
| Over 90 days | 2,000 | 15 | 300 |
| | $60,000 | | $2,340 |

Further assume that the Allowance for Uncollectible Accounts has a balance of $1,200 at June 30. Using the accounts receivable aging method, the balance would need to be adjusted by $1,140 = ($2,340 – $1,200). The required entry would be

| June 30, 2xxx | Uncollectible Accounts Expense | 1,140 | |
| | Allowance for Uncollectible Accounts | | 1,140 |

The balance sheet would show the following net realizable value of Accounts Receivable:

| Accounts Receivable | $60,000 |
| Less: Allowance for Uncollectible Accounts | 2,340 |
| | $57,660 |

Note that the accounts receivable aging method focuses on the balance sheet, since it bases its estimates on the accounts in the ending Accounts Receivable balance. It estimates how much of the end of accounting period Accounts Receivable balance will not be collected and adjusts the Allowance for Uncollectible Accounts to bring Accounts Receivable to its net realizable value.

### Percentage of Total Accounts Receivable Method

An alternative to the accounts receivable aging method that focuses on the balance sheet is the percentage of total accounts receivable method. This method works by applying a percentage to the total ending balance of the Accounts Receivable and adjusting the Allowance for Uncollectible Accounts to bring its balance into agreement with the amount determined by applying the percentage to the ending total balance. The journal entries would be like the aging method described previously, except the amount of adjustment would be based on the percentage of the ending Accounts Receivable balance.

## Recovery of an Accounts Receivable

Suppose that a customer whose accounts receivable was written off subsequently decides to pay off the amount that he owes. For example, XYZ Company had such a customer and the amount paid was $1,000 on February 1, 2xxx. The account would be restored as follows:

| | | | |
|---|---|---|---|
| February 1, 2xxx | Accounts Receivable | 1,000 | |
| | Allowance for Uncollectible Accounts | | 1,000 |
| February 1, 2xxx | Cash | 1,000 | |
| | Accounts Receivable | | 1,000 |

## Promissory Notes Receivable

As stated previously, a promissory note may be used when companies sell products or services to a customer. Use of promissory notes can arise from selling very expensive equipment or when the customer has a poor credit history and the selling company wants a legal instrument that is enforceable in a court of law. Of course, there could be other reasons for using promissory notes. Typically, these types of notes are interest bearing, as they represent an investment of funds by the business, and good management requires a reasonable return on any investment.

The standard method for computing interest is based a 360-day year. The formula for computing interest is:

$$\text{Interest} = \text{Principal} \times \text{Interest rate} \times \text{Time in days}$$

The principal is the face value of the note; the interest rate is stated as an annual rate; and the time is the fraction of a year represented by the note. For example, a company issues a $1,000, 90-day note, at 6 percent interest. At the end of the period the interest would be computed as follows:

$$\$1,000 \times .06 \times \frac{90}{360} = \$15$$

As an example of the accounting for a note receivable, assume that on November 1, 2xxx, XYZ Company sells $5,000 worth of goods and accepts a promissory note for that amount at a 6 percent interest rate, payable in six months (180 days). Also, assume that XYZ's accounting year ends on December 31. Prepare journal entries for

**a.** November 1, 2xxx, when the note is issued

**b.** The adjusting entry on December 31, 2xxx

**c.** The journal entry when the note is paid off on April 30, 2xxx

The solution is

| a. | November 1, 2xxx | Notes Receivable | 5,000 | |
|---|---|---|---|---|
| | | Sales | | 5,000 |

(To record the issuance of a notes receivable for sold goods)

| b. | December 31, 2xxx | Interest Receivable | 50 | |
|---|---|---|---|---|
| | | Interest Revenue | | 50 |

$$\text{(To accrue interest} = \$5,000 \times .06 \times \frac{60}{360} = \$50)$$

| April 30, 2xxx | Cash | 5,150 | |
| c. | Interest Receivable | | 50 |
| | Interest Income | | 100 |
| | Notes Receivable | | 5,000 |

(To record collection of note: interest for 120 days = $5,000 \times .06 \times \dfrac{120}{360} = \$100$, additional interest revenue on notes receivable)

## Uncollectible Notes Receivable

If a company accepts a significant number of notes receivable, then an Allowance for Uncollectible Notes Receivable account should be established in order to compute the net realizable value of notes receivable at the end of the accounting period. The procedures for estimating the bad debt expense and the journal entries would be exactly like those for accounts receivable.

## Dishonored Notes Receivable

Suppose the following: a business does not have a significant number of notes receivable, does not use the allowance method, and has a customer that does not pay off the note at maturity. In this case, the Notes Receivable is moved to Accounts Receivable and the amount of interest is recognized as Interest Revenue, because the interest was still earned, even if it was not collected. Using the computations from the preceding example, the journal entries at April 30 would be

| April 30, 2xxx | Accounts Receivable | 5,150 | |
| | Interest Receivable | | 50 |
| | Interest Income | | 100 |
| | Notes Receivable | | 5,000 |
| | (To record a dishonored/ note) | | |

# QUIZ

1. **A company that uses the direct write-off method computes and recognizes the uncollectible accounts expense:**
   A. By aging the accounts receivable and computes a percentage for each tier
   B. As a percentage of net credit sales during the period
   C. In the period in which the account amounts are actually written off
   D. As a percentage of accounts receivable balance at the end of the period

2. **XYZ Company had $20,000 in sales on account, and it gave the customer a $1,000 allowance because there was a defect in some of the items. The correct journal entry would be:**
   A. A debit to Accounts Receivable for $19,000, a debit to Sales Returns and Allowances for $1,000, and a credit to Sales for $20,000
   B. A debit to Accounts Receivable for $20,000, a credit to Sales Returns and Allowances for $1,000, and a credit to Sales for $19,000
   C. A debit to Accounts Receivable for $19,000, a debit to Defect Expense $1,000, and a credit to Sales for $20,000
   D. None of the above

3. **(True or false?) When a company sells products under warranty, a provision must be made for warranty expense when the products are sold by debiting Warranty Expense and crediting Estimated Warranty Liability.**

   The following information pertains to problems 4–6. A company uses the percentage-of-sales method to estimate the amount of uncollectible expense during the accounting period. It had sales of $80,000, with 80 percent being on credit. The company estimates that 4 percent of credit sales will be uncollectible.

4. **If the end of the accounting period ended on December 31, what would be the journal entry at that date?**
   A. A debit to Uncollectible Accounts Expense of $3,200, and a credit to Allowance for Doubtful Accounts for $3,200
   B. A debit to Uncollectible Accounts Expense of $2,560, and a credit to Allowance for Doubtful Accounts for $2,560
   C. A debit to Allowance for Doubtful Accounts for $3,200, and a credit to Uncollectible Accounts Expense for $3,200
   D. None of the above

5. **(True or false?) The net realizable value of Accounts Receivable on the balance sheet at December 31 would be $80,000.**

6. Suppose a customer's account of $500 is declared uncollectible. The correct journal entry would be

   A. A debit to Allowance for Uncollectible Accounts for $500, and a credit to Accounts Receivable Expense for $500

   B. A debit to Allowance for Uncollectible Accounts for $500, and a credit to Accounts Receivable for $500

   C. A debit to Uncollectible Accounts Expense for $500, and a credit to Accounts Receivable

   D. None of the above

7. Jones Company sold $50,000 of merchandise on credit using credit cards on a given date. The servicing bank charges a service fee of 5 percent on all credit card sales processed. Which of the following statements is correct, assuming the bank credits Jones's bank account for collections on the day it processes each charge?

   A. Jones would make a journal entry crediting Sales for $50,000.

   B. Jones would make a journal entry debiting Bankcard Servicing Fee for $2,500.

   C. Jones would make a journal entry debiting Cash for $47,500.

   D. All of the above are correct.

8. (True or false?) The use of the percentage of the accounts receivable method in estimating the allowance for doubtful accounts emphasizes the balance sheet in valuing accounts receivable.

9. (True or false?) If a written-off account is subsequently recovered, the correct journal entry is always to debit Accounts Receivable for the full amount written off and credit Allowance for Doubtful Accounts for the same amount.

The following information pertains to problems 10 to 12. On June 1, 2xxx, Peterson Company accepts a 60-day, 6 percent promissory note for the sale of an expensive product in the amount of $20,000.

10. The entry at the date of sale would be

    A. A debit to Notes Receivable for $20,000, and a credit to Sales for $20,000

    B. A debit to Accounts Receivable for $20,000, and a credit to Sales for $20,000

    C. A debit to Notes Receivable for $17,900, and a credit to Sales for $17,900

    D. None of the above

11. Assume Peterson's accounting period ends on June 30. What would be the amount of interest recognized as interest revenue on that date?

    A. $200

    B. $300

    C. $400

    D. $100

12. **If at the end of July 31 the note is paid off, which of the following statements would *not* be true?**

   A. Notes receivable would be credited for $20,000.
   B. Interest revenue of $100 would be recognized in the month of July.
   C. Interest revenue of $200 would be recognized in the month of July.
   D. None of the above

   The following schedule pertains to problems 13 and 14. Assume the following accounts receivable aging schedule and the estimated uncollectible percentages of accounts receivable.

**EXHIBIT 7.2**  Accounts Receivable Aging Schedule

| Age of Account | End of Accounting Period Balance of Accounts Receivable | Estimated Uncollectible Percentage | Amount Needed in Allowance Account at End of Period |
|---|---|---|---|
| 1–30 Days | $10,000 | 1 | $100 |
| 31–60 Days | 30,000 | 4 | 1,200 |
| 61–90 Days | 8,000 | 8 | 640 |
| Over 90 days | 2,000 | 15 | 300 |
| | $50,000 | | $2,240 |

13. **Further assume that the Allowance for Doubtful Accounts has a balance of $1,000 at June 30, the end of the accounting period. Using the accounts receivable aging method, what would be the journal entry at June 30?**

   A. Debit Uncollectible Accounts Expense for $2,240, and credit Allowance for Doubtful Accounts for $2,240.
   B. Debit Uncollectible Accounts Expense for $1,240, and credit Allowance for Doubtful Accounts for $1,240.
   C. Debit Uncollectible Accounts Expense for $2,240, and credit Accounts Receivable for $2,240.
   D. None of the above

14. **(True or false?) The net realizable value of Accounts Receivable on the balance sheet on June 30 would be:**

| | |
|---|---|
| Accounts Receivable | $50,000 |
| Less: Allowance for Uncollectible Accounts | 2,240 |
| | $47,760 |

15. Johns Company partially recovered an accounts receivable that had been previously written off in the amount of $2,000. The amount recovered was $800. If Johns Company uses the accounts receivable aging method, which of the following statements is incorrect regarding the journal entry to record the recovery?

   A. Debit Accounts receivable for $800.
   B. Credit Allowance for Uncollectible Accounts for $800.
   C. Debit Cash for $800, and credit Accounts Receivable for $800.
   D. Debit Accounts Receivable for $2,000, and credit Allowance for Doubtful Accounts for $2,000.

chapter **8**

# *Accounting for Inventories*

## CHAPTER OBJECTIVES

*The purposes of this chapter are to*

- Define and compare inventories for merchandising and manufacturing companies
- Explain the purchasing and recording of inventory
- Explain methods for inventory accounting
  - The perpetual inventory method
  - The periodic inventory method
- Explain how inventories are valued
  - Specific identification method
  - Weighted average method
  - First-in, first-out (FIFO) method
  - Last-in, last-out (LIFO) method
  - Gross profit method

# Inventories in Merchandising and Manufacturing Companies

There are basically three types of businesses in the United States: merchandising, manufacturing, and service. Since service businesses have virtually no inventory held for resale, they will not be a part of this discussion. A **merchandising company**, such as Nordstrom, purchases ready-to-sell merchandise for resale, and its inventory consists of unsold items on hand at the end of an accounting period. As inventory is sold during the period, the value of that inventory is charged to Cost of Goods Sold.

A **manufacturing company**, on the other hand, purchases raw materials and adds labor and overhead to manufacture a finished product for sale. Thus, its inventories include raw materials, work in process, and finished goods. The finished goods inventory is analogous to a merchandise inventory in a retail company. The cost flow in a manufacturing company would be like that shown in Exhibit 8.1.

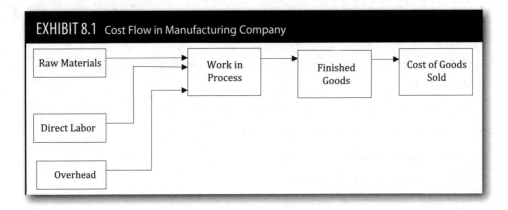

**EXHIBIT 8.1**   Cost Flow in Manufacturing Company

On the balance sheet the inventories of a merchandising company and a manufacturing company would look like those shown in Exhibit 8.2a and Exhibit 8.2b.

Note: detailed accounting procedures for manufacturing inventories are not covered in this book.[1]

---

[1]See Berry, Leonard Eugene: *Management Accounting Demystified*, McGraw-Hill, 2005, a companion text to this book.

**EXHIBIT 8.2a**  XYZ Merchandising Company
Balance Sheet December 31, 2xxx

| Current Assets: | |
| --- | --- |
| Cash and cash equivalents | $105,000 |
| Receivables | 80,000 |
| Inventories | 520,000 |
| Prepaid expenses | 40,000 |
| Total current assets | $745,000 |

**EXHIBIT 8.2b**  ABC Manufacturing Company
Balance Sheet December 31, 2xxx

| Current Assets: | | |
| --- | --- | --- |
| Cash and cash equivalents | | $105,000 |
| Receivables | | 80,000 |
| Inventories: | | |
| Raw Materials | $205,000 | |
| Work in process | 300,000 | |
| Finished goods | 400,000 | |
| | | 905,000 |
| Prepaid expenses | | 40,000 |
| Total current assets | | $1,050,000 |

# Purchasing and Recording Inventory

For most businesses, the acquisition of inventory starts with a purchase order from the purchasing department. The purchase order is a record of the order details of a request to a vendor for inventory. Internally, copies of the purchase order usually go to these places:

- To the receiving department, where they are compared to the shipping documents and physical items when they are received. The receiving department will notify accounts payable when all items have been received. In most large companies, these actions are computerized, where a scanner is used to report items received to the accounts payable department.

- To the accounts payable department, where they are compared to the vendor's invoice and the receiving report from the receiving department. These documents support payment for the goods received.

## What Are the Costs Included in the Purchased Inventory?

In determining the cost of purchased goods a question arises as to when the title passes and who should pay the freight. The answer depends on the **FOB** (free on board) terms.

> **FOB destination** means that the title passes when the purchaser receives the goods and the seller is responsible for the cost of freight. **FOB shipping point** means that title passes at the point of shipment and the purchaser is responsible for the cost of the freight (freight-in). Therefore, the cost of the goods purchased should include the purchase cost (invoice price) and the cost of the freight-in.

## Purchase Returns and Allowances

Purchasers may return goods to the vendor because of ordering or receiving the wrong item, slight damage to the goods, or ordering too much inventory. Such returns are recorded separately as Purchasing Returns and deducted from the cost of the inventory. Recording of Purchasing Returns is the opposite of the recording of Sales Returns by a seller. Assume that XYZ Company purchased $10,000 of inventory and it paid $100 freight. Also, assume that it returns $500 of goods purchased because it ordered too many items. The following would be the journal entries:

| At purchase: | Merchandise Inventory | 10,000 | |
|---|---|---|---|
| | Freight-in | 100 | |
| | Accounts Payable | | 10,100 |
| Goods returned: | Accounts Payable | 500 | |
| | Purchases Returns and Allowances | | 500 |

The balance sheet would show the following:

| | | |
|---|---|---|
| Beginning Inventory Balance | | $0 |
| Add: | Purchases | 10,000 |
| | Freight-in | 100 |
| Less: | Purchasing Returns and Allowances | (500) |
| Cost of Goods Available for Sale | | $9,600 |

Purchasers may receive goods that are defective or damaged but decide to keep them, if the seller provides a reasonable allowance. The accounting for an allowance is handled exactly the same as purchase returns and is deducted from Cost of Goods on the balance sheet.

## Purchase Discounts

A **purchase discount** is a reduction in the purchase price by the seller for prompt payment of a receivable. The discount is usually shown in the following format: 3/10, n/30. This notation means that the vendor will give a 3 percent discount if the purchaser pays within 10 days. If the purchaser does not pay by then, the full amount is due in 30 days. A purchaser must carefully manage its payments to make sure that discounts are taken, as failure to do so may result in a significant unnecessary expense.

There are two options in record purchase discounts: (1) inventory purchases may be recorded as net of discounts (e.g., the purchase cost is recorded net of purchase discounts), and (2) alternatively, the inventory purchases may be recorded at gross cost, ignoring discounts, and a separate account called Purchase Discounts is used to record the discount.

## Consigned Goods

**Consigned goods** are items that are possessed by one party (the consignee) but owned by another. The consignee normally acts as a sales agent to sell the items that have been received from the consignor. For example, a clothing store may accept clothing items from a seller on consignment. The consignee does not make any entries in the inventory records for goods received under consignment. However, the consignee must be careful to segregate consigned items from the regular inventory so as not to get the two mixed up and included in the regular inventory. When consigned items are sold, the consignee will keep a percentage of the sold items as a fee and remit the balance to the consignor. For example, assume that Jones Clothing Stores sold $1,000 of clothing from a client and charged a fee of 10 percent for acting as the seller. Jones also spent $100 on advertising the clothing. The journal entry would be

| | | |
|---|---|---|
| Receivable from Consignor | 100 | |
|     Cash | | 100 |
| (To record advertising for consignor) | | |
| Cash | 1,000 | |
|     Payable to Consignor | | 1,000 |
| (To record sale of consigned goods) | | |

*(Continued)*

| Payable to Consignor | 1,000 | |
|---|---|---|
|     Receivable from Consignor | | 100 |
|     Commission Fee | | 100 |
|     Cash | | 9,800 |
| (To record payment to consignor) | | |

# Inventory Cost Flow Methods

Thus far, we have assumed that when inventory is purchased it is posted (debited) to a merchandising inventory account, and when items are sold they are directly posted (credited) to the same inventory account. The cost flow of the inventory is shown in Exhibit 8.3.

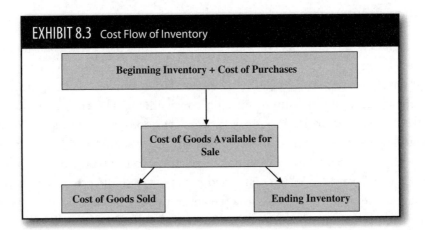

**EXHIBIT 8.3**  Cost Flow of Inventory

Beginning Inventory + Cost of Purchases

Cost of Goods Available for Sale

Cost of Goods Sold

Ending Inventory

As the illustration shows, a company usually starts with a beginning inventory and adds purchases during the period, arriving at goods available. Costs of goods available for sale are assigned to either Cost of Goods Sold or Ending Inventory. But how is this done? It depends on which inventory system that the company uses: the perpetual inventory system or the periodic inventory system.

A **perpetual inventory system** requires real-time updating of the inventory records each time there is a purchase, sale, or return. Prior to the improvements in computer technology this system was not popular, since it required manually updating the inventory each time there was an inventory transaction. However, with current computer technology and point-of-sale systems, a company can more easily use the perpetual inventory system. The perpetual inventory system has the following features:

- All purchases are debited to the Inventory account, not to the Purchases account.
- Freight-in is debited directly to the Inventory account.
- After each sale, the Cost of Goods Sold account is debited and the inventory is credited.
- A physical inventory is normally taken once each year to determine the accuracy of the merchandising inventory's ending balance. Any errors are charged to an Inventory Over or Short account. The offsetting debit or credit is posted to the Inventory account.

A **periodic inventory system** requires that the value of the inventory be determined periodically via a physical count, usually at the end of the accounting period. This system has the following features:

- All purchases are debited to a Purchases account, which is adjusted for returns, allowances, and discounts, as discussed previously.
- The purchases during the period are added to the Beginning Inventory to get Cost of Goods Available for sale.
- A physical inventory is taken at the end of the accounting period. The value of this inventory is deducted from Cost of Goods Available for Sale to determine Cost of Goods Sold (Beginning Inventory + Purchases − Ending Inventory = Cost of Goods Sold). Due to the cost of taking a full physical inventory, it is normally done at the end of an accounting period, typically once per year.

A summary of the journal entries for the two different systems are illustrated in Exhibit 8.4b using the data in Exhibit 8.4a.

| EXHIBIT 8.4a  Illustrative Inventory Data | |
| --- | --- |
| Beginning inventory | 1,000 units @ $10 = $10,000 |
| Purchases | 5,000 units @ $10 = $50,000 |
| Sales | 4,500 units @ $15 = $67,500 |
| Ending inventory | 1,500 units @ $10 = $15,000 |

**EXHIBIT 8.4b** Journal Entries: Perpetual vs. Periodic Inventory Systems

| | Perpetual | | | Periodic | | |
|---|---|---|---|---|---|---|
| Purchases | Inventory | 50,000 | | Purchases | 50,000 | |
| | Accounts Payable | | 50,000 | Accounts Payable | | 50,000 |
| Sales | Accounts Receivable | 67,500 | | Accounts Receivable | 67,500 | |
| | Sales | | 67,500 | Sales | | 67,500 |
| | Cost of Goods Sold | 45,000 | | (No cost of goods sold until the end of the period) | | |
| | Inventory | | 45,000 | | | |
| End-of-period–close-outs | (No entry since inventory is kept real time. However, an inventory should be taken to test the accuracy of the inventory balance.) | | | Inventory (ending inv) | 15,000 | |
| | | | | Cost of Goods Sold | 45,000 | |
| | | | | Purchases | | 50,000 |
| | | | | Inventory (Beg.) | | 10,000 |
| | | | | (Adjusting entry at end of accounting period) | | |

# Inventory Valuation Methods

So far in this chapter we have assumed that all purchases have been made at the same price. Rarely is that the case. Thus, a valuation method must be adopted that results in a systematic approach for assigning costs to the various items on hand that were purchased at different prices. The following are the typical valuation methods used:

- Specific identification method
- Weighted average method
- First-in, first out (FIFO) method
- Last-in, last out (LIFO) method
- Retail method

## Specific Identification Method

The **specific identification method** keeps track of each item in the inventory and each item sold. That is, it specifically identifies each item sold and assigns the actual cost paid when the item was purchased. Obviously, this method requires effort and is normally used in situations were there are small numbers of items that are easily distinguishable. The ending inventory value will be the same under either the perpetual or the periodic inventory systems. Two good examples are jewelry and automobiles. For example, using the inventory data for XYZ Retail Company (assume net of purchase returns, allowances, and discounts) as shown in Exhibit 8.5.

| **EXHIBIT 8.5**  Purchases and Goods Available for Sale before Sales | | | | | | |
|---|---|---|---|---|---|---|
| **Date** | **No. of Units** | | **Unit Cost** | | **Total Cost** | |
| January 1(Beg Inv) | | 800 | $5.90 | | | $4,720 |
| January 10 | 2,000 | | $6.00 | $12,000 | | |
| February 15 | 2,000 | | $6.10 | $12,200 | | |
| March 12 | 3,000 | | $6.15 | $18,450 | | |
| Total purchases | | 7,000 | | | | 42,650 |
| Total goods available for sale | | 7,800 | | | | $47,370 |

SALES: Assume that 2,000 units were sold on January 20, 1,500 units were sold on February 15, and 2,500 units were sold on March 15. Total sales = 6,000 units.

Using the data in Exhibit 8.5, what is the value of the ending inventory and cost of goods sold using the specific identification method of costing?

One way to compute these two numbers is to compute the cost of each sale based on the unit cost in each tier of purchases. However, the easier way is to "back into the ending inventory" and "squeeze" the cost of goods sold. If all 1,800 items in the Ending Inventory came from the last purchase of 3,000 units at $6.15, which they did, then the Ending Inventory must be $6.15 × 1,800 = $11,070. The Cost of Goods Sold is determined as follows:

| | |
|---|---|
| Cost of Goods Available | $47,370 |
| Deduct: Ending inventory | 11,070 |
| Cost of Goods Sold | $36,300 |

The journal entries would be (assuming the periodic inventory system):

| | | |
|---|---|---|
| Cost of Goods Sold | 36,300 | |
| Inventory (ending) | 11,070 | |
| Inventory (beginning) | | 4,720 |
| Purchases | | 42,650 |

However, if the specific identification method uses the perpetual inventory system, the inventory would be updated after each sale and charged to Cost of Goods Sold. This would result in the inventory records showing a "real-time running balance."

Note that under the specific identification method the cost flow matches the physical flow of goods. While the specific identification method can be more accurate, it has the weaknesses of being costly to maintain and users may manipulate net income by selecting the unit prices that best favor the cost of goods sold to achieve the net income desired.

## Weighted Average Method

The **weighted average method** determines the units and cost of the goods available for sale and uses that to compute an average cost per unit, which is then used to value both cost of goods sold and the ending inventory.

Using the data in Exhibit 8.5, the average cost per unit is: $\dfrac{\$47,370}{7,800} = \$6.073$.

Thus, the cost of goods sold and ending inventory would be

$$\text{Cost of goods sold } (6{,}000 \times \$6.073) = \$36{,}440$$

$$\text{Ending inventory } (\$1{,}800 \times \$6.073) = \$10{,}930$$

The journal entries would be (assuming the periodic inventory system):

| | | |
|---|---|---|
| Cost of Goods Sold | 36,440 | |
| Inventory (ending) | 10,930 | |
| Inventory (beginning) | | 4,720 |
| Purchases | | 42,650 |

The weighted average method has the advantage of being simple to apply and is less subject to income manipulation. Note that the previous example assumed that the periodic inventory system had been used. If the perpetual inventory system were used, a new weighted average would have to be computed each time a purchase or sale was made. This can get very complicated when there are a large number of different items involved. Companies that use the perpetual system with the weighted average usually have sophisticated computer technology that can perform these computations.

## First In, First Out Method

The **first in, first out (FIFO)** method assumes that the first items purchased are the first items sold. Thus, it is assumed that the last items purchased must be the items in the ending inventory. Under the FIFO method the cost of goods sold and ending inventory will be the same under both the periodic and perpetual inventory systems. This is because the same costs will always be first in and first out under both and what is left after sales are deducted is the ending inventory.

To illustrate the FIFO method, look at the data on Exhibit 8.5. Using the *periodic inventory system* and FIFO, the Ending Inventory would be as shown in Exhibit 8.6.

| EXHIBIT 8.6 | | | |
|---|---|---|---|
| **Date** | **No. of Units** | **Unit Cost** | **Total Cost** |
| March 12 | 1,800 | $6.15 | $11,070 |

| Cost of Goods Available for Sale | $47,370 |
|---|---|
| Less: Ending Inventory: 1,800 × $6.15 | 11,070 |
| Cost of Goods Sold | $36,300 |

The journal entries would be:

| Cost of Goods Sold | 36,300 | |
|---|---|---|
| Inventory (ending) | 11,070 | |
| Inventory (beginning) | | 4,720 |
| Purchases | | 42,650 |

To illustrate the **perpetual inventory system** using FIFO, the Ending Inventory would be as shown in Exhibit 8.7.

## EXHIBIT 8.7

| Date | Purchased | Sold | Balance |
|---|---|---|---|
| Beginning | 800 @ $5.90 = $4,720 | 0 | 800 @ $5.90 = **$4,720** |
| January 10 | 2,000 @ $6.00 = 12,000 | | 800 @ $5.90 = $4,720<br>2,000 @ $6.00 = $12,000<br>Total **$16,720** |
| January 20 | | 800 @ $5.90 = $4,720<br>1,200 @$6.00 = $7,200 | 800 @ $6.00 = **$4,800** |
| February 15 | 2,000 @ $6.10 = $12,200 | 800 @ $6.00 = $4,800<br>700 @ $6.10 = $4,270 | 1,300 @ $6.10 = **$7,930** |
| March 12 | 3,000 @ $6.15 = $15,375 | | 1,300 @ 6.10 = $7,930<br>3,000 @ $6.15 = $18,450<br>Total **$26.380** |
| March 15 | | 1,300 @ $6.10 = $7,930<br>1,200 @ $6.15 = $7,380 | 1,800 @ $6.15 = **$11,070** |

The Cost of Goods Sold would be

| Cost of Goods Available for Sale | $47,370 |
|---|---|
| Less: Ending Inventory (computed above) | 11,070 |
| Cost of Goods Sold | $36,300 |

The ending inventory is the same under the perpetual inventory system and the periodic system using FIFO. Also, the ending inventory and cost of goods sold is the same as the specific identification method. This will always be true if the specific identification method follows the physical flow of costs in assigning costs to ending inventory. However, the latter is not always true.

The following is a summary of the journal entries using the perpetual inventory system under FIFO:

| | | |
|---|---|---|
| Cost of Goods Sold | 36,300 | |
| Inventory | | 36,300 |

The FIFO method has the advantage of following the physical flow of costs. However, in a time of rapidly changing prices it does not match the most current costs to income. It charges the oldest costs against more current sales prices on the income statement, which may distort net income for the period.

## Last In, Last Out Method

The **last in, last out (LIFO)** method assumes that the most recent (last) purchases were the first sold during the period. This means that this method assigns the last costs to Cost of Goods Sold and the earliest purchases are assigned to Ending Inventory.

To illustrate the LIFO method using the *periodic inventory system* and the data in Exhibit 8.5, the ending inventory would be calculated as shown in Exhibit 8.8.

### EXHIBIT 8.8

| Date | No. of Units | Unit Cost | Total Cost |
|---|---|---|---|
| Beginning inventory | 800 | $5.90 | $4,720 |
| January 10 | 1,000 | 6.00 | 6,000 |
| | | | $10,720 |

| | |
|---|---|
| Cost of Goods Available for Sale | $47,370 |
| Less: Ending Inventory, as computed above | 10,720 |
| Cost of Goods Sold | $36,650 |

The journal entries would be:

| | | |
|---|---|---|
| Cost of Goods Sold | 36,650 | |
| Inventory (ending) | 10,720 | |
| Inventory (beginning) | | 4,720 |
| Purchases | | 42,650 |

To illustrate the LIFO method using the *perpetual inventory system* using the data in Exhibit 8.5, the ending inventory would be calculated as shown in Exhibit 8.9.

## EXHIBIT 8.9

| Date | Purchased | Sold | Balance |
|---|---|---|---|
| Beginning | 800 @ $5.90 = $4,720 | 0 | 800 @ $5.90 = **$4,720** |
| January 10 | 2,000 @ $6.00 =12,000 | 0 | 800 @ $5.90 = $4,720 |
| | | | 2,000 @ $6.00 = $12,000 |
| | | | **Total Balance $16,720** |
| January 20 | 0 | 2,000 @ $6.00 = $12,000 | **Bal 800 @ $5.90 = $4,720** |
| February 15 | | | 800 @ 5.90 = $4,720 |
| | 2,000 @ $6.10 = $12,200 | | $2,000 @ $6.10 = $12,200 |
| | | | **Total Balance $16,920** |
| February 15 | | 1,500 @ $6.10 = $9,150 | 800 @ $5.90 = $4,720 |
| | | | 500 @ $6.10 = $3,050 |
| | | | **Total Balance $7,770** |
| March 12 | | 0 | 800 @ 5.90 = $4,720 |
| | | | 500 @ $6.10 = $3,050 |
| | 3,000 @ $6.15 = $18,450 | | 3,000 @ $6.15 = $18,450 |
| | | | **Total Balance $26,220** |
| March 15 | | 2,500 @ $6.15 = $15,375 | 800 @ 5.90 = $4,720 |
| | 0 | | 500 @ $6.10 = $3,050 |
| | | | 500 @ $6.15 = $3,075 |
| | | | **Total Balance $10,845** |

The Cost of Goods Sold would be

| Cost of Goods Available for Sale | $47,370 |
| Less: Ending Inventory, as computed above | 10,845 |
| Cost of Goods Sold | $36,525* |

*Note that the cost of goods sold could have been computed by adding the total cost of sales in the "sold" column in Exhibit 8.9 but the answer would have been the same.

Note that the Ending Inventory of $10,845 and the Cost of Goods Sold of $36,525 under the perpetual inventory system are different than that of the periodic inventory system ($10,720 and $36,650).

A summary entry of all the journal entries made during the period under the perpetual inventory system for LIFO would be

| Cost of Goods Sold | 36,525 | |
| Inventory | | 36,525 |

The strongest advantage of the LIFO method for valuing the inventory is that it results in the more current costs being matched with current revenues. Thus, many people claim LIFO to be superior to FIFO during a time of rising prices.

Variations of the LIFO method are found in accounting practice. For example, a so-called LIFO reserve can be used when values reported for external purposes differ from values used for internal reporting purposes. Most companies use LIFO for external reporting but may use FIFO or weighted average for internal purposes. The LIFO reserve is used to account for the difference in the two. LIFO reserve is not covered in this book, but the topic can be found in a more advanced accounting text.

## Lower-of-Cost-or-Market Adjustments

Although a company may make every attempt to present financial statements that reflect the current value of its inventory, there may be situations where the inventory may still be overvalued. For example, the inventory may contain items that are obsolete or defective, or they may have suffered major price declines. When that happens, the accountant will employ the concept of **conservatism** to assure that the inventories are valued at the lower of cost or market. The lower-of-cost-or-market (LCM) rule states that inventory should be carried at the lower of its cost or market value (replacement cost) on the date of the balance sheet. Note that replacement cost is not necessarily the same as the selling price. Each group of items in the inventory is assessed and if the total cost carried on the accounting records is greater than the replacement cost, an account entitled Loss for Decline in Market Value would be debited and the offsetting credit would be to Inventory. Exhibit 8.10 is an illustration of the application of the LCM rule.

**EXHIBIT 8.10**  Illustration of the Lower-of-Cost-or-Market Rule

| Item | Inventory in Units | Unit Cost | Unit Replacement Cost | Total Cost | Total Replacement Cost | Lower of Cost or Market |
|------|--------------------|-----------|-----------------------|------------|------------------------|-------------------------|
| A | 1,000 | $1.00 | $.90 | $1,000 | $900 | $900 |
| B | 1,200 | $2.00 | $2.10 | 2,400 | 2,520 | 2,400 |
| C | 2,500 | $1.50 | $1.30 | 3,750 | 3,250 | 3,250 |
| Total | | | | $7,150 | $6,670 | $6,550 |

Adjustments to the inventory using the LCM rule can be made using individual items or in aggregate. Using the aggregate approach the adjustment would use $6,670 ($6,670 vs. $7,150). Using the item-by-item approach the adjustment would use $6,550 ($6,550 vs. $6,670). The difference between either of these two values and the carrying cost of the inventory ($7,150) would be used to make the journal entry in the books. Most companies use the item-by-item method for adjusting inventories, as it gives the most conservative valuation. Why? Because the aggregate approach results in market values higher than costs offsetting market values lower than cost. Another reason for using the item-by-item approach is that the Internal Revenue Service requires it, and keeping two sets of records is costly.

Using the data above, the item-by-item approach would require the following journal entry:

| | | |
|---|---|---|
| Loss for Decline in Market Value | 600 | |
| Inventory | | 600 |
| ($7,150 − $6,550 = $600) | | |

Once the inventory has been adjusted, the new valuation becomes the basis for valuation and reporting purposes during the next cycle.

Use of the LCM rule can get more complicated. GAAP states that inventory market values should not exceed its net realizable value (NRV). NRV = Selling Price – Completion and Disposal Costs. This establishes a ceiling value. For example, if the replacement costs were $1,500 and the net realizable value was $1,400, then the $1,400 value would be used to determine LCM. GAAP also states that the replacement value should not be less than a floor amount: the net realizable less a normal profit margin. For example, if the replacement cost was $2,400 and the floor value was $2,200, then $2,200 would be used to determine LCM.

## Estimating Inventory Values: The Gross Profit Method

The discussion up to this point has been based on the assumption that inventory valuations and adjustments will be made at the end of the accounting year. It has also assumed that a physical inventory would be taken once each year and adjustments made based on that count. This is true whether the company uses the periodic inventory system or the perpetual inventory system. However, most companies issue interim financial statements, usually quarterly. It would be impractical and expensive to conduct a physical inventory each quarter. To overcome this necessity many companies will use an estimation method to estimate the ending inventory for quarterly reporting. These methods are also to be used in case of a catastrophic event, such as a fire, to estimate the inventory.

One estimating method is the **gross profit method,** which means that the company's historical gross profit percentage (gross profit as a percentage of sales) is used to estimate the amount of gross profit and cost of goods sold. From these computations the ending inventory is estimated. As an example, assume XYZ Company has a beginning inventory of $20,000, net purchases of $100,000, and net sales of $200,000.

**Step 1.** *Determine gross profit percentage.* Assume that sales were most recently $200,000 and gross profit was $120,000. Thus, the gross profit percentage was 60 percent ($120,000/$200,000).

**Step 2.** *Compute Cost of Goods Sold.* $200,000 × (100% – 60%) = $80,000.

**Step 3.** *Use the income statement format to fill in the ending inventory* as shown in Exhibit 8.11.

**EXHIBIT 8.11**  Partial Income Statement

| | | |
|---|---|---|
| Net Sales | | $200,000 |
| Less:Cost of goods sold | | |
| Beginning inventory | $20,000 | |
| Net purchases | $100,000 | |
| Cost of goods available | $120,000 | |
| Less: Ending inventory | ???? | |
| Cost of goods sold | | 80,000 |
| Gross profit on sales | | $120,000 |
| (60% × $200,000) | | |

Using the formula Cost of Goods Available less Ending Inventory = Cost of Goods Sold, the Ending Inventory is $120,000 – Ending Inventory = $80,000. Ending Inventory = $40,000.

# QUIZ

1. The replacement cost of an inventory item is $10, the actual cost of that item is $9.50, the net realizable value is $11, and the floor value is $10.50. Using the lower-of-cost-or-market rule, what is the inventory valuation for that item?
   A. $10.00
   B. $10.50
   C. $9.50
   D. None of the above

2. (True or false?) When the terms of sale for goods are FOB destination, ownership of the goods changes at the point of shipment.

3. Which of the following inventories would most likely not be found in a manufacturing company?
   A. Merchandise Inventory
   B. Finished Goods
   C. Work in Process
   D. Raw Materials

4. A company had $10,000 in beginning inventory, $50,000 in purchases, $11,000 in the ending inventory (before any sales), and sales at a cost of $10,000. Assuming the periodic inventory system and the LIFO method, which layer of inventory would be used to charge to Cost of Goods Sold?
   A. The $10,000 in the beginning inventory would be charged first.
   B. $10,000 of the ending inventory would be charged first.
   C. $10,000 of the purchases would be charged first.
   D. None of the above

5. During a period of rising inflation, which cost flow method produces the highest net income?
   A. Weighted average method
   B. Gross profit method
   C. LIFO
   D. FIFO

6. According to GAAP, the term "market" in "lower-of-cost-or-market," means:
   A. Replacement cost
   B. Net realizable value
   C. Ceiling price
   D. Floor price

*Use the data in the following income statement to answer questions 7 and 8.*

| Partial Income Statement | | |
|---|---|---|
| Net Sales | | $100,000 |
| Less: Cost of goods sold | | |
| Beginning inventory | $10,000 | |
| Net purchases | 50,000 | |
| Cost of goods available | $60,000 | |
| Less: Ending inventory | ????? | |
| Cost of goods sold | | ?????? |
| Gross profit on sales | | $60,000 |

7. **Using the gross profit method, what is the cost of goods sold?**
   A. $36,000
   B. $24,000
   C. $20,000
   D. $40,000

8. **Using the gross profit method, what is the ending inventory?**
   A. $36,000
   B. $20,000
   C. $40,000
   D. $24,000

*Use the data in the following table to answer questions 9 and 11.*

| Item | Inventory in Units | Unit Cost | Unit Replacement Cost | Total Cost | Total Replacement Cost | Lower of Cost or Market |
|---|---|---|---|---|---|---|
| A | 1,000 | $11.00 | $10.50 | $11,000 | $10,500 | $10,500 |
| B | 1,200 | $12.00 | $12.50 | 14,400 | 15,000 | 14,400 |
| C | 2,500 | 11.50 | 11.30 | 28,750 | 28,250 | 28,250 |
| Total | | | | $54,150 | $53,750 | $53,150 |

9. Using the lower-of-cost-or-market aggregate method, what would be the Inventory adjustment?
   A. $1,000
   B. $0
   C. $400
   D. None of the above

10. **Using the lower-of-cost-or-market item-by-item method, what would be the Inventory adjustment?**
    A. $1,000
    B. $0
    C. $400
    D. None of the above

11. **A business that sells high-priced jewelry would most likely use which of the following cost flow methods?**
    A. FIFO
    B. LIFO
    C. Gross profit method
    D. Specific identification method

*Use the following data for questions 12 through 14:*

| Date | No. of Units Purchased | Unit Cost | Total Cost |
|---|---|---|---|
| January 1(Beg Inv) | 1,000 | $10.00 | $10,000 |
| January 11 | 3,000 | 11.00 | 33,000 |
| February 15 | 2,000 | 11.50 | 23,000 |
| March 12 | 3,000 | 12.00 | 36,000 |
| Total purchases | 8,000 | | 92,000 |
| Total goods available for sale | 9,000 | | $102,000 |

**SALES:** Assume that that 2,000 units were sold on January 20, 1,500 units were sold on February 15, and 2,500 units were sold on March 15. Total sales = 7,000 units.

12. Using LIFO and the perpetual inventory system, what is the value of the ending inventory on January 21?

A. $22,000
B. $21,000
C. $21,500
D. None of the above

13. Using FIFO and the periodic inventory system, what is the Cost of Goods Sold at the end of the period?

A. $78,000
B. $79,000
C. $80,000
D. None of the above

14. Using the weighted average method and the perpetual inventory system, what would Ending Inventory be after January 21?

A. $22,000
B. $21,000
C. $21,500
D. None of the above

15. The inventory cost flow method that would most likely result in manipulation of income is:

A. LIFO
B. FIFO
C. Weighted average method
D. Specific identification method

## chapter 9

# Accounting for Long-Term Assets

## CHAPTER OBJECTIVES

*The purposes of this chapter are to*

- Define plant, property, and equipment and how they are valued
- Explain the depreciation of plant and equipment
- Explain the accounting for plant and equipment disposals
- Explain the accounting for intangible assets

## What Are Plant, Property, and Equipment?

Plant, property, and equipment are tangible fixed assets acquired for operational use over a long term that are not for resale. They are used in the productive operation of a business and include land, buildings (offices, retail structures, factories, and warehouses), and equipment (furniture, computers, machinery, vehicles, tools, etc.). Intangible assets are not included in this category; they will be covered later in this chapter. Note that "productive operations" would exclude land held for future use (or for speculation) and idle facilities. The latter should be included under Long-Term Investments.

## Acquisition of Plant, Property, and Equipment

A business will acquire plant, property, and equipment (PP&E) based on its long-term strategies. Each year, after the company reviews its strategies and selects the ones that are most appropriate for success, the business will normally prepare a long-term capital budget based on these strategies. Once the capital budget is approved, the business will acquire any needed assets through competitive procurement procedures.

The basis for recording long-term assets into the accounting records is **historical cost** using the historical cost principle (see Chapter 2). This would include the purchase price, shipping costs, and any costs expended in readying the assets for operational use. The term "capitalization" is often used to describe the recording of costs of assets in the accounting records. Items included in cost of a long-term asset are further discussed in the following paragraphs.

### Land

The following are typical costs included in land acquisition:

- Purchase price
- Real estate commissions
- Closing costs
- Attorney's fees
- Recording fees
- Costs associated with preparing the land for use—for example, clearing the land by removing old buildings, grading, filling, and landscaping
- Special assessments for local improvements (e.g., paving and sewers)

Improvements with limited lives (e.g., fences and parking lots) should not be recorded as cost of land; instead, they should be recorded as Land Improvements and depreciated over their useful lives.

### Buildings

These are typical costs included in a finished building acquisition:

- The purchase price of a finished building
- Real estate commissions
- Closing costs

- Attorney's fees
- Recording fees

These are typical costs included in constructed buildings:

- Architectural fees
- Building permits
- Other professional fees
- Excavation costs
- Materials, labor, and overhead costs incurred during construction

## Equipment

The following are typical costs included in the purchase of equipment:

- Purchase price (net of discounts)
- Sales taxes and permits
- Freight or delivery costs, including insurance in transit
- Normal assembling and installation costs, including test runs
- Interest to finance the purchase of long-term assets

Training costs necessary to learn to operate the new plant or equipment are *not* included in the acquisition costs. These items are normally expensed in the period in which they are incurred.

For example, assume a company purchased a manufacturing building for $1,500,000, including all associated costs. The journal entry would be

| | | |
|---|---|---|
| Buildings | 1,500,000 | |
| Cash | | 1,500,000 |
| (To record purchase of a building) | | |

## Bundled Acquisitions

Sometimes a business may purchase land, buildings, and equipment for one lump-sum price. In this situation, it is necessary to allocate the cost among the individual assets acquired. The business should use the **relative fair market value method** for this purpose, which means that a business should obtain an appraisal for each asset when a valid value cannot be otherwise determined. For example, assume a company purchases a building, equipment, and land for one price of $600,000. Further assume that the building was appraised for $400,000, the land for $200,000, and the equipment for $200,000. Buildings would be debited as

$$\frac{400,000}{800,000} \times 600,000 = 300,000$$

Land would be debited as

$$\frac{200,000}{800,000} \times 600,000 = 150,000$$

Equipment would be debited as

$$\frac{200,000}{800,000} \times 600,000 = 150,000$$

# Depreciation of Plant and Equipment

As businesses use operational assets, they will undergo loss of value due to wear and tear, obsolescence, and other factors. (Note that depreciation does not apply to land, as it is not a depreciable asset.) Said another way, **depreciation** describes any method of spreading the purchase price of an asset over its useful life, as an expense, due to wear and tear and other factors. It is a process of cost allocation that attempts to determine how much of an asset should be expensed for its use during a period, which is then matched with the revenue generated during the same period. Keep in mind that any method of depreciation is arbitrary in that it is impossible to determine the actual amount of an asset that is used up during a period. What is important is that there be a rationale for a depreciation method and that it be systematically determined and applied. There are three major types of depreciation methods:

- Straight-line depreciation
- Units-of-output depreciation (activity)
- Declining balance depreciation, which is further broken down as follows:
  - Double declining balance depreciation
  - Sum-of-the-years'-digits depreciation

Some common depreciation terminology is summarized in Exhibit 9.1.

| EXHIBIT 9.1   Depreciation Terminology | |
|---|---|
| Acquisition cost, or historical cost | The purchase price for an asset, including any associate costs necessary to get the asset to an operation state. It also includes any improvements that extend the future service potential of the asset. |
| Service life | The anticipated useful life of an asset measured in years or units of output. |
| Salvage value, or residual value | An estimate of the amount that the business anticipates receiving at the end of the asset's useful life. |
| Depreciable base | The cost of the asset less its salvage value. |
| Carrying value, or net book value | The historical cost of the asset less its accumulated depreciation. |

## Steps in Recording Depreciation Expense

The amount of depreciation to be expensed and recorded each period is determined by the following steps:

**Step 1**: *Estimate the useful life of the asset.* This determination is a matter of judgment but is usually determined when the asset is new. Consulting experts, such as construction engineers or equipment engineers, can be helpful.

**Step 2**: *Estimate the salvage value.* Again, this is a judgment call and should be determined at the time of purchase. The salvage value may need to be revised during the useful life of the asset.

**Step 3**: *Compute the depreciation expense* using one of the methods described in this chapter. Note that, except for the double declining method, the salvage value is deducted from the cost of the asset to obtain the depreciable base before the amount of the expense is computed.

**Step 4**: *Make the journal entry.* Note that the asset account is not credited. Instead a contra-asset account called Accumulated Depreciation is credited. This account provides information on how much depreciation has been accumulated over the asset's life instead of having the depreciation expense netted against the asset account.

# Straight-Line Depreciation Method

**Straight-line depreciation** is the simplest of the depreciation methods in that it is determined by dividing the depreciable base by the expected useful life measured in time. It assumes that the using up of an asset is a function of time rather than a function of usage. The major advantages of this method are its simplicity and they way it may mirror significant obsolescence that is the same from period to period. The major disadvantage is the assumption that the loss of usefulness is the same from period to period. Many assets suffer peak usage and obsolescence in the early years of service. Surveys have shown that, despite its disadvantages, the straight-line method is the most widely used method of depreciation for reporting purposes.

As an example of the straight-line method, assume the XYZ Company purchases a lathe for $190,000 for use in its production process; it also incurs $10,000 in costs to get the machine operational ready. Also, assume that its useful life is 10 years and it will have a salvage value of $50,000 at the end of 10 years. What is the annual depreciation expense? Using the above steps, the computations are

$$\left(\frac{\$190,000 + 10,000 - 50,000}{10}\right) = \$15,000 \text{ annual depreciation expense}$$

The journal entry would be at the end of the accounting period (assuming one full year):

| | | |
|---|---|---|
| Depreciation Expense | 15,000 | |
| Accumulated Depreciation | | 15,000 |

The **accumulated depreciation** is an asset-offset or contra-asset account that reflects the accumulated depreciation expense over the life of an asset. It is deducted from the historical cost of the asset on the balance sheet to get a net book value. The balance in this account is deducted from the original cost of the asset on the balance sheet.

What happens if an asset is purchased and put in service at times other than the beginning of the account period? The amount of depreciation under the straight-line method is determined as a fraction of the year. Using the previous example, say that XYZ acquired the lathe at the end of the second month of a new accounting year. The depreciation expense would be determined as follows:

$$\left(\frac{\$190,000 + 10,000 - 50,000}{10}\right)\$15,000 \times \frac{10}{12} = \$12,500$$

## Units-of-Output Method

The **units-of-output method** assumes that the depreciation of an asset is a function of its use or production instead of the passage of time. The computation is similar to the straight-line method, except the estimated number of units of output is used rather than the estimated number of years of usage.

To illustrate using the XYZ Company data discussed previously, assume that the lathe will produce an estimated 300,000 units during its lifetime. Also, assume that company produced 29,000 units during its first full year's use of the lathe. What is the annual depreciation expense? The computations are as follows:

$$\left(\frac{\$190,000 + 10,000 - 50,000}{300,000}\right) = \$.50 \, \text{per unit}$$

The first year's depreciation expense would be

$$29,000 \times \$.50 = \$14,500.$$

The journal entry would be

| Depreciation Expense | 14,500 | |
|---|---|---|
| Accumulated Depreciation | | 14,500 |

## Declining Balance Methods

The *declining balance methods* (an *accelerated depreciation method*) charge more depreciation expense in the early years of an asset's life than do other methods. The rationale is that a business uses up more of the asset in its earlier years, because the asset is more productive during that period. With respect to repair and maintenance, assets tend to have less repair and maintenance in their earlier years and more in the later years of their usage. Thus, the declining balance methods tend to mesh with this phenomenon better than do other methods. The two common types of declining balance methods are the double declining method and the sum-of-the-years'-digits method.

The **double declining balance method** is an accelerated depreciation method based on the declining book value of the asset. The double declining method simply takes twice the straight-line rate to compute the annual depreciation expense. The declining balance method *initially ignores salvage value.* There are two ways to compute the annual rate: (1) simply compute the straight-line expense and double it, or (2) compute the expense using the formula

$$\text{Book value} \times (2/\text{Estimated Useful Life})$$

To illustrate using the earlier XYZ Company example, the first-year computation would be

$$(\$190,000 + \$10,000) \times 2/10 = \$40,000$$

The book value at the end of the first year would be $200,000 – 40,000 = $160,000.

At the end of the second year the computation for depreciation would be

$$\$160,000 \times 2/10 = \$32,000$$

Exhibit 9.2 depicts the depreciation charge over the useful life of the asset.

**EXHIBIT 9.2**  Depreciation Schedule—Double Declining Balance Method (All numbers are rounded)

| Year 1 | Depreciable Rate (Beg. of Year) 2 | Depreciation Rate 3 | Depreciation Expense 4 | Accumulated Depreciation (End of Year) 5 | Book Value (End of Year) (200,000 – Col. 6) 6 |
|---|---|---|---|---|---|
|   | $200,000 | 2/10 | $40,000 | $40,000 | $160,000 |
| 1 | $160,000 | 2/10 | 32,000 | 72,000 | 128,000 |
| 2 | 128,000 | 2/10 | 25,600 | 97,600 | 102,400 |
| 3 | 102,400 | 2/10 | 20,480 | 118,080 | 81,920 |
| 4 | 81,920 | 2/10 | 16,384 | 134,464 | 65,536 |
| 5 | 65,536 | 2/10 | 13,109 | 147,571 | 52,429 |
| 6 | 52,429 | 2/10 | 2,429 | 150,000 | 50,000 |
| 7 | 50,000 | 2/10 | 0 | 150,000 | 50,000 |
| 8 | 50,000 | 2/10 | 0 | 150,000 | 50,000 |
| 9 | 50,000 | 2/10 | 0 | 150,000 | 50,000 |
| 10 |   |   |   |   |   |

Note from Exhibit 9.2 that depreciation expense in year six is only $2,429, so the ending book value equals the salvage value of $50,000.

*Sum-of-the-years'-digits depreciation method* is an accelerated depreciation method that uses the number of years of expected life as a fraction. The numerator is the number of years of estimated life remaining as of the beginning of the year, and the denominator is the sum of all digits and is the same for each annual computation. In the XYZ Company illustration, the useful life is 10 years. Thus, the sum-of-the-years'-digits is $10 + 9 + 8 + 7 + 6 + 5 + 4 + 3 + 2 + 1 = 55$. Under this method, the depreciable base would be the cost less the salvage value, which would remain the same throughout the useful life. For the XYZ Company example, the depreciable base would be $200,000 - 50,000 = $150,000$. The first year's depreciation would be

$$\$150,000 \times 10/55 = \$27,273$$

The second year's depreciation would be

$$\$150,000 \times 9/55 = \$24,545$$

Exhibit 9.3 depicts the depreciation expense over the life of the asset. Note that no further depreciation is taken after the salvage value is reached in the ninth year.

**EXHIBIT 9.3**  Depreciation Schedule—Sum-of-the-Years'-Digits Depreciation Method (All numbers are rounded)

| Year 1 | Depreciation Base 2 | Remaining Years 3 | Depreciation Rate 4 | Depreciation Expense (Col. 2 x 4) 5 | Accumulated Depreciation (Col. 6 + 5) 6 | Book Value (200,000 – Col. 6) 7 |
|---|---|---|---|---|---|---|
| 1 | 150,000 | 10 | 10/55 | 27,272 | 27,273 | 172,727 |
| 2 | 150,000 | 9 | 9/55 | 24,544 | 51,818 | 148,183 |
| 3 | 150,000 | 8 | 8/55 | 21,818 | 73,636 | 126,364 |
| 4 | 150,000 | 7 | 7/55 | 19,091 | 92,727 | 107,273 |
| 5 | 150,000 | 6 | 6/55 | 16,364 | 109,091 | 90,909 |
| 6 | 150,000 | 5 | 5/55 | 13,363 | 122,727 | 77,273 |
| 7 | 150,000 | 4 | 4/55 | 10,909 | 138,636 | 61,264 |
| 8 | 150,000 | 3 | 3/55 | 8,182 | 146,818 | 138,736 |
| 9 | 150,000 | 2 | 2/55 | 3,182 | 150,000 | 150,000 |
| 10 | 150,000 | 1 | 1/55 | 0 | 150,000 | 150,000 |

## Impact of Depreciation on Tax Laws

The objective of a business is to minimize the amount of taxes paid to governments. The tax laws have unique regulations when it comes to depreciation, and these features usually do not agree with generally accepted accounting principles (GAAP). So, it is not uncommon to find companies applying GAAP for financial reporting purposes and the tax law for preparation of their tax return, which usually do not agree and necessitates two sets of books. There is nothing sinister or illegal with having two sets of books.

The reason for these differences is that GAAP has a different objective than the tax laws. Financial reporting has to do with measuring economic activity and matching revenues and expenses for a given period. Whereas, tax laws have two objectives: (1) to collect revenue for the government, and (2) to stimulate the economy. Generally, a company will choose accelerated depreciation methods for tax purposes (they give the greatest tax deductions) and may choose the straight-line depreciation method or another method for financial reporting purposes.

## Disposal of Plant and Equipment

Companies may decide to sell an asset that is no longer useful or needed in the operation of the business. This may be done for several reasons:

- The asset is no longer useful to the company, even though it may still have productive capacity remaining.
- A newer model is on the market that is more efficient than the old one.
- The asset is worn out from wear and tear and is sold for scrap.
- The asset has become obsolete.

Usually, there is a gain or loss associated with the sale of an asset. To determine a gain or loss, the proceeds from the sale are compared to the book value of the asset. If the proceeds exceed the book value, there is a gain. If the proceeds are less than the book value, there is a loss. Of course, if the proceeds are the same as the book value, there is no gain or loss. After the gain or loss is determined, the accountant will make a journal entry that records the cash received, recognizes the gain or loss, and removes the asset's historical cost and the accumulated depreciation from the books.

To illustrate, assume that XYZ Company sold a machine for $25,000 cash that cost $100,000 and had $80,000 accumulated depreciation. Determine the gain or loss and make the necessary journal entry to remove the asset from the books.

Computation of gain or loss: $25,000 – ($100,000 – 80,000) = $5,000 gain.

The journal entry would be

| Cash | 25,000 | |
|---|---|---|
| Accumulated Depreciation | 80,000 | |
| Gain on Sale Asset | | 5,000 |
| Machinery | | 100,000 |

If an asset were simply scraped with no proceeds received, the amount of the remaining book value would be the loss. For example, in the previous illustration, assume that the machine was totally obsolete and the company could not sell it and it was scrapped and removed for the removal costs. The journal entry would be

| Accumulated Depreciation | 80,000 | |
|---|---|---|
| Loss on Disposal of Equipment | 20,000 | |
| Machinery | | 100,000 |

Again, the tax treatment for gains and losses are usually different than that using GAAP for financial reporting purposes.

## Trading in of Plant and Equipment

A company may trade in an asset for a new one rather than dispose it. Statement of Financial Standard No. 153 states that the exchange must be assessed to determine if the trade has commercial substance, which essentially means that the company must assess whether the exchange will cause a significant change in the configuration of future cash flows.[1] Assuming that the transaction

---

[1] The determination and impact of "economic substance" is much more involved than discussed in this introductory text. See Statement of Financial Accounting Standard No. 153, Financial Accounting Standards Board, for a full discussion.

has commercial substance, the new asset must be recorded at fair value. The recording of the trade-in would involve the following:

- The book value of the old asset would be compared to its fair value. If the fair value is in excess of the book value of the old asset, a gain arises.
- If the fair value is less than book value of the old asset, a loss would be recognized.
- The new asset would be recorded at its fair value.
- The old asset and accumulated depreciation would be removed from the books.

For example, assume the data in Exhibit 9.4 for the trade of a piece of equipment and that it is determined that it has commercial substance.

| EXHIBIT 9.4   Trading-in of an Old Asset | |
|---|---:|
| **Old Equipment:** | |
| Historical cost | $100,000 |
| Accumulated depreciation through end of last year | $80,000 |
| Depreciation expense since end of year to date of trade-in | $3,000 |
| Fair value of old asset | $27,000 |
| **New Equipment:** | |
| Cost | $150,000 |
| Fair value of new equipment | $150,000 |
| Trade-in allowance | $27,000 |
| Cash paid | $123,000 |

**Step 1.** *Record the depreciation since the end of last year.*

| | | |
|---|---|---|
| Depreciation Expense | 3,000 | |
| Accumulated Depreciation | | 3,000 |

**Step 2.** *Determine gain or loss.*

| | |
|---|---|
| Fair value of old asset | $27,000 |
| Less: Book value of old equipment | 17,000 |
| Gain on trade-in | $10,000 |
| (Book value = $100,000 – 83,000 = $17,000) | |

**Step 3.** *Record the trade.*

| | | |
|---|---|---|
| Accumulated Depreciation | 83,000 | |
| Equipment (new) | 150,000 | |
| Equipment (old) | | 100,000 |
| Cash | | 123,000 |
| Gain on Trade-in of Asset | | 10,000 |

What happens when there is a loss on the trade in? Using the above data, except the fair value of the old asset is $15,000 instead of $27,000. The cash payment would become $150,000 – 15,000 = $135,000. The depreciation expense since the beginning of the year would be recorded the same as above. The journal entries would be

| | | |
|---|---|---|
| Accumulated Depreciation | 83,000 | |
| Equipment (new) | 150,000 | |
| Loss on Trade-in of Equipment | 2,000 | |
| Equipment (old) | | 100,000 |
| Cash | | 135,000 |

# Accounting for Intangible Assets

In addition to tangible assets (plant, property, and equipment), most companies will have intangible assets. **Intangible assets** are nonmonetary assets that cannot be seen, touched, or physically measured. There are two major types of intangibles:

- *Rights granted by a government or by another company.* Examples of rights granted by a government are trademarks, patents, and copyrights. Examples of a right granted by another company are franchises, customer lists, and Internet domains.
- *Internally generated intangibles.* Examples are organization costs, goodwill, and leasehold improvements.

Some intangibles are amortized over their legal life or useful life. **Amortization** means to reduce the value of the intangible by spreading its cost over a period of years. Intangible assets may have an Accumulated Amortization account or not. If the Accumulated Amortization account is not used, the Intangible Assets account is directly reduced. For example, a patent (discussed further below) is defended in court, which cost $50,000 in legal fees. The patent is amortized over 20 years. The legal fees where the accumulated amortization is not used would be recorded as follows:

| Patents | 50,000 | |
|---|---|---|
| Cash | | 50,000 |

The first year's amortization would be

| Patent Amortization Expense | 2,500 | |
|---|---|---|
| Patents | | 2,500 |

If the Accumulated Amortization account were used, the first year's amortization journal entry would be

| Patent Amortization Expense | 2,500 | |
|---|---|---|
| Accumulated Amortization | | 2,500 |

## Valuation of Intangibles

An intangible can only be recorded in the accounting records when it is purchased from another party in an arm's-length transaction. Typical costs that are capitalized include the intangible's purchase price, legal fees incurred in acquiring the intangible, and other incidental expenses. What about stock or other assets that are given in exchange for the intangible? The cost of the intangible to be recorded is the fair market value of the asset given or the fair market value of the intangible, whichever is most valid.

Research and development and other costs associated with internally generated intangibles are normally written off as an expense in the period in which they occurred. An exception is a direct cost associated with developing the intangible, such as legal costs. These are usually capitalized.

Major intangibles are discussed further in the paragraphs that follow.

# Goodwill

**Goodwill** is the excess of cost over the fair value of net assets of a purchased company. For example, suppose that Microsoft purchased a small software development company for $20 million but all of the assets of this software company were appraised at $16 million. The difference of $4 million would be recorded as goodwill. Microsoft paid more than the appraised value of the assets because the software company had developed unique software not possessed by any other company and Microsoft needed it immediately to enhance its product offerings.

The cost of the goodwill is *not* amortized as an expense, since it is assumed to have an indefinite life. An exception is when the goodwill has been significantly impaired. This occurs later on, when the fair value of the acquired unit is less than its carrying value. To determine impairment, the fair value of the acquired unit is first compared to its carrying value, including goodwill. If the fair value of the acquired unit exceeds the carrying value, then nothing is done, as goodwill has not been impaired.

| | |
|---|---|
| Cash | $100,000 |
| Net receivables | 200,000 |
| Merchandise inventory | 500,000 |
| Plant, property, and equipment net of depreciation | 800,000 |
| Goodwill | 700,000 |
| Less: Current and long-term liabilities | (500,000) |
| Net assets | $1,800,000 |

However, if the fair value of the acquired unit is less than its carrying value, the following step is performed: the amount by which the fair value of the acquired unit exceeds the net identifiable assets (excluding goodwill) is the amount of implied goodwill. This amount is then compared to the carrying value of the Goodwill account. If the carrying value is greater than the implied value of goodwill, the difference is written off. For example, assume that a company has the following assets listed on the balance sheet:

Through an appraisal, the company determines that the business is worth $1,900,000. Since the fair value of the business exceeds the carrying amount of the net assets, there is no impairment of goodwill. However, assume that the appraisal was for $1,700,000 rather than $1,900,000. First the net identifiable assets, excluding goodwill, are compared to the fair value of the company:

| | |
|---|---|
| Fair value of company | $1,700,000 |
| Net identifiable assets, less goodwill ($1,800,000 - 700,000) | 1,100,000 |
| Implied goodwill | $ 600,000 |

Since the carrying value of goodwill is $700,000 and the implied goodwill is $600,000, the impaired goodwill of $100,000 would be written off as follows:

| | | |
|---|---|---|
| Goodwill Impairment Expense | 100,000 | |
| Goodwill | | 100,000 |

# Copyrights

A **copyright** is a federally granted legal protection to authors, musicians, painters, sculptors, and other creations and expressions. The copyright is granted for the life of the creator plus 70 years. Costs of acquiring the copyright are recorded along with any costs in defending the copyright. Costs of a copyright are amortized, using the straight-line method, over its legal or useful life, whichever is shorter.

# Patents

A *patent* is a property right granted by the federal government that gives the holder exclusive right to use, manufacture, and sell a product or process for a period of 20 years without infringement by others. All costs associated with acquiring the patent are capitalized, including costs to defend the patent. However, costs associated with research and development of a product or process is expensed in the period that they occur. Patent costs are amortized over the legal life or useful life of the patented item, whichever is shorter.

## Trademarks

A **trademark** is a distinctive sign or symbol, word, or phrase used by an individual business, or any other legal entity that distinguishes the company's product or service from another. The trademark is registered with the U. S. Patent and Trademark Office, and it grants ten years of protection, which is renewable. Trademarks are not amortized.

## QUIZ

1. A company purchased another company for $10 million cash, but the assets were appraised for $8 million. The company would record the purchase as:
   A. A debit to Goodwill for $2,000,000.
   B. A debit to Loss on Purchase of Subsidiary for $2,000,000.
   C. No entry would be made, as Goodwill is not recorded into the accounting records.
   D. None of the above

2. Which of the following is not a distinguishing feature of plant, property, and equipment?
   A. They are long-term assets and are subject to depreciation.
   B. They are tangible assets.
   C. They are acquired for use in operations.
   D. All of the above are correct.

3. Gains that result from trade-ins are:
   A. Recognized as a gain in the period in which it occurred
   B. Never recognized
   C. Recognized to the extent that the gain is recorded as a reduction of the cost basis of the new asset
   D. None of the above

4. A machine used in production was acquired for $20,000, plus $1,000 to set up the machine to get it operational. The asset has a useful life of 10 years and a salvage value of $1,000. Using straight-line depreciation, what is the depreciation charge in the second year of use?
   A. $1,900
   B. $2,000
   C. $2,100
   D. $2,200

5. Refer to the facts in question 4. Assume that the machine will produce 200,000 units of output over its useful life. Assume further that the machine produced 18,000 units during the first year of use. What would be the depreciation expense during that first year?
   A. $20,000
   B. $1,710
   C. $1,890
   D. $1,800

6. Refer to the facts in question 4. Assume that the company uses the sum-of-the-years'-digits depreciation method. What would be the second year's depreciation expense?
   A. $3,273
   B. $3,109
   C. $3,436
   D. None of the above

7. Each of the following would be classified as plant, property, and equipment in a manufacturing company, except:
   A. Machinery
   B. Raw materials inventory
   C. Patents on products owned
   D. Land on which the manufacturing plant is located

8. A company expends $100,000 to defend a copyright. Which account would be debited for this amount?
   A. Legal Expenses
   B. Accumulated Amortization
   C. Copyrights
   D. None of the above

9. (True or false?) A company may use different depreciation methods for reporting purposes than it uses for filing its tax returns.

10. When a piece of equipment is being disposed, the journal entry recording the disposal would always include:
    A. Recognition of a loss
    B. A credit to the Asset account for the book value of the asset
    C. A credit to the Accumulated Depreciation account for the book value of the asset
    D. A debit to the Accumulated Depreciation account for the accumulated depreciation

11. Which of the following is not an intangible asset?
    A. Purchase of an Internet domain for cash
    B. Leasehold improvement
    C. A franchise
    D. Customer lists
    E. All of the above are intangible assets.

12. Assume that XYZ Company sold a machine for $50,000 cash that cost $200,000 and had $130,000 accumulated depreciation. What is the gain or loss on the sale?
    A. Loss of $20,000
    B. Loss of $70,000
    C. Gain of $20,000
    D. None of the above

13. Refer to question 12. Which of the following would not be part of the journal entry to record the disposal?
    A. Debit to Cash for $25,000
    B. Debit to Accumulated Depreciation for $130,000
    C. Credit to Machinery for $200,000
    D. Credit to Machinery Improvements

14. (True or false?) Research and development costs of developing a process are capitalized as a patent and expensed over 20 years.

15. (True or false?) Sum-of-the-years'-digits method and double declining method are examples of accelerated depreciation methods.

## chapter 10

# Accounting for Liabilities

*The purposes of this chapter are to*

- Define the types of current liabilities and explain how they are recorded
- Define the types of long-term liabilities
- Explain the accounting for long-term and short-term notes payable
- Define the types of bonds
- Explain the accounting for the issuance of bonds
- Explain the accounting for interest on bonds payable
- Summarize the accounting for leases

## Introduction

Liabilities are obligations of a business enterprise arising from past transactions or events. They require settlement by making future payment of cash or other resources. Liabilities may be current, noncurrent, or long term. Current and long-term liabilities will now be discussed in more detail.

# Current Liabilities

**Current liabilities** are debts and obligations of the business that are typically settled by expending cash or another current asset within the next year or operating cycle, whichever period is longer. Typical current liabilities are shown in Exhibit 10.1. Accounts Payable, Notes Payable, and payroll-related payables are discussed and illustrated further in the paragraphs that follow.

**EXHIBIT 10.1** A Summary of the Types of Current Liabilities

| Type | Definition | Examples |
|---|---|---|
| Accounts payable | Obligations that arise from the purchase of goods or services that have been charged on an open account | Suppliers, wholesalers, consulting services, and insurance |
| Notes payable | An unconditional written agreement to pay a sum of money within up to one year, with interest, to the bearer on a specific date | Notes from borrowing money at banks. Notes from acquiring goods or fixed assets payable within one year |
| Payroll related | Expenses or withholdings related to employee payroll owed to federal or state governments, unions, and other parties | Involuntary taxes withheld from employees. Employer match for FICA and Medicare, currently (2011), 6.2% and 1.45%, respectively. Federal and state unemployment taxes. Union dues withheld. Group insurance deductions |
| Accrued expenses | Liabilities resulting from expenses incurred but not paid | Interest payable, wages payable, and taxes payable |
| Unearned or deferred revenue | Liabilities resulting from revenue received in advance but not earned. Settlement requires the business to deliver goods or services within the next year | Unearned subscription revenue, rental revenue, or fees revenue |

# Accounts Payable

Accounts payable is a record of unpaid invoices, bills, or statements for services rendered by outside vendors, contractors, or professionals. The accounting for Accounts Payable is rather simple: the asset acquired or the service received is debited, and Accounts Payable is credited. For example, suppose XYZ

Company purchased $10,000 worth of inventory on account. The following entry would be made:

| Inventory (or Purchases) | 10,000 | |
| Accounts Payable | | 10,000 |

Accounts Payable may be extensive in some companies that have a large number of suppliers and vendors, such as The Home Depot. In such situations, subsidiary ledgers of vendors and suppliers should be kept to ensure that bills are paid on time. Often, companies are offered discounts for paying accounts by a specific date. The company should establish controls to ensure that these discounts are taken.

## Notes Payable

One of the most common examples of notes payable is when the company decides to borrow money from the bank to meet short-term needs. To illustrate the accounting for short-term notes payable, assume the following: On December 1, 2xxx, a company needs short-term cash and borrows $10,000 from a bank at 6 percent interest for six months by signing a note. The company's fiscal year ends on December 31. Make the necessary journal entries to record the loan, make any adjusting entries at December 31, and record the payment of the loan on May 30.

On December 1 the following entry would be made:

| Cash | 10,000 | |
| Notes Payable | | 10,000 |
| (To record a bank loan) | | |

On December 31, the following adjusting entry would be made:

| Interest Expense | 50 | |
| Accrued Interest Payable | | 50 |
| (To accrue interest on Notes Payable) | | |
| (Computations: $10,000 \times \dfrac{1}{12} \times .06 = \$50$) | | |

Note that Accrued Interest Payable is an example of an accrued expense incurred but not paid.

On May 30 the loan would be paid off with interest:

| | | |
|---|---|---|
| Notes Payable | 10,000 | |
| Interest Expense | 250 | |
| Accrued Interest Payable | 50 | |
| Cash | | 10,300 |
| (Record payment of loan and interest) | | |
| (Computation of additional interest: | | |
| $\$10,000 \times \dfrac{5}{12} \times .06 = \$250$) | | |

## Payroll-Related Payables

Assume that a company has a monthly payroll for 10 employees that totals $40,000. Federal income tax withheld was $8,000; social security and Medicare was $3,069 (6.2 percent + 1.45 percent respectively); group medical insurance was $3,000. The journal entry for payment of the salaries and the withholdings would be

| | | |
|---|---|---|
| Salaries Expense | 40,000 | |
| Federal Income Taxes Payable | | 8,000 |
| Social Security Taxes Payable | | 3,069 |
| Medical Insurance Payable | | 3,000 |
| Cash | | 25,931 |
| (To record the payroll) | | |

The following is the record of the matching social security taxes ($3,069 from above) and unemployment insurance of $1,200 that are expenses to the company:

| | | |
|---|---|---|
| Payroll Taxes Expense | 4,269 | |
| Social Security Taxes Payable | | 3,069 |
| Unemployment Taxes Payable | | 1,200 |
| (To record payroll tax expense) | | |

Federal taxes withheld and social security taxes are paid quarterly to the Internal Revenue Service, and the unemployment taxes are paid to the federal and state authority as appropriate.

# Long-Term Liabilities

Long-term liabilities arise from a company's need for financing that is to be repaid over a period longer than one year. These needs may arise from the purchasing of equipment, construction of buildings, or for other operational purposes when sufficient cash has not been provided by operations or the company does not want to issue additional stock to raise the necessary funds. Typical long-term liabilities are listed in Exhibit 10.2.

## Long-Term Notes Payable

Long-term notes payable may have different repayment options:

- It may not be repaid until its maturity along with interest as stated in the loan contract.

**EXHIBIT 10.2**  Summary of the Types of Long-Term Liabilities

| Type | Definition | Examples |
|---|---|---|
| Long-term notes payable | An unconditional written agreement to repay the face amount of the note in one lump sum at some time beyond one year in the future or repay with a series of payments over the life of the note. | Bank loan for operating needs. Purchase of property and equipment, when collateral is not required. Notes payable are further discussed below. |
| Mortgage payable | Mortgage payable is a form of notes payable as described above, except the borrowing party must put up collateral to acquire the loan. The written agreement gives the lender claim on the property, if the borrower does not make timely payments on the loan. | Loan to purchase property or equipment when collateral is required |
| Bonds payable | An interest-bearing, written agreement that is issued by corporations and other organizations to acquire funds for long–term capital needs. The agreement specifies the face amount of the bond, the stated rate of interest, and the term of the bond. Bonds are further discussed later in this chapter. | Corporate bonds, municipal Revenue bonds, and U.S. Treasury bonds |

- It may be repaid with periodic payments over the life of the note, much as an individual would repay a mortgage on a house.
- It may be issued with no interest or at an interest rate that differs from that of the market rate. These procedures would be covered in a more advanced accounting text. However, they are similar to repayment of bonds payable, which is discussed later on.

We will deal with the first two options.

### Lump-Sum Repayment of Notes Payable

This is a note payable that is paid in full when the note is due. It is accounted for as a current liability notes payable would be. The major difference is that the long-term notes payable usually involves additional repayment periods: annually, semiannually, or monthly, which include interest and principal. For example, a company signs a note for equipment purchased on January 1 for $5,000 to be repaid in full in three years at an annual rate of 6 percent with interest payable each year. The company pays interest only at the end of each year. The journal entries are as follows:

When note is signed:

| Equipment | 5,000 | |
|---|---|---|
| Notes Payable | | 5,000 |

At the end of the first year:

| Interest Expense | 300 | |
|---|---|---|
| Cash | | 300 |
| ($5,000 × .06) | | |

At the end of two years:

| Interest Expense | 300 | |
|---|---|---|
| Cash | | 300 |

At the end of three years when the note is due:

| Notes Payable | 5,000 | |
|---|---|---|
| Interest Expense | 300 | |
| Cash | | 5,300 |

## Periodic Payments on Notes Payable

In the previous example, assume that the company had to make annual payments at the end of each period. Also, assume that the amount of the payment was not known. How would the payment be computed? How much of the payment would be interest, and how much would be principal?

Since the making of annual payments is an annuity (payments made at the end of each year for three years) the solution would require discounting the note to compute the present value of an annuity. **Discounting** means to compute the present value of future cash flows. (Note: Readers who are not familiar with discounting using the time value of money should read the appendix to this chapter before proceeding.)

The accounting for each payment can be accomplished in three steps.

**Step 1.** *Find the annual payment.*

In the appendix we see that the formula for present value of an annuity is

$$PVA = \text{Payment/Receipt } (PVIFA_{i,n})$$

where

$$PVIFA = \text{present value interest factor of an annuity}$$
$$i = \text{interest rate}$$
$$n = \text{number of periods}$$

If we insert what is known into the equation (including the interest factor from Table 10A-2 on 6 percent), we have:

$$\$5,000 = \text{Payment} \times 2.673$$

Solving for the unknown payment:

$$\text{Payment} = \frac{\$5,000}{2.673} = \$1,870.56$$

**Step 2.** *Find the amount of interest and principal embedded in each payment.* The easiest way to do this is construct a table as shown in Exhibit 10.3.

**Step 3.** Make journal entries.

Using year 1 as an example, the journal entry would be:

| | | |
|---|---|---|
| Interest Expense | 300.00 | |
| Loan Payable | 1,570.56 | |
| Cash | | 1,870.56 |

**EXHIBIT 10.3**  Computation of Interest and Principal

| 1 Year | 2 Loan Balance Beginning of Year | 3 Interest on Beginning Balance | 4 Amount of Payment | 5 Principal Reduction (4 − 3) | 6 Balance End of Year (2−5) |
|---|---|---|---|---|---|
| 1 | $5,000.00 | $300.00 | $1,870.56 | $1,570.56 | $3,429.44 |
| 2 | 3,429.44 | 205.77 | 1,870.56 | 1,664.79 | 1,764.65 |
| 3 | 1,764.65 | 105.88 | 1,870.56 | 1,764.65 | 0.00 |

Similar entries would be made in years 2 and 3.

# Mortgage Payable

A mortgage payable is a form of a note payable. The differences are that mortgages are usually for real estate and require collateral to be put up for the loan. Also, mortgages usually require periodic payments, often monthly. Thus, the accounting for mortgages is essentially the same as long-long term notes payable.

# Bonds Payable

A **bond** is a formal interest-bearing contract known as a bond indenture that is issued by large organizations for the purpose of raising capital to carry out organizational strategies. Bonds are used instead of notes payable when banks and other lenders will not loan the large amount of money for the length of time needed. Bonds can be secured with collateral or be unsecured. A *debenture bond* is an unsecured bond. Among other stipulations, the written bond certificate contains the following:

- Interest rate (called the stated rate or face rate)
- Amount of the bond (usually called the face amount or par value)
- Term of the bond in years

Although the bond contains a stated interest rate, which is the rate that must be paid to the bondholder, the interest rate in the market will almost always differ from that. This gives rise to bonds being sold at a discount or premium. Specifically, when a bond is sold in the market, three situations may occur:

1. *Bonds are sold at par.* They are sold at the face value stated in the bond certificate. The stated interest rate is the same as the market interest rate.

2. *Bonds are sold at a discount.* This means that the market interest rate is greater than the stated interest rate. This situation occurs because an investor will not buy a bond that pays interest less than the market. Thus, selling the bond at less than face value is a way to compensate for this difference.

3. *Bonds are sold at a premium.* With this type of sale, the stated interest rate is greater than the market interest rate. This situation occurs because the seller of the bond will not sell when the stated amount of interest to be paid is greater than what is being paid in the market. Selling at a premium is a way of compensating for the difference.

### More Information on Bond Premiums and Discounts

**Why doesn't the company just include the market rate on the bonds and not have to deal with the accounting for premiums and discounts?** The company and the investment banker that handles the sale of bonds do try to anticipate the market rate. However, there may be a considerable time lapse from the time that the interest rate estimate is made to time of printing and the eventual sale. Also, market interest rates change frequently, even daily. So, it is impossible to predict the actual market rate of interest when selling bonds.

## Types of Bonds

The following are typical bonds sold on the market:

- **Coupon (bearer) bonds** have detachable coupons that are cashed in at specific dates. They are easily transferred on the open market. Very few bonds are now issued as coupon bonds.

- **Registered bonds** are issued in the name of the owner and require the surrender of the bond certificate at time of maturity. With modern technology, most bonds are registered to the owner.

- **Serial bonds** are issued to mature at dates spread over time. This bond is often used to avoid having to establish a sinking fund. A *sinking fund* is a type of escrow account where monies are periodically transferred to pay off bonds at maturity.

- **Convertible bonds** are bonds that can be exchanged by the holder for a specified number of shares of corporate stock, usually common stock.

- **Callable bonds** give the company the option of buying back the bonds at a specified price before the bonds' maturity date. The company will exercise this option when the market interest drops significantly below the stated rate of the bonds.

# Accounting for Bonds

## Bonds Issued at Par

If bonds are sold at par, the accounting for bonds is similar to the accounting for notes payable: the Cash account is debited for the amount of the sale, and the Bonds Payable account is credited for the same amount. Each interest date, Interest Expense is debited for the amount of interest paid (the stated rate times the face value of the bond), and Cash is credited for the same amount. For example, assume that XYZ Company issues a five-year, $100,000 group of 6 percent bonds at par or face value on January 1, 2010. The following entries would be made:

On January 1, 2010 the following entry would be made:

| Cash | 100,000 | |
| Bonds Payable | | 100,000 |

At the end of June 2010 the following interest entry would be made, and the same entry would be made each six months until the end of five years:

| Interest Expense | 3,000 | |
| Cash | | 3,000 |
| (Computations: $100,000 \times \dfrac{6}{12} \times .06 = \$3,000$) | | |

At the end of five years the following entry would be made:

| Interest Expense | 3,000 | |
| Bonds Payable | 100,000 | |
| Cash | | 103,000 |

But things are not that simple. As stated previously, usually bonds are sold at a premium or discount. Thus, each of these situations must be explained in more detail.

## Bonds Issued at a Premium

A bond issued at a premium occurs when the market interest rate is less than the stated rate on the bond. This means that the interest paid on the face value of the bond must be adjusted to determine the effective interest expense. Why? Since the market rate is less than the stated rate and the stated rate is what must be paid to bondholders, the amount of interest paid is greater than what should be charged as interest expense, which is called the effective amount of interest.

### Still Confused?

**Financial pages list bonds at 101 or 98, what does that mean?** Normally, the sale of bonds is stated as a percentage of par value. For example, if a bond is sold at 101, it is at 101 percent of par. If it were sold at 98, it would be sold at 98 percent of par. For example, if a $1,000 bond were sold for 101, the proceeds would be $10,100 less any expenses associated with the sale.

Some of the premium must be offset against the paid interest. This is accomplished through amortization of the premium. There are two methods for amortization of a premium or discount: The straight-line method and the effective interest method.

The *straight-line method* amortizes a constant amount of a premium or a discount each period over the period that the bonds are outstanding. For example, assume that XYZ Company issues a five-year, $100,000 group of 6 percent bonds for 103 or $103,000 on January 1, 2010. Record the sale and the interest at the first semiannual interest payment.

Journal entry at date of sale:

| Cash | 103,000 | |
|---|---|---|
| Premium on Bonds Payable | | 3,000 |
| Bonds Payable | | 100,000 |

Using the straight-line method, the premium would be amortized over 20 semiannual periods (10 years × 2). The semiannual amortized amount would be $\left(\dfrac{\$3,000}{20}\right) = \$150$.

Journal entry at first interest payment:

| Interest Expense | 2,850 | |
|---|---|---|
| Amortization of Premium on Bonds Payable | 150 | |
| Cash | | 3,000 |
| $\left(\$100,000 \times \dfrac{6}{12} \times .06 = \$3,000\right)$ | | |
| ($3,000 – 150) = $2,850 = Interest Expense | | |

The *effective interest method* is theoretically the more correct method for amortizing the premium or discount. It recognizes the interest expense as a constant percentage of the bond's carrying value rather than as an equal dollar amount each year as the does the straight-line method. This approach also aligns with the effective rate of interest on which the bonds were priced.

Assume that XYZ Company issues $200,000 of 8 percent bonds on January 1, 2010 due in five years. Assume also that the effective rate of interest (market rate) is 6 percent. There are three steps to amortizing a premium or discount under the effective interest method and making the journal entries:

**Step 1.** *Compute the amount of premium to be amortized.* How this is accomplished is illustrated in Exhibit 10.4. Note that the computed premium is the difference between the total principal at maturity and the proceeds from the sale (present value of the principal at maturity plus the present value of all the interest payments over the life of the bond).

**Step 2.** *Prepare an amortization schedule to determine the interest expense and the amount of the premium to be amortized.* How this is done is illustrated in Exhibit 10.5.

| EXHIBIT 10.4 Computation of Premium to Be Amortized | | |
|---|---|---|
| Total principal of bonds payable at maturity | | $200,000 |
| Proceeds from the sale of the bonds: | | |
| **Present value of principal:** | | |
| $200,000 due in 5 years, $n = 10$, $i = 3\%$ semianually | | |
| (Table 10A.1): $200,000 × 07.44 = | $148,800 | |
| **Present value of interest payments:** | | |
| Present value of $8,000 interest | | |
| ($200,000 × 4\% = $8,000, $n = 10$, $i = 3\%$ semiannually | | |
| (Table 10A.2): $8,000 × 8.530 = | <u>68,240</u> | |
| Proceeds from the sale of bonds | | <u>217,040</u> |
| Premium on sale of bonds | | $17,040 |

| EXHIBIT 10.5 Computation of Interest Expense and Amortization of Premium | | | | |
|---|---|---|---|---|
| Date 1 | Interest Paid 2 | Interest Expense 3 | Premium Amortized 4 | Carrying Amount of Bonds 5 |
| 1/1/2010 | | | | $217,070 |
| 7/1/2010 | $8,000[a] | $6,512[b] | $1,488[c] | 215,582[d] |
| 1/1/2011 | 8,000 | 6,467 | 1,533 | 214,049 |
| 7/1/2011 | 8,000 | 6,421 | 1,579 | 212,470 |
| 1/1/2012 | 8,000 | 6,374 | 1,626 | 210,844 |
| 7/1/2012 | 8,000 | 6,325 | 1,675 | 209,169 |
| 1/1/2013 | 8,000 | 6,275 | 1,725 | 207,444 |
| 7/1/2013 | 8,000 | 6,223 | 1,777 | 205,667 |
| 1/1/2014 | 8,000 | 6,170 | 1,830 | 203,837 |
| 7/1/2014 | 8,000 | 6,115 | 1,885 | 201,952 |
| 1/1/2015 | 8,000 | 6,048 | 1,952 | 200,000 |

[a]$200,000 × .08 × 6/12
[b]$217,070 × .06 × 6/12
[c]Column 2 − 3
[d]Column 5 − 4

**Step 3.** *Make journal entries.* Limit entries to January 1, 2010 and July 1, 2010.

Journal entry at date of sale, January 1, 2010:

| Cash | 217,070 | |
| Premium on Bonds Payable | | 17,070 |
| Bonds Payable | | 200,000 |

Journal entry at first interest payment, July 1, 2010:

| Interest Expense | 6,512 | |
| Amortization of Premium on Bonds Payable | 1,488 | |
| Cash | | 8,000 |
| (Refer to Exhibit 10.5) | | |

## Bonds Issued at a Discount

A bond issued at a discount occurs when the market interest rate is greater than the stated rate on the bond. As with bonds issued at a premium, the interest paid on the face value of the bond must be adjusted to determine the effective interest expense.

The *straight-line method* amortizes a constant amount of the discount each period over the period that the bonds are outstanding. For example, assume that XYZ Company issues a 10-year, $100,000 group of 6 percent bonds for 97 on January 1, 2010. Record the sale and the interest at the first semiannual interest payment:

Journal entry at date of sale:

| Cash | 97,000 | |
| Discount on Bonds Payable | 3,000 | |
| Bonds Payable | | 100,000 |

Using the straight-line method, the discount would be amortized over 20 semiannual periods (10 years × 2). The amount amortized would be $\left(\dfrac{\$3,000}{20}\right) = \$150$.

Journal entry at first interest payment:

| | | |
|---|---|---|
| Interest Expense | 3,150 | |
|    Amortization of Discount on Bonds Payable | | 150 |
|    Cash | | 3,000 |
| $\left( \$100,000 \times \dfrac{6}{12} \times .06 = \$3,000 \right)$ | | |
| ($3,000 + 150) = $3,150 = Interest Expense | | |

The *effective interest method* is computed using the steps previously explained:

**Step 1.** *Compute the amount of discount to be amortized.* Assume that XYZ Company issues a 10-year, $200,000 group of 8 percent bonds when the effective (market) rate is 10 percent on January 1, 2xxx. The amount of the discount is computed in Exhibit 10.6. Note that the computed discount is the difference between the total principal at maturity and the proceeds from the sale (present value of the principal at maturity plus the present value of all the interest payments over the life of the bond).

**EXHIBIT 10.6**  Computation of Discount to Be Amortized

| | | |
|---|---|---|
| Total principal of bonds payable at maturity | | $200,000 |
| Proceeds from the sale of the bonds: | | |
| **Present value of principal:** | | |
| $200,000 due in 5 years, $n = 10$, $i = 5\%$ semianually | | |
| (Table 10A.1): $200,000 × 0. 614 = | $122,800 | |
| **Present value of interest payments:** | | |
| Present value of $8,000 interest | | |
| $200,000 × 4% = $8,000, $n = 10$, $i = 5\%$ semiannually | | |
| (Table 10A.2): $8,000 × 7.722 = | <u>61,776</u> | |
| Proceeds from the sale of bonds | | <u>184,576</u> |
| Discount sale of bonds | | $15,424 |

**Step 2.** *Prepare an amortization schedule to determine the interest expense and the amount of the discount to be amortized.* This is done in Exhibit 10.7.

**EXHIBIT 10.7**  Computation of Interest Expense and Amortization of Discount

| Date 1 | Interest Paid 2 | Interest Expense 3 | Discount Amortized 4 | Carrying Amount of Bonds 5 |
|---|---|---|---|---|
| 1/1/2010 | | | | $184,576 |
| 7/1/2010 | $8,000[a] | $9,229[b] | $1,229[c] | 185,805[d] |
| 1/1/2011 | 8,000 | 9,290 | 1,290 | 187,095 |
| 7/1/2011 | 8,000 | 9,355 | 1,355 | 188,450 |
| 1/1/2012 | 8,000 | 9,423 | 1,423 | 189,873 |
| 7/1/2012 | 8,000 | 9,494 | 1,494 | 191,367 |
| 1/1/2013 | 8,000 | 9,568 | 1,568 | 192,935 |
| 7/1/2013 | 8,000 | 9,647 | 1,647 | 194,582 |
| 1/1/2014 | 8,000 | 9,729 | 1,729 | 196,311 |
| 7/1/2014 | 8,000 | 9,816 | 1,816 | 198,127 |
| 1/1/2015 | 8,000 | 9,873 | 1,873 | 200,000 |

[a]$200,000 \times .08 \times 6/12$
[b]$184,576 \times .10 \times 6/12$
[c]Column 2 − 3
[d]Column 5 + 4

**Step 3.** *Make journal entries.* Limit entries to January 1, 2010 and July 1, 2010.

Journal entry at date of sale, January 1, 2010:

| | | |
|---|---|---|
| Cash | 184,576 | |
| Discount on Bonds Payable | 15,424 | |
| Bonds Payable | | 200,000 |

Journal entry at first interest payment, July 1, 2010:

| | | |
|---|---|---|
| Interest Expense | 9,229 | |
| Amortization of Discount on Bonds Payable | | 1,229 |
| Cash | | 8,000 |
| (Refer to Exhibit 10.7 for computations) | | |

### Bonds Issued between Interest Payment Dates

When bonds are issued they have the issue date printed on the certificate. Interest is usually paid semiannually, the first payment being six months from the issue date. Thus, if they are sold between the established interest payment dates, the purchaser must pay the interest that has been accrued from the last interest payment date (or in the case of a new issue, from the printed issue date). This is necessary because the full amount of interest must be paid at the next interest payment date. For example, assume that on April 1, 2010 a company issues $100,000 of 10-year, 6 percent bonds at face value, dated January 1, 2010. Interest is payable on January 1 and July 1 each year. Record the sale and the first interest payment on July 1.

At date of issuance, April 1, 2xxx:

| Cash | 101,500 | |
|---|---|---|
|     Bonds Payable | | 100,000 |
|     Interest Expense (or Payable) | | 1,500 |
| $\left( \$100,000 \times \dfrac{3}{12} \times .06 = \$1,500 \right)$ | | |

The interest paid in advance by the purchaser is credited to interest expense, which will offset against the full $3,000 interest paid on July 1 (see next entry).

On July 1 interest payment date:

| Interest Expense | 3,000 | |
|---|---|---|
|     Cash | | 3,000 |
| $\left( \$100,000 \times .06 \times \dfrac{6}{12} = \$3,000 \right)$ | | |

Note that the credit of $1,500 at issuance date will offset the $3,000 debit on July 1 giving the correct amount of interest expense of $1,500.

When bonds are issued at a premium or discount between interest dates, the amount of premium or discount must be adjusted accordingly.

## Other Long-Term Liabilities: Leases

It is very common for a business to lease long-term assets rather than buy them for a variety of reasons. The accounting for leases—particularly capital leases—is somewhat complex and is not covered in detail in this book. The reader should consult an intermediate financial accounting text or "Accounting for Leases," Statement of Financial Accounting Standard No. 13 (and related standards) (Stamford, CT: FASB, 1976). However, a brief summary of lease accounting is presented below.

There are two types of lease options in accounting parlance:

- **Operating lease** in which the lessor (owner) transfers only the right to use the property to the lessee, who does not assume any risk of ownership. The property is returned to the lessor at the end of the lease period. The lease payment is called a *lease expense* and is treated as an expense on the income statement.

- **Capital lease** in which the lessee assumes some of the risks of ownership and enjoys some of the benefits. Thus, the lease is capitalized as an asset (present value of the lease payments) on the balance sheet with an offsetting liability on the balance sheet. Each year the lessee has the right to deduct depreciation on the asset and the interest expense component of the lease payment. A lease is a capital lease when at least one of the following four criteria is met:

    - The title is transferred to the lessee at the end of the lease term.
    - There is a "bargain price" option for the lessee to purchase the asset at the end of the lease term.
    - The life of the lease is 75 percent or more of the life of the property.
    - The present value of the lease payments, discounted at an appropriate discount rate, exceeds 90 percent of the fair market value of the asset.

# Appendix: Time Value of Money

A dollar to be received in the future does not have the same value as a dollar possessed today, and vice versa. A person who has won a lottery that it is to be paid out in an equal sum each year over 20 years would rather have all of the money right now. But, as we shall see, the value of the lump-sum payment right now is much less than the sum of the payments received over 20 years. A person who invests in a five-year certificate of deposit with a bank would expect to receive a higher amount at the end of five years than he or she invested today. Why are both these situations true? They both have to do with the time value of money. Why does money change over time? There are several factors involved:

- If we hold money over a period of time, the length of time and the timing of the cash flows are important.

- If we hold money over time, part of its value will be lost due to inflation.

- If an investor invests in a risk security, that person will want a higher return due to the risk associated with the investment.

- If an investor is dealing with several investment opportunities and selects one of them, that person will want a return for excluding the other investments. This is called an opportunity cost. **Opportunity costs** are the costs associated with giving up the next best opportunity in an investment decision.

Notice that two key variables in the preceding factors are an interest rate and timing of the cash flows. The first factor in the list relates to timing. The next three factors relate to the interest rate assigned to a decision that one is considering. Thus, the interest rate and the timing of cash flows involved are key elements in dealing with the issue of time value of money.

As previous chapters have shown, the interest rate affects an investment or a loan. If the interest is computed only on the principal, it is called simple interest. If the interest is computed on the principal plus any interest that has been accumulated but not paid, it is called compound interest. Either simple interest or compound interest may come into play with the time value of money.

To summarize, there are three key variables relating to the time value of money:

- Interest rate (symbolically: $i$)
- Number of periods involved (symbolically: $n$)
- The type of time value of money involved (see the next four categories)

There are four major categories of time value of money:

- Present value of a lump sum (symbolically: PV).
- Present value of an annuity (symbolically: PVA).
- Future value of a lump sum (symbolically: FV).
- Future value of an annuity (symbolically: FVA).

# Present Value of a Lump Sum

The present value of a lump sum is the opposite of future value of a lump sum. The formula is as follows:

$$PV = \frac{FV}{(1+i^n)}$$

where:

    PV = Present value

    FV = Future value

      $i$ = Interest rate (sometimes called the discount rate)

     $n$ = Number of periods

Let us assume that a person is to inherit $20,000 in 10 years when she becomes 25 years of age. However, the person wants the money now and contracts with a company that will pay her for her inheritance now in return for an agreement for the company to receive her inheritance at age 25. However, the company desires a 5 percent return on the advance payment. How much would the individual receive? Asked another way, what is the present value of that amount, if the going rate of interest is 5 percent? We can insert this data into the equation, but the computations would become cumbersome. Instead, Exhibit 10.A1 is a present value table that will provide us a present value factor that we can insert into the equation. The above equation would be changed to become

$$PV = FV \ (PVIF_{i,n})$$

where:

    PV = Present value

  PVIF = Present value interest factor

     $i$ = Interest or discount rate

    $n$ = Number of periods

To obtain the present value factor, look in Exhibit 10.A1 under 5 percent and at 10 years, where we find the PVIF to be 0.614. Inserting this into our equation we have

$$PV = \$20,000 \ (0.614) = \$12,280$$

Thus, the company will pay the individual $12,280 now in return for the right to receive the $20,000 inheritance in 10 years.

## Present Value of an Annuity

**Present value of an annuity** computes the present value of a series of equal payments or receipts made periodically over equally spaced periods of time, usually at the end of such periods. If the payments or receipts do occur at the end of the period, they are called ordinary annuities. For example, assume that a person won a lottery and will receive $100,000 at the end of each year for

10 years. However, the individual has the option of receiving the money in one lump sum now. Assume a market interest rate of 7 percent. How much would the individual receive in the lump-sum payment?

Again, the computations necessary to find this answer would be very complex. However, the solution could easily be computed using Excel or by referring to a table presenting interest factors for a present value of an annuity. To do this the formula would be as follows:

$$PVA = \text{Payment/Receipt } (PVIFA_{i,n})$$

where:

$\quad$ PVA = Present value of an annuity

$\quad$ PVIFA = Present value interest factor of an annuity

$\qquad i$ = Interest or discount rate

$\qquad n$ = Number of periods

The solution to the above problem, using Exhibit 10A.2, would be:

$$PVA = \$100,000 \times (7.024) = \$702,400$$

## Future Value of a Lump Sum

(Note: Future value of money is not used in this text but the following is a description for contrast to present value and for information purposes.)

Future value of a lump sum answers the question: "How much will I have if I invest a lump at a given interest rate for a specific period of time?" The following is the formula for this computation:

$$FV = PV \, (1 + i)^n$$

where:

$\quad$ FV = Future value of a lump sum

$\quad$ PV = Present value of the lump sum being invested

$\qquad n$ = Number of periods involved

$\qquad i$ = Interest rate

For example, assume that one purchased a certificate of deposit (CD) for $1,000 that will mature in three years at an interest rate of 5 percent. How much would the CD be worth at the end of three years? The answer:

$$FV = \$1,000 \, (1 + .05)^3$$

$$FV = \$1,000 \, (1 + .05) \, (1 + 1.05) \, (1 + 1.05) = \$1,000 \times 1.1576 = \$1,157.63$$

If there are a large number of periods involved, the computations become cumbersome. Tables of future value factors are available on the Internet or in advanced accounting texts. Also, future value of a lump sum can be calculated with computer software such as Excel.

# Future Value of an Annuity

**Future value of an annuity** computes the future value of a series of payments or receipts made at specific time periods at a given interest rate. For example, a person decides to deposit $1,000 in a savings account at the beginning of each quarter for two years at an interest rate of 8 percent. How much would be in the account at the end of two years? The formula for this calculation is complicated, and most accountants use software such as Excel for this purpose. Alternatively, tables showing future value of an annuity may be used for this purpose; they can be found on the Internet. These tables present interest factors for a given interest rate and number of periods. Using FVA tables, the formula would be

$$FVA = \text{Payment } (FVIFA)_{i,n}$$

where:

$\quad$ FVA = Future value of an annuity

FVIFA = Future value interest factor of an annuity

$\quad\quad i$ = Interest rate

$\quad\quad n$ = Number of interest periods

The number of periods would be 8 (4 quarters per year × 2). The interest rate would be 2 percent (8 percent annual rate divided by 4 quarters). Using these variables, the FVIFA from a table, taken from the Internet (not presented in this book), would be 8.2857. Using the formula the answer to the problem would be as follows:

$$FVA = 1,000 \times 8.2857 = \$8,286 \text{ (rounded)}$$

# Time Value Table

**EXHIBIT 10A.1** Present Value of \$1 (Lump Sum) $PVIF_{i,n} = \dfrac{1}{(1+i^n)}$

| Periods (n) | 1% | 2% | 3% | 4% | 5% | 6% | 7% | 8% | 9% | 10% | 12% | 14% |
|---|---|---|---|---|---|---|---|---|---|---|---|---|
| 1 | 0.990 | 0.980 | 0.971 | 0.962 | 0.952 | 0.943 | 0.935 | 0.926 | 0.917 | 0.909 | 0.893 | 0.877 |
| 2 | 0.980 | 0.961 | 0.943 | 0.925 | 0.907 | 0.890 | 0.873 | 0.857 | 0.842 | 0.826 | 0.797 | 0.769 |
| 3 | 0.971 | 0.942 | 0.915 | 0.889 | 0.864 | 0.840 | 0.816 | 0.794 | 0.772 | 0.751 | 0.712 | 0.675 |
| 4 | 0.961 | 0.924 | 0.888 | 0.855 | 0.823 | 0.792 | 0.763 | 0.735 | 0.708 | 0.683 | 0.636 | 0.592 |
| 5 | 0.951 | 0.906 | 0.863 | 0.822 | 0.784 | 0.747 | 0.713 | 0.681 | 0.650 | 0.621 | 0.567 | 0.519 |
| 6 | 0.942 | 0.888 | 0.837 | 0.790 | 0.746 | 0.705 | 0.666 | 0.630 | 0.596 | 0.564 | 0.507 | 0.456 |
| 7 | 0.933 | 0.871 | 0.813 | 0.760 | 0.711 | 0.665 | 0.623 | 0.583 | 0.547 | 0.513 | 0.452 | 0.400 |
| 8 | 0.923 | 0.853 | 0.789 | 0.731 | 0.677 | 0.627 | 0.582 | 0.540 | 0.502 | 0.467 | 0.404 | 0.351 |
| 9 | 0.914 | 0.837 | 0.766 | 0.703 | 0.645 | 0.592 | 0.544 | 0.500 | 0.460 | 0.424 | 0.361 | 0.308 |
| 10 | 0.905 | 0.820 | 0.744 | 0.676 | 0.614 | 0.558 | 0.508 | 0.463 | 0.422 | 0.386 | 0.322 | 0.270 |

# Time Value Table

EXHIBIT 10A.2  Present Value of Annuity $PVIFA_{i,n} = \sum_{t=1}^{n} \frac{1}{(1+i)^n}$

| Periods (n) | 1% | 2% | 3% | 4% | 5% | 6% | 7% | 8% | 9% | 10% | 12% | 14% |
|---|---|---|---|---|---|---|---|---|---|---|---|---|
| 1 | 0.990 | 0.980 | 0.971 | 0.962 | 0.952 | 0.943 | 0.935 | 0.926 | 0.917 | 0.910 | 0.893 | 0.880 |
| 2 | 1.970 | 1.942 | 1.914 | 1.886 | 1.859 | 1.833 | 1.810 | 1.783 | 1.759 | 1.736 | 1.690 | 1.647 |
| 3 | 2.940 | 2.884 | 2.830 | 2.780 | 2.723 | 2.673 | 2.624 | 2.580 | 2.531 | 2.487 | 2.402 | 2.322 |
| 4 | 3.902 | 3.808 | 3.717 | 3.630 | 3.546 | 3.465 | 3.387 | 3.312 | 3.240 | 3.170 | 3.037 | 2.914 |
| 5 | 4.853 | 4.714 | 4.580 | 4.452 | 4.330 | 4.212 | 4.100 | 3.993 | 3.900 | 3.791 | 3.605 | 3.433 |
| 6 | 5.796 | 5.601 | 5.417 | 5.242 | 5.076 | 4.917 | 4.767 | 4.623 | 4.486 | 4.355 | 4.111 | 3.889 |
| 7 | 6.728 | 6.472 | 6.230 | 6.002 | 5.786 | 5.582 | 5.389 | 5.206 | 5.033 | 4.868 | 4.564 | 4.288 |
| 8 | 7.652 | 7.326 | 7.020 | 6.733 | 6.463 | 6.210 | 5.971 | 5.747 | 5.535 | 5.335 | 4.968 | 4.639 |
| 9 | 8.566 | 8.162 | 7.786 | 7.434 | 7.108 | 6.802 | 6.515 | 6.247 | 5.995 | 5.760 | 5.328 | 4.946 |
| 10 | 9.471 | 8.983 | 8.530 | 8.111 | 7.722 | 7.360 | 7.024 | 6.710 | 6.418 | 6.145 | 5.650 | 5.216 |

# QUIZ

1. **All of the following are current liabilities, except:**
   A. Taxes payable
   B. Accounts payable
   C. Bonds payable
   D. Unearned income

2. **Bonds issued with a stated interest rate that is higher than the prevailing market rate are issued at:**
   A. Par
   B. Premium
   C. Discount
   D. None of the above

3. **Employer payroll taxes include all of the following except:**
   A. State income taxes
   B. Federal unemployment taxes
   C. State unemployment taxes
   D. FICA (social security) taxes

4. **On January 1, 2010, the XYZ Company issued bonds maturing in 10 years with a face value of $800,000 and a stated rate of 10 percent. XYZ received $708,240 in cash proceeds from the sale. How much cash will the XYZ Company pay bondholders on the first semiannual payment?**
   A. $35,412
   B. $42,494
   C. $48,000
   D. $40,000

5. **XYZ Company hired an administrative assistant for a salary of $3,000 per month. Assume that income tax is withheld at 20 percent of the salary; FICA is withheld at 6.2 percent of the salary; Medicare is withheld at 1.45 percent of the salary. What is XYZ's total salary expense for the administrative assistant's salary for one month?**
   A. $3,000.00
   B. $229.50
   C. $3,186.00
   D. $3,229.50

6. XYZ Company issued 10-year 6 percent bonds with a face value of $200,000 for 98 on January 1, 2xxx. Which of the following would not be recorded on the date of issuance?

A. Debit Interest Expense for $6,000
B. Debit Cash for $196,000
C. Debit Discount on Bonds Payable for $4,000
D. Credit Bonds Payable for $200,000

7. Refer to question 6. What would be the total bond interest expense on July 1, 2xxx, assuming the bond discount is amortized using the straight-line method?

A. $6,200
B. $6,000
C. $5,800
D. None of the above

8. A $10,000 bond was issued by XYZ Company with a stated rate of 5 percent when the market rate was 6 percent. How much interest payment will the bond-holders receive each year?

A. $600
B. $500
C. $100
D. None of the above

9. Assume that a company signs a note for a computer system costing $5,000 to be repaid in full in three years at an annual rate of 6 percent with interest payable each year. Assume that the terms of the note require an annual payment of $1,871. How much interest expense is charged on the note at the end of year one?

A. $1,871
B. $1,571
C. $300
D. None of the above

10. Refer to question 9. How much principal reduction would occur at the end of year 1?

A. $300
B. $1,871
C. $150
D. $1,571

11. Assume that on January 1, 2010, a company issues $10,000 of bonds due in five years with a stated rate of interest of 7 percent when the market (effective) rate of interest is 6 percent. Also assume that the interest is payable semiannually. If the present value interest factor of a lump sum $\left( n = 10, i = \dfrac{6}{12} \times 6\% \right)$ is 0.744) and the present value interest factor of an annuity $\left( n = 10, i = \dfrac{6}{12} \times 6\% \right)$ is 8.530, what is the total proceeds from the sale of the bonds?

    A. $10,426
    B. $10,600
    C. $10,700
    D. $10,750

12. Refer to question 11. What is the premium on the sale of the bonds?

    A. $350
    B. $426
    C. $300
    D. None of the above

13. Refer to question 11. What is the interest expense on July 1, 2010?

    A. $313
    B. $300
    C. $350
    D. None of the above

14. Refer to question 11. How much of the bond premium is amortized on July 1, 2010?

    A. $50.00
    B. $21.30
    C. $37.00
    D. None of the above

15. Refer to question 11. What is the carrying value of the bonds payable at December 31, 2010?

    A. $9,935
    B. $10,389
    C. $10,365
    D. None of the above

## chapter 11

# Accounting for Stockholders' Equity

## CHAPTER OBJECTIVES

*The purposes of this chapter are to*

- Define the corporate form of organization
- Define common terminology relating to stockholders' equity
- Explain the accounting for the major components of stockholders' equity
- Explain the accounting for treasury stock
- Explain the accounting for dividends and stock splits
- Explain the accounting for retained earnings

## The Corporate Form of Organization

The **corporation** is a legal entity having existence separate and distinct from its stockholder owners. It is often described as an artificial being created by law with an indefinite life. The corporation is incorporated in an individual state where it must submit an application, including articles of incorporation, to the relevant state official, usually the secretary of state. **Articles of incorporation** state such things as the purpose of the corporation and how it will be governed.

After approval of the application, the state will issue a charter that recognizes the corporation as a legal entity, after which it is allowed to begin operation. The incorporators will then make their initial common stock investment or acquire investors for this purpose. The final step will be for the new stockholders to hold a meeting to adopt bylaws and elect a board of directors, who then will appoint the corporate officers so that the corporation can commence business.

These are the *advantages* of the corporate form of organization:

- If the corporation fails, shareholders normally stand to lose only their investment, as they are not liable for debts that remain owing to the corporation's creditors.
- Corporate stock of publicly traded companies is easily transferable from one person to another or on an organized stock exchange. Because their shares are publicly traded, corporations are subject to certain regulatory registration and reporting requirements that serve to protect the investor.
- Corporations have perpetual existence, which means that they don't cease to exist if there is a change in ownership or if an owner dies.
- Given its indefinite life, a corporation can raise significant amounts of funds from the public through the sale of stock or bonds.

There are some significant *disadvantages* to the corporate form of organization:

- Corporate taxes are high.
- There is double taxation to stockholders, because the corporation itself is taxed and then the stockholders are taxed again when dividends are distributed.
- The cost of compliance with governmental regulations pertaining to corporate affairs can be heavy.
- The costs of filing financial reports with the Securities and Exchange Commission and the loss of information to outsiders stated therein also can be high.

# Common Terminology

The following terms are common to the issuance and accounting for stock in a corporation:

- **Authorized shares of stock** are the maximum of shares of stock that can be issued by a corporation as established in its charter.

- **Board of directors** is a body of individuals, elected or appointed, who oversee the governance of a corporation as defined in the corporation's bylaws. Duties of the board may include establishing broad goals and policies; ensuring that the company has adequate financial resources; appointing and reviewing the performance of the chief executive officer and other senior officers; approving capital and annual budgets; and reporting the performance of the company to its stakeholders.

- **Contributed capital** is stock purchased by stockholders at par or stated value, plus capital in excess of par, donated stock, and the resale of treasury stock.

- **Issued shares** are the number of authorized shares of stock that have been sold by the corporation.

- **Outstanding shares** are the number of shares of stock actually owned by stockholders, which equals issued shares less shares of treasury stock.

- **Par value** is the nominal value of a stock that is assigned by the corporation upon its issuance. Par value is unrelated to its market value. If the company sells the stock at a price greater than par, the difference is recorded as additional paid-in capital. If the company sells shares at less than par value, the difference is recorded as discount on common stock.

- **Stockholder** (also called shareholder) is an individual who or another organization that owns one or more shares of stock in a corporation.

- **Common-stock holders** are the owners of the company; they have the following rights:

  - To vote on important matters such as the election of the board of directors and issuance of additional shares of stock

  - To share in the distribution of the company's income through dividends

  - To purchase new shares issued by the company

      – To share in the distribution of the company's assets in the event of liquidation; however, these rights are subordinate to the rights of the company's creditors

- **Subscribed stock** shares are stock that has been sold with a down payment, with the remaining amount being deferred. Subscribed shares are not issued until the subscription has been paid.

## Accounting for Common Stock

**Common stock** is the most widespread type of ownership in a corporation and entitles the owners to certain rights:

- To share in the corporation's profits through dividends that are declared by the board of directors.
- To vote for members of the board of directors
- To maintain their fractional ownership in the corporation by being allowed to purchase a proportional share of future shares issued by the corporation; this is known as a **preemptive right**
- To share in assets left over after liquidation and all creditors and other priority claims have been settled
- To receive periodic financial reports on corporate performance

### Issuance of Common Stock

Assume that XYZ Company has just started business and has one million shares of authorized common stock. Also, assume that XYZ issues 100,000 shares of $1 par value stock for $20 per share. Make the necessary journal entry to record this sale.

| | | |
|---|---|---|
| Cash | 2,000,000 | |
|     Common Stock | | 100,000 |
|     Additional Paid-In Capital—Common Stock | | 1,900,000 |
| (To record sale of 100,000 shares of common stock) | | |

    Exhibit 11.1 shows how the information would appear on the balance sheet.

| EXHIBIT 11.1 Contributed Capital | |
|---|---|
| Common stock (par value $1 per share); one million shares authorized; 100,000 shares issued and outstanding | $100,000 |
| Additional paid-in capital | 1,900,000 |
| Total stockholders' equity | $2,000,000 |

## Accounting for Preferred Stock

**Preferred stock** gets its name from the fact that it is paid dividends before common-stock holders and is preferred to common-stock holders in the event of liquidation of company assets. Dividends on preferred shares are paid as percentage of par value, which is stated in the stock contract. Preferred-stock holders do not have voting rights. There are several types of preferred stock:

- **Callable preferred stock** means that the preferred-stock holders can be forced to sell their stock back to the company at the *call price* in the stock contract. The price is usually a percentage of par value. For example, 103 would mean that the company would have to pay the stockholders 103 percent of par value.

- **Convertible preferred stock** means that the preferred-stock holders can convert preferred shares to common stock shares at a ratio stipulated in the stock contract.

- **Cumulative preferred stock** means that when the company does not pay the preferred-stock holders an annual dividend the dividend that would have been paid is cumulative, and all cumulative dividends must be paid before any dividends are paid to common-stock holders.

- **Noncumulative preferred stock** means that annual dividends that are not paid to preferred-stock holders are lost.

## Issuance of Preferred Stock

Assume that the XYZ Company from the preceding example was authorized to issue 500,000 shares of 6 percent, cumulative preferred stock, par value of $100. Also, assume that XYZ issued 100,000 shares of this stock at $110. Make the necessary journal entry to record this sale.

| | | |
|---|---|---|
| Cash | 11,000,000 | |
| Preferred Stock | | 10,000,000 |
|    Additional Paid-In Capital—Preferred Stock | | 1,000,000 |
| (To record sale of 100,000 shares of preferred stock at $110 per share.) | | |

After the sale, including the common stock in the preceding example, the balance sheet would show the information as in Exhibit 11.2.

| EXHIBIT 11.2 Contributed Capital | |
|---|---|
| Preferred stock (par value $100, 6%, cumulative); 500,000 shares authorized; 100,000 shares issued and outstanding | $10,000,000 |
| Common stock (par value $1 per share); one million shares authorized; 100,000 shares issued and outstanding | 100,000 |
| Additional paid-in capital—Preferred Stock | 1,000,000 |
| Additional paid-in capital—Common Stock | 1,900,000 |
| Total stockholders' equity | $13,000,000 |

# Accounting for Subscribed Common Stock

Common stock shares may be sold on an installment plan. The corporation will require a specified down payment—say, 25 percent of sales price—and will also usually require periodic payments until the subscriptions are paid off. The stock is not issued until the subscription has been fully paid. The balance due is recorded as Subscriptions Receivable and is listed in the current assets section of the balance sheet. To illustrate, assume that XYZ Company sold 5,000 shares of its common stock, with a par value of $1, for $20 per share to a board member who paid 30 percent down on the sale. The journal entry would be as follows:

| | | |
|---|---|---|
| Cash | 30,000 | |
| Subscriptions Receivable | 70,000 | |
|    Common Stock Subscribed | | 5,000 |
|    Additional Paid-in Capital—Common Stock | | 95,000 |
| (Sale of 5,000 shares of subscribed stock) | | |

After the sale, including sales of common and preferred stock as described in the preceding examples, the balance sheet would show the information as in Exhibit 11.3.

| EXHIBIT 11.3 Contributed Capital | |
|---|---|
| Preferred stock (par value $100, 6%, cumulative); 500,000 shares authorized; 100,000 shares issued and outstanding | $10,000,000 |
| Common stock (par value $1 per share); one million shares authorized; 100,000 shares issued and outstanding | 100,000 |
| Common Stock Subscribed | 5,000 |
| Additional paid-in capital—Preferred Stock | 1,000,000 |
| Additional paid-in capital—Common Stock | 1,995,000 |
| Total stockholders' equity | $13,100,000 |

Assume that six months later the board member paid the remaining subscriptions receivable. The entry would be:

| | | |
|---|---|---|
| Cash | 70,000 | |
| Common Stock Subscribed | 5,000 | |
| Subscriptions Receivable | | 70,000 |
| Common Stock | | 5,000 |
| (To record payment of subscription and issuance of common stock) | | |

# Accounting for Treasury Stock

**Treasury stock** simply means that the company has repurchased its own shares from current stockholders and has not retired the stock. The shares are considered treasury stock until they are resold or retired. Treasury stock owned by the company does not have a right to dividends or to vote on corporate matters. Companies purchase their own stock for several reasons:

- *Shares are selling at a significantly low price.* By purchasing these shares the company will support the stock's market value, since the number of shares outstanding will decrease resulting in the earning per share increasing and usually the share price increases.

- *Shares are needed to distribute to employees for compensation plans.* When a company gives employees shares of its stock as a part of a compensation plan, it normally uses treasury stock for this purpose.

- *As a defense against a hostile takeover.* Purchasing treasury stock and reselling it to purchasers who would resist the takeover is a strategy often used by corporations to prevent a hostile takeover.

## The Purchase of Treasury Stock

Treasury stock is shown in the accounting records as an offset or contra account after retained earnings in the stockholders' equity section of the balance sheet. That is, it is a reduction of contributed capital in some way. There are two methods for recording treasury stock into the accounting records. The *cost method* records the purchase at total acquisition cost with a journal entry that debits Treasury Stock and credits Cash. This method deducts the recorded amount from total paid-in capital *and* retained earnings on the balance sheet. The *stated value method* records the purchase of treasury shares at their stated or par value and deducts the recorded amount as a deduction from capital stock only. GAAP accepts either of these methods, but the cost method is the most widely used in practice and will be used in the following example. The stated value method can be found in any intermediate accounting textbook.

To illustrate the purchase of its shares of stock using the cost method, assume that the XYZ Company from the previous example purchased 10,000 shares of its stock for $22 per share. The entry in the accounting records would be

| | | |
|---|---|---|
| Treasury Stock | 220,000 | |
| Cash | | 220,000 |
| (To record the purchase of 22,000 shares of XYZ Co. stock at $22 per share.) | | |

At the end of the year, assume that XYZ Company had retained earnings of $200,000. The XYZ Company balance sheet would show the information as shown in Exhibit 11.4.

| EXHIBIT 11.4 Contributed Capital | |
|---|---:|
| Preferred stock (par value $100, 6%, cumulative); 500,000 shares authorized; 100,000 shares issued and outstanding | $10,000,000 |
| Common stock (par value $1 per share); one million shares authorized; 100,000 shares issued and 90,000 shares outstanding[a] | 100,000 |
| Common Stock Subscribed | 5,000 |
| Additional paid-in capital—Preferred Stock | 1,000,000 |
| Additional paid-in capital—Common Stock | 1,995,000 |
| Total contributed capital | $13,100,000 |
| Retained Earnings | 200,000 |
| Total contributed capital and retained earnings | $13,300,000 |
| Less: Cost of Treasury Stock (10,000 shares) | (220,000) |
| Total stockholders' equity | 13,080,000 |

[a]Note that the 10,000 shares of treasury stock are deducted from shares outstanding.

## Accounting for the Sale of Treasury Stock

When treasury stock is reissued, there are two situations to deal with:

- *Reissue of Treasury Stock above Cost:* In this case, the difference is *not* recognized as a gain but is credited to Paid-in Capital from Treasury Stock. For example, assume that XYZ Company sold the 10,000 shares of treasury stock illustrated previously for $23 (the purchase price was $22). The journal entry would be

| Cash | 230,000 | |
|---|---|---|
| Treasury Stock | | 220,000 |
| Paid-in Capital from Treasury Stock | | 10,000 |
| (To record the sale of 10,000 shares of treasury stock at $23.) | | |

- *Reissue of Treasury Stock below Cost:* In this case, the difference is *not* recognized as a loss but is debited to Paid-in Capital from Treasury Stock. If there is no credit balance in the Paid-in Capital from Treasury Stock account, then the difference is debited to Retained Earnings. For example, instead of the preceding sale of treasury stock for $23, assume that XYZ

Company sold the treasury stock for $20. The difference between the $22 paid for the purchase and the $20 sold would be debited to Retained Earnings ($23 − 22) × 10,000 = $20,000), since there is no balance in Paid-in Capital from Treasury Stock:

| Cash | 200,000 | |
| Retained Earnings | 20,000 | |
| Treasury Stock | | 220,000 |

If there were a partial sale of treasury stock at a loss, the difference would be debited to Paid-in Capital from Treasury Stock. When all shares of treasury stock have been sold and there is a remaining credit balance in the Paid-in Capital from Treasury Stock, the balance is debited to Retained Earnings when the transaction is recorded, as shown previously.

# Dividends

Dividends are a form of payment to stockholders from retained earnings. Retained earnings may be retained in the business to meet operational and strategic needs, or they can be paid out in dividends to the stockholders. When paid, dividends are stated as an amount per share. For common-stock holders the board of directors determines whether there is to be a cash dividend—both preferred and common—and the amount per share. For preferred-stock holders the amount per share is stated in the stock contract as a percent of par value. Preferred dividends are usually paid each year, especially if the preferred stock is cumulative. The board of directors determines the amount of common stock dividends. There are usually three types of common stock dividends: cash dividends, property dividends, and stock dividends.

## Cash Dividends

A board of director's resolution votes dividends on common stock on a given date, which is the *date of declaration*. Since there is a delay in payment of these dividends, because the company must compile a list of eligible payees and make arrangements for payment, the eligible payees will be determined on the *date of record*. Finally, the *payment date* is a few days after that. Once the dividend is declared it becomes a current liability to the company. For example, assume that XYZ Company declared a cash dividend of $0.60 per share on January 10 for payment on February 1. Assume further that there were 100,000 common shares outstanding on January 23, the date of record. The following entries would be made:

At date of declaration, January 10:

| | | |
|---|---|---|
| Retained Earnings (or Cash Dividends) | 60,000 | |
| Dividends Payable | | 60,000 |
| (To record cash dividends declared) | | |

If the Cash Dividends account is used, it must be closed against Retained Earnings during the closing process at the end of the year.

At date of record, January 23:
No entry required.

At date of payment, February 1:

| | | |
|---|---|---|
| Dividends Payable | 60,000 | |
| Cash | | 60,000 |
| (Payment of cash dividends) | | |

What happens when there is preferred stock on a company's balance sheet? Generally, the board of directors will decide on a total amount of cash dividends to be paid to both preferred- and common-stock holders. Remember that the preferred-stock holders must be paid first, including any dividends in arrears on cumulative preferred stock. For example, using the XYZ Company balance sheet shown previously, assume that the company did not pay the preferred-stock holders cash dividends in the previous year. Since this a cumulative preferred stock, it has $600,000 ($10,000,000 \times .06$) of preferred dividends in arrears. Before it can pay $60,000 to common-stock holders it must pay the $600,000 in arrears to the preferred-stock holders. The board of directors must decide whether the company can afford to pay both dividends.

# Property Dividends

**Property dividends** are payments to stockholders in a form other than in cash, which is a rare event. An example of this type of dividend is the distribution of shares of stock held in a subsidiary company. The value of the dividend is the fair market value of the asset at the date of declaration. To record the property dividend at the date of declaration, Retained Earnings would be debited and Property Dividend Payable would be credited. At the date of payment the Property Dividend Payable would be debited and the relevant asset account would be credited.

## Stock Dividends

A **stock dividend** is an issuance of additional shares of stock to existing stockholders on a pro rata basis without receiving any payment for them. Basically, a stock dividend involves the capitalization of part of retained earnings to contributed capital. The company does not distribute any assets—only additional shares of stock. Thus, the stockholder maintains his or her proportionate interest in the company. The accounting for the stock dividend depends on the size of the stock dividend:

*A small (ordinary) stock dividend (less than 20 to 25 percent of existing shares outstanding)* is valued at the market price of existing stock on the declaration date.

*A large stock dividend (greater than 20 to 25 percent of existing shares outstanding)* is valued at par value. To illustrate these two cases, assume that the XYZ Company has 100,000 shares of common stock at $1 par value. The market price of the stock is $25 on the date of declaration and issued. The entry for both of the above cases is as follows:

Small stock dividend: Assume XYZ issues a 10 percent stock dividend.

| | | |
|---|---|---|
| Retained Earnings | 2,500,000 | |
| Common Stock | | 100,000 |
| Additional Paid-in Capital—Common Stock | | 2,400,000 |
| (10 percent stock dividend of 100,000 shares outstanding × $25) | | |

Large stock dividend: Assume XYZ issues a 30 percent stock dividend.

| | | |
|---|---|---|
| Retained Earnings | 30,000 | |
| Common Stock | | 30,000 |
| (30 percent stock dividend of 100,000 shares outstanding × $1 par value) | | |

# Stock Splits

A **stock split** is the issuance of a significant number of shares of stock by simply reducing its par value and issuing a proportionate number of shares. For example, a two-for-one stock split would double the number of shares outstanding and cut the par value of the stock in half. No formal entry is made in the accounting records. However, a memorandum is maintained of stock splits to keep track of the number of shares outstanding and the related par value. Also, the new number of shares outstanding would be reported on the balance sheet.

# Retained Earnings

**The retained earnings** balance is the amount of income earned since the company's inception less any net losses and less any dividends paid to stockholders. Companies may appropriate retained earnings for a specific purpose, such as contingencies, a sinking fund required by a bond covenant, or plant expansion. The amount of appropriation is unavailable for dividend payments. For example, XYZ Company appropriates $200,000 for a plant expansion. The journal entry would be:

| | | |
|---|---|---|
| Retained Earnings | 200,000 | |
| Appropriated Retained Earnings | | 200,000 |

When the appropriation is no longer needed the appropriation is reversed.

Companies may also restrict retained earnings without a journal entry in order to retain a certain retained earnings balance for purposes like those listed previously. In this case, the restriction should be disclosed in a footnote to the balance sheet.

# QUIZ

1. **Treasury stock is:**
   A. A company's stock that is issued but not outstanding
   B. A company's stock that is purchased and added to its investment account and used for trading
   C. An increase to assets and a decrease to stockholders' equity, when it is purchased
   D. None of the above

2. **Which of the following is *not* a right of a stockholder?**
   A. To share proportionately in company assets in the event of liquidation
   B. To share proportionately in any new issue of common stock
   C. To share proportionately in any earnings of the company
   D. To share proportionately in all management decisions

3. **Stockholders' equity includes all of the following, except:**
   A. Common stock
   B. Stock owned in a subsidiary
   C. Additional paid-in capital
   D. Retained earnings

4. **A company issued 5,000 shares of $10 par value common stock at $30. Which of the following entries would *not* be made?**
   A. Debit cash for $150,000.
   B. Credit Common Stock for $50,000.
   C. Credit Subscribed Stock for $50,000.
   D. Credit Additional Paid-in Capital for $100,000.

5. **A company issued a 10 percent stock dividend when it had 500,000, $1 par value, shares of stock outstanding. The current market price of the stock is $50 on the date the dividend is declared and issued. Which of the following is incorrect?**
   A. Credit Common Stock for $50,000.
   B. Credit Paid-in Capital in Excess of Par for $2,450,000.
   C. No entry is made, but a memorandum is made of the stock dividend.
   D. Retained Earnings is debited for $2,500,000.

6. **When treasury stock is reissued for more than the company paid for it, the difference is:**
   A. Credited to an Additional Paid-in Capital account
   B. Given to the stockholders in a dividend
   C. Included as a gain on the income statement
   D. None of the above

7. **Which of the following dividends do not decrease stockholders' equity?**
   A. Liquidating dividends
   B. Stock dividends
   C. Property dividends
   D. None of the above

8. **A company declared a two-for-one stock split when it had 100,000 shares outstanding. The stock has a par value of $1 and a market value of $10. Which of the following is correct?**
   A. Common Stock is credited for $100,000.
   B. A memorandum entry is made of the stock split.
   C. Common Stock is credited for $1,000,000.
   D. Additional Paid-in Capital is credited for $900,000.

9. **A company sold 10,000 shares of its $1 par value common stock subscriptions at $10 per share to someone who paid 20 percent down on the sale and the balance was to be paid later. Which of the following journal entries is incorrect?**
   A. Debit to Cash for $20,000.
   B. Debit to Subscriptions Receivable for $80,000.
   C. Credit to Additional Paid-in Capital for $90,000.
   D. Credit to Common Stock for $10,000.

10. **A company declares a property dividend. How much should Retained Earnings be reduced?**
    A. Cost of the property
    B. Cost of the property less accumulated depreciation
    C. Fair value of the property
    D. Carrying value of the property

11. **Which of the following preferred-stock holders would usually receive the largest amount of cash dividends?**
    A. Cumulative and fully participating
    B. Noncumulative and fully participating
    C. Cumulative and nonparticipating
    D. Noncumulative and nonparticipating

12. **Common Stock Dividends Payable would be reported on the balance sheet as:**
    A. A current liability
    B. A reduction of total stockholders' equity
    C. An offset to common stock
    D. An addition to additional paid-in capital

13. **Which of the following is not a characteristic of preferred stock?**
    A. It is preferred as to dividends.
    B. It is preferred when liquidating assets.
    C. It receives a dividend based on its par value.
    D. It is allowed to vote on corporate matters.

14. **(True or false?) Convertible preferred stock means that the preferred-stock holders can convert preferred shares to common stock shares at a ratio stipulated in the stock contract.**

15. **The balance of the Retained Earnings account is affected by which of the following?**
    A. Losses from operations since the inception of the company
    B. Profit from the inception of the company
    C. Dividends paid from the inception of the company
    D. All of the above

# Statement of Cash Flows

*The purposes of this chapter are to*

- Describe the purpose and importance of the statement of cash flows
- Describe the classification of cash flows from operating, investing, and financing activities
- Describe the difference between the direct method and the indirect method of preparing the statement of cash flows
- Explain how to prepare the statement of cash flows

## Purpose and Importance of the Statement of Cash Flows

The basic purpose of the statement of cash flows is to provide information on the cash receipts (inflows) and cash payments (outflows) of a business. This information is organized around the business entity's operating, investing, and financing activities. The statement cash flows is important because it provides information to do the following:

- Determine whether cash has been generated from operations, financing (e.g., borrowing), or from investment (e.g., sale of buildings and equipment) activities.
- Determine where cash has been spent.
- Explain the differences between net income and net cash flow from operating activities. The income statement is based on accrual accounting, which incorporates many noncash transactions into arriving at net income (e.g., depreciation expense). A business could have a positive net income but still have a shortage of cash to meet its needs. Knowing the differences between net income and net cash flows will be very helpful in planning operating, investing, and financing activities.
- Determine whether there will be sufficient future cash flows to pay dividends and cash obligations of the business. This involves predicting the amounts and timing of cash flows.
- Assess and plan the sources and uses of cash so that cash will be available when needed. With this information a business can prevent a cash shortage by establishing a line of credit with a bank, borrowing money from other sources, or cutting expenses to save cash.

### What Is the True Meaning of Cash?

The Financial Accounting Standards Board recommends that the statement of cash flows use cash and cash equivalents as the definition of cash. Cash equivalents are short-term, highly liquid investments that are readily convertible to cash and have maturity dates of three months or less. Examples are Treasury bills, commercial paper, and money market funds.

## Statement of Cash Flows Classifications

The statement of cash flows will include all cash flows for the three classifications of activities, as shown in Exhibit 12.1.

| EXHIBIT 12.1 Classification of Cash Flows | | | |
|---|---|---|---|
| Types of Activities | Types of Transactions | Examples of Cash Inflows | Examples of Cash Outflows |
| Operating | Cash transactions relating to the everyday operations of the business | —Collections from customers<br>—Receipts of dividends from investments | —Payments to vendors<br>—Payments to employees<br>—Payments for taxes |
| Investing | Cash transactions relating to acquiring and disposing of long-term assets | —Proceeds from sale of land or building<br>—Proceeds from sale of investments in securities | —Purchase of buildings or equipment<br>—Acquiring additional stock in a subsidiary |
| Financing | Cash transactions relating to long-term debt and stockholders' equity (contributed capital) | —Proceeds from a new stock issue<br>—Proceeds from a sale of bonds<br>—Proceeds from a long-term loan | —Payment of dividends to stockholders<br>—Payment to redeem callable bonds |

# Two Methods for Preparing the Statement of Cash Flows

As discussed in earlier chapters, businesses must use accrual accounting, which requires that revenues be recognized in the accounts when they are earned and expenses be recognized when they are incurred. Thus, the basic approach in preparing the statement of cash flows is to convert accrual revenues and expenses to a cash basis along with identifying cash flows from investing and financing activities. There are two basic methods for preparing the statement of cash flows: the direct method and the indirect method; both are acceptable under GAAP. The indirect method will be covered first.

## Indirect Method

The Financial Accounting Standards Board suggests that companies use the direct method for preparing the statement of cash flows. However, surveys of companies show that the vast majority (well over 90 percent) uses the indirect method. Why? Simply stated, the indirect method is easier and less expensive to prepare. Also, the indirect method provides a better reconciliation from accrual-based reported net income to cash provided by operations.

The **indirect method** starts with net income reported on the income statement and adjusts this figure for items that did not affect cash. For example, depreciation expense does not affect cash flow, so the amount reported on the income statement is added back to Net Income on the statement of cash flows.

| EXHIBIT 12.2  Format of the Statement of Cash Flows Using the Indirect Method | |
|---|---|
| **Net income reported on income statement** | **XXX** |
| **Cash Flow from Operating Activities (Selected Accounts)** | |
| Adjustments to reconcile net income to net cash provided by operating activities: | |
| Add: Depreciation and amortization | +XXX |
| (Increase)/decrease in accounts receivable | −/+XXX |
| (Increase)/decrease in inventories | −/+XXX |
| (Increase)/decrease in prepaid expenses | −/+XXX |
| Increase/(decrease) in interest payable | +/XXX |
| Increase/(decrease) in accounts payable | +/−XXX |
| Increase/(decrease) in taxes payable | <u>+/− XXX</u> |
| Net cash provided by operating activities | +/−XXX |
| **Cash Flow from Investing Activities (Selected Accounts)** | |
| Purchase of buildings and equipment | −XXX |
| Purchase of additional shares in subsidiary | −XXX |
| Proceeds from sale of land | +XXX |
| Proceeds from sale of equipment | <u>+XXX</u> |
| Net cash provided by investing activities | +/−XXX |
| **Cash Flow from Financing Activities (Selected Accounts)** | |
| Payment of dividends | −XXX |
| Payment of long-term debt | −XXX |
| Proceeds from sale of bonds | −XXX |
| Proceeds from sale of common stock | <u>−XXX</u> |
| Net cash provided by financing activities | <u>+/−XXX</u> |
| **Increase (Decrease) in Cash** | +/−XXX |
| Add: Cash at the beginning of the year | <u>+XXX</u> |
| Cash at the end of the year | <u>XXX</u> |

Exhibit 12.2 depicts the cash flow statement format using the indirect method.

## Steps in Preparing the Statement of Cash Flows

**Step 1.** *Determine the change in cash.*

This involves subtracting the ending cash balance as reported on the balance sheet from the beginning cash balance for the period being reported (e.g., ending of year balance less beginning of year balance). This will act as the check figure for comparison to the increase or decrease in cash found on the statement of cash flows.

**Step 2.** *Determine cash flows from operating activities.*

This essentially involves the elimination of noncash transactions that do not increase or decrease cash from operating activities as depicted in Exhibit 12.2. This is first accomplished by adding back depreciation or amortization expense as they do not involved cash. Next, the beginning and ending balances for each current asset and current liability account on the balance sheet are compared for changes. Generally, the following rules apply in analyzing these accounts, which synchronize with the format depicted in Exhibit 12.2:

- *An increase in a current asset account is a use of cash.* For example, an increase in Accounts Receivable would signify that some of the sales reported on the income statement included sales that have not been collected. Thus, this increased amount, in effect, decreases the reported cash flow from sales. The sales figure on the income statement would, in effect, be adjusted downward to show the actual cash inflow from customers.

- *A decrease in a current asset account is a source of cash.* For example, a decrease in Prepaid Insurance would signify that the company paid less cash for insurance than was reported on the income statement as an expense. Prepaid insurance reported on the income statement would be adjusted downward to show the actual cash flow for payment for insurance, thus reducing the amount of cash outflow from what was reported on the income statement.

- *An increase in a current liability account is a source of cash.* For example, an increase in Accounts Payable would signify that the company paid less to vendors for operating expenses (inventory, etc.) than is reported on the income statement. Thus, Cash Paid for Operating Expenses on the income statement would, in effect, be adjusted downward to reduce the amount of actual cash paid to vendors.

- *A decrease in a current liability account is a use of cash.* For example, a decrease in Taxes Payable would signify that the company paid more to the tax authorities than the tax expense reported on the income statement, that is, it paid down taxes owned from a previous period. Thus, the Taxes Paid to Tax Authorities would be adjusted upward to show the actual cash paid.

**Step 3.** *Determine the cash flows from investing activities.*

The next step is to compare the beginning and ending balances of long-term assets to determine if the changes affected cash flow. The rules listed previously for changes in current asset and current liability accounts also apply to long-term assets and liabilities accounts. Transactions for each of these accounts should be reviewed to identify any offsetting transactions.

**Step 4.** *Determine the cash flows from financing activities.*

The next step is to compare beginning and ending balances for long-term liabilities and stockholders' equity to determine if the changes affected cash flow. The rules above for liabilities also apply here. In addition, the rules for stockholders' equity are

- An increase in a stockholders' equity account is a source of cash. For example, the company sold common stock for cash, which increases the Common Stock account.

- A decrease in a stockholders' equity account is a use of cash. For example, the company pays dividends, which decreases Retained Earnings.

**Step 5.** *Prepare the statement of cash flows.*

Use the format shown in Exhibit 12.2.

*An example using the indirect method:* Assume that XYZ Company started business in 2009 and had the comparative ending balance sheets shown in Exhibit 12.3 for 2009 and 2010.

Assume that XYZ Company had the income statement shown in Exhibit 12.4 for the year ended December 31, 2010.

Additional information: XYZ paid $18,000 in cash dividends during the year.

Prepare a statement of cash flows using the *indirect method*.

**EXHIBIT 12.3**  XYZ Company Comparative Balance Sheet December 31, 2010

|  | 2010 | 2009 | Change Increase/ Decrease |
|---|---|---|---|
| **Assets** | | | |
| Cash | $37,000 | $49,000 | $12,000 decrease |
| Accounts Receivable | 26,000 | 36,000 | 10,000 decrease |
| Prepaid Expenses | 6,000 | 0 | 6,000 increase |
| Investment in Stock | 500 | 1,000 | 500 decrease |
| Land | 70,000 | 0 | 70,000 increase |
| Buildings | 200,000 | 0 | 200,000 increase |
| Accumulated Depreciation—Buildings | (11,000) | (0) | 11,000 increase |
| Equipment | 68,000 | 0 | 68,000 increase |
| Accumulated Depreciation—Equipment | (10,000) | (0) | 10,000 increase |
| Total Assets | $386,500 | $86,000 | |
| **Liabilities and Stockholders' Equity** | | | |
| Accounts Payable | $40,500 | $6,000 | $34,500 increase |
| Bonds Payable | 300,000 | 0 | $300,000 increase |
| Common Stock | 60,000 | 60,000 | $0 |
| Retained Earnings | 136,000 | 20,000 | $116,000 increase |
| Total | $386,500 | $86,000 | |

**EXHIBIT 12.4**  XYZ Company Income Statement for the Year Ended December 31, 2010

| | | |
|---|---|---|
| Revenues | | $492,000 |
| Less: | | |
| Total Operating Expenses (excluding depreciation) | $269,000 | |
| Depreciation Expense | 21,000 | |
| Total Operating Expenses | | 290,000 |
| Income from Operations | | $202,000 |
| Less: Income Tax Expense | | (68,000) |
| Net Income | | $134,000 |

**EXHIBIT 12.5**  Cash Flows from Operating Activities

| | | |
|---|---:|---:|
| Depreciation Expense | $21,000 | |
| Decrease in Accounts Receivable | 10,000 | |
| Increase in Prepaid Expenses | (6,000) | |
| Increase in Accounts Payable | 34,500 | |
| Net Cash Flow Provided by Operating Activities | | $59,500 |

**Step 1.** *Determine the change in cash.*

The cash balance at the end of 2009 was $49,000, and the cash balance at the end of 2010 was $37,000. Thus, there was a decrease in cash of $12,000.

**Step 2.** *Determine cash flows from operating activities.*

The cash flows from operating activities are computed as shown in Exhibit 12.5.

**Step 3.** *Determine the cash flows from investing activities.*
The cash flows from investing activities are as shown in Exhibit 12.6.

**EXHIBIT 12.6**  Cash Flows from Investing Activities

| | | |
|---|---:|---:|
| Sale of stock (investment) | $500 | |
| Purchase of land | (70,000) | |
| Purchase of Buildings | (200,000) | |
| Purchase of equipment | (68,000) | |
| Net cash outflow from investing activities | | ($337,500) |

**Step 4.** *Determine the cash flows from financing Activities.*

Cash flows from financing activities are shown in Exhibit 12.7.

**Step 5.** *Prepare the statement of cash flows.*

The statement of cash flows is shown in Exhibit 12.8.

**EXHIBIT 12.7**  Cash Flows from Financing Activities

| | | |
|---|---:|---:|
| Sale of bonds | $150,000 | |
| Payment of dividends | (18,000) | |
| Net cash flow provided by financing activities | | $132,000 |

| EXHIBIT 12.8  XYZ Company Statement of Cash Flows for the Year Ended December 31, 2010 | | |
|---|---:|---:|
| Net income reported on the income statement | | $134,000 |
| **Cash Flow from Operating Activities** | | |
| Adjustments to reconcile net income to net cash provided by operating activities: | | |
| Depreciation expense | $21,000 | |
| Additional cash received from customers | 10,000 | |
| Additional cash paid for operating expenses (prepaid items) | (6,000) | |
| Less cash paid to vendors than expensed | 34,500 | 59,500 |
| Net cash flow provided by operating activities | | $193,500 |
| **Cash Flow from Investing Activities** | | |
| Sale of stock | $500 | |
| Purchase of land | (70,000) | |
| Purchase of buildings | (200,000) | |
| Purchase of equipment | (68,000) | |
| Net cash outflow from investing activities | | (337,500) |
| **Cash Flow from Financing Activities** | | |
| Sale of bonds | $150,000 | |
| Payment of dividends | (18,000) | |
| Net cash flow provided by financing activities | | 132,000 |
| **Increase (Decrease) in Cash** | | ($12,000) |
| Add: Cash at the beginning of the year | | 49,000 |
| Cash at the end of the year | | $37,000 |

## Direct Method

Compared to the indirect method, the **direct method** reports cash receipts (inflows) and cash disbursements (outflows) from *operating* activities in detail. Each operating activity account must be analyzed. The cash flow from investing and financing activities are reported just as they are using the indirect method. The format of the statement of cash flow using the direct method is depicted in Exhibit 12.9.

*An illustration using the direct method:* Taking the preceding data from XYZ Company, the statement of cash flows is shown in Exhibit 12.10:

**EXHIBIT 12.9** Format of the Statement of Cash Flows Using the Direct Method

| Cash Flow from Operating Activities (Selected Examples) | Affect on Cash Flow | Net Effect |
|---|---|---|
| Net Sales + Beg. A/R - End. A/R = Cash from Customers | +XXX | |
| Net Merchandise Purchases + Beg. A/P - End. A/P = Cash Inv. Purchases | -XXX | |
| Salary Expense + Beg. Salaries Payable - End. Salaries Payable = Cash Salaries | -XXX | |
| Insurance Expense + End. Prepaid Insurance - Beg. Prepaid Insurance = Cash Paid for Insurance | -XXX | |
| Income Tax Expense + Beg. Income Taxes Payable - End. Income Taxes Payable = Cash Paid for Income Taxes | <u>-XXX</u> | |
| Net Cash Provided by Operating Activities | | +/-XXX |
| **Cash Flow from Investing Activities** | | |
| Proceeds from Sale of Buildings and Equipment | +XXX | |
| Proceeds from the Sale of Investments | +XXX | |
| Purchase of Buildings and Equipment | -XXX | |
| Purchase Stock in Subsidiary | -XXX | |
| Net Cash Provided by Investing Activities | | +/-XXX |
| **Cash Flow from Financing Activities** | | |
| Payments of Long-Term Debt | -XXX | |
| Dividends Paid | -XXX | |
| Purchase of Treasury Stock | -XXX | |
| Proceeds from Issuance of Long-Term debt | +XXX | |
| Proceeds from Issuance of Common Stock | <u>+XXX</u> | |
| Net Cash Provided by Financing Activities | | <u>+/-XXX</u> |
| **Increase (Decrease) in Cash** | | <u>+/-XXX</u> |
| Add: Cash at the beginning of the Year | | +XXX |
| Cash at the end of the Year | | <u><u>XXX</u></u> |

**EXHIBIT 12.10** XYZ Company Statement of Cash Flows for the Year Ended December 31, 2010

| | | |
|---|---|---|
| **Cash Flow from Operating Activities** | | |
| Cash received from customers | $502,000[a] | |
| Cash payments for total operating expenses | (234,500)[b] | |
| Cash payments relating to prepaid expenses | (6,000)[c] | |
| Cash payment for taxes | (68,000)[d] | |
| Net cash flow provided by operating activities | | $193,500 |
| **Cash Flow from Investing Activities** | | |
| Sale of stock | $500 | |
| Purchase of land | (70,000) | |
| Purchase of buildings | (200,000) | |
| Purchase of equipment | (68,000) | |
| Net cash outflow from investing activities | | (337,500) |
| **Cash Flow from Financing Activities** | | |
| Sale of bonds | $150,000 | |
| Payment of dividends | (18,000) | |
| Net cash flow provided by financing activities | | $132,000 |
| **Increase (Decrease) in Cash** | | ($12,000) |
| Cash at the beginning of the year | | 49,000 |
| Cash at the end of the year | | $37,000 |

[a]Net Sales + Beg. A/R – End. A/R = $492,000 + 36,000 – 26,000 = $502,000.
[b]Operating Expense + Beg. A/P – End. A/P = $269,000 + 6,000 – 40,500 = $234,500.
[c]Since Prepaid Expenses had no beginning balance, the prepayments were made during the year.
[d]Since there is no Taxes Payable account, the total tax expense was paid in cash.

# QUIZ

1. Classify each of the following cash transactions as a cash flow from: (O) operating activities, (I) investing activities, or (F) financing activities.
   A. Payment for purchase of new equipment
   B. Payment of employee salaries
   C. Paid dividends to stockholders
   D. Payment to redeem callable bonds
   E. Payment of accounts payable to vendors

2. In computing net cash flows, all of the following adjustments are added to net income from operating activities except:
   A. An increase in Prepaid Insurance.
   B. A decrease in Accounts Receivable.
   C. Depreciation Expense.
   D. An increase in Accounts Payable.

3. Issuing common stock for cash would be reported as:
   A. A decrease in net income
   B. An investing activity
   C. A financing activity
   D. Both an investing and financing activity

4. A company purchased a building for $300,000 cash. This transaction would be reported on the statement of cash flows as:
   A. A decrease in net income
   B. As a use of cash in the financing activity section
   C. As a use of cash in the operating activities section
   D. As a use of cash in the investing activity section

5. For each of the following events indicate whether it will increase or decrease net income from operating activities to arrive at net cash flows from operations:
   A. Amortization of a copyright
   B. Increase in accounts receivable
   C. Decrease in prepaid insurance
   D. Decrease in wages payable
   E. Increase in inventory

6. A company declared $50,000 in stock dividends. How would this affect the cash flow statement?
   A. It would show an increase in Cash in the financing section.
   B. It would show an increase in Cash in the investing section.
   C. It would not affect the statement, as it does not affect cash flow.
   D. None of the above

7. The last items to be included in the statement of cash flows are:
   A. Each current asset account's beginning balance
   B. The beginning and ending balances in the Cash account at the bottom of the statement
   C. The changes in stockholders' equity
   D. Each current asset and current liability accounts' beginning and ending balance

8. A company purchased equipment for $50,000; issued stock for $60,000 in cash; declared dividends of $20,000; charged $25,000 to depreciation expense; and sold investments for $10,000 in cash. What would be the net cash flows from investing activities?
   A. Net increase of $25,000
   B. Net decrease of $50,000
   C. Net increase of $35,000
   D. Net decrease of $40,000

9. (True or false?) The indirect method for preparing the statement of cash flows starts with net income reported on the income statement and adjusts this figure for items that did not affect cash.

10. A company had net income of $200,000 for the year, depreciation expense of $20,000 for the year, sale of equipment for $30,000, and an increase in prepaid expenses of $10,000 for the year. What would be the net cash flows from operating activities for the year?
    A. $190,000
    B. $210,000
    C. $200,000
    D. $220,000

11. A company had net cash inflows from financing activities of $20,000, net cash inflows of $30,000 from investing activities, and a net increase in cash of $25,000 for the year. How much was the cash flows from operating activities?
    A. Net cash outflow of $25,000
    B. Net cash inflow of $50,000
    C. Net cash inflow of $10,000
    D. None of the above

12. (True or false?) While the indirect method provides more information, most companies use the direct method for preparing the statement of cash flows.

13. Cash from the sale of treasury stock:
    A. Would be included in investing activities section
    B. Would be included in financing activities section
    C. Would be included in operating activities section
    D. None of the above

14. **A company sold a computer system for $5,000 cash that had a cost of $15,000 and accumulated depreciation of $12,000. The sale would be reported in the statement of cash flows in the:**
    A. Operating section as a loss of $3,000
    B. Financing section as a net cash inflow of $5,000
    C. Investing section as a gain of $3,000
    D. Investing section as a net cash inflow of $5,000

15. **The Financial Accounting Standards Board recommends that cash be defined as:**
    A. Cash
    B. Short-term investments readily convertible to cash
    C. Highly liquid investments
    D. Maturity date of 90 days or less
    E. All of the above

## chapter 13

# Financial Statement Analysis

*The purposes of this chapter are to*

- Explain why financial statement analysis is important to users of financial statements
- Explain horizontal analysis and its uses
- Explain vertical analysis and its uses
- Explain ratio analysis and its uses

## Who Needs to Analyze Financial Statements?

This book has presented the principles and procedures for the preparation of financial statements and the meaning of the items and concepts contained therein. Shouldn't an understanding of the basic statements be enough to evaluate the company being reported on? The answer is that the basic statements themselves do go a long way to evaluate a company. Yet they basically present raw data. Thus, different users of the statements will need to subject these statements to further analysis in order to fully evaluate a business. The type of analysis will depend on the needs of a particular user. The following list shows those users and some of their needs:

- *Stockholders and prospective investors* have similar needs in evaluating financial statements. Their primary concern is the past and future profit performance of the business. Why? Because performance of the business in terms of earnings is a major factor in determining the stock price of the business. Thus, these users will be primarily interested in the profitability ratios and ability to pay dividends .computed from the financial statements.

- *Short-term creditors,* such as banks and vendors, are interested in the ability of the business to pay liabilities coming due during the current operating cycle. These users would be interested in short-term solvency measures computed from the relationship of current assets to current liabilities.

- *Long-term creditors,* such as bondholders, are interested in the ability of the business to pay its long-term obligations. These users would be interested in such things as the long-term profitability prospects of the business so that they can evaluate whether the company will be able to pay interest when due. Also, they would be interested in the company's present capital structure (the extent of total liabilities compared to other components of the balance sheet).

- *Internal managers* are mainly interested in the performance trends of the business in terms of profitability. They are also interested in the capital structure and its impact on future financing needs of the firm.

## Horizontal Analysis

**Horizontal analysis** compares each item on a financial statement with that same item on statements from previous periods. While one could simply compare raw dollar amounts, it is better to also compare amounts from one period to another period on a percentage basis. For example, XYZ Company had sales of $1,000,000 in 2009 and $1,200,000 in 2010. The change in percentages would be

$$\frac{1,200,000 - 1,000,000}{1,000,000} = .20$$

This indicates that XYZ had an increase in sales, year over year, of 20 percent. It is best to look at the change both in percentage terms and in dollar amounts. That is because small dollar amount changes could result in a high-percentage change when the base figure is also small. For example, a change in interest expense from $1,000 to $1,500 would be a 50 percent increase but, because of the small number involved, it may not be significant.

In addition to computing simple percentages, when one is comparing several years of comparative data, it is better to also compute the percentages using a

**EXHIBIT 13.1** The XYZ Company Comparative Balance Sheet December 31, 2008, 2009, and 2010 (in Thousands of Dollars)

| | 2010 | 2009 | 2008 |
|---|---|---|---|
| **Assets** | | | |
| Current Assets | | | |
| Cash | $150.0 | $175.0 | $175.0 |
| Accounts Receivable | 100.0 | 75.0 | 50.0 |
| Inventory | 100.0 | 75.0 | 100.0 |
| Other Current Assets | 250.0 | 225.0 | 175.0 |
| Total Current Assets | $600.0 | $550.0 | $500.0 |
| Plant, Property, and Equipment | 500.0 | 450.0 | 425.0 |
| Total Assets | $1,100.0 | $1,000.0 | $925.0 |
| **Liabilities** | | | |
| Accounts Payable | $100.0 | $90 | $105.0 |
| Taxes Payable | 90.0 | 100.0 | 95.0 |
| Other Current Liabilities | 87.0 | 60.0 | 60.0 |
| Total Current Liabilities | $277.0 | $250.0 | $260.0 |
| Long-Term Liabilities | 400.0 | 375.0 | 350.0 |
| Total Liabilities | $677.0 | $625.0 | $610.0 |
| **Stockholders' Equity** | | | |
| Contributed Capital | $225.0 | $225.0 | $225.0 |
| Retained Earnings | 198.0 | 150.0 | 90.0 |
| Total Stockholders' Equity | $423.0 | $375.0 | $315.0 |
| Total Liabilities and Stockholders' Equity | $1,100.0 | $1,000.0 | $925.0 |

**EXHIBIT 13.2** The XYZ Company Comparative Balance Sheet December 31, 2008, 2009, and 2010 (Percentage Index—Base 2008)

|  | 2010 | 2009 | 2008 |
|---|---|---|---|
| **Assets** | | | |
| Current Assets | | | |
| Cash | 85.7 | 100.0 | 100 |
| Accounts Receivable | 200.0 | 150.0 | 100 |
| Inventory | 100.0 | 75.0 | 100 |
| Other Current Assets | 142.9 | 128.6 | 100 |
| Total Current Assets | 120.0 | 110.0 | 100 |
| Plant, Property, and Equipment | 117.7 | 105.9 | 100 |
| Total Assets | 118.9 | 108.1 | 100 |
| **Liabilities** | | | |
| Accounts Payable | 95.3 | 86.8 | 100 |
| Taxes Payable | 94.3 | 105.3 | 100 |
| Other Current Liabilities | 145.0 | 100.0 | 100 |
| Total Current Liabilities | 106.5 | 96.2 | 100 |
| Long-Term Liabilities | 114.3 | 107.1 | 100 |
| Total Liabilities | 111.0 | 102.5 | 100 |
| **Stockholders' Equity** | | | |
| Contributed Capital | 100.0 | 100.0 | 100 |
| Retained Earnings | 220.0 | 166.7 | 100 |
| Total Stockholders' Equity | 134.3 | 119.1 | 100 |
| Total Liabilities and Stockholders' Equity | 118.9 | 108.1 | 100 |

base year. To illustrate consider the balance sheet in Exhibit 13.1, which shows raw data. In Exhibit 13.2 the balance sheet has been recast into comparative percentages. How were these comparative percentage indexes computed? Each item in the base year (2008) was assigned an index of 100. Then each value in the comparative year(s) was divided by the base year amount (2008) and multiplied by 100. Using percentage indexes allows a company to compare its financial positions and performance for a given item to indexes of competitors or other companies in the same industry.

One can easily see the advantage of evaluating trends on a balance sheet. For example, the Accounts Receivable balances of XYZ Company shows a significant increase over a three-year period. This may suggest that the company's credit policies are too lax and should be evaluated.

# Vertical Analysis

**Vertical analysis** is a technique whereby a significant item on a financial statement is selected as a base value and all other related items on the statement are expressed as a percentage of that amount. Thus, the analysis involves evaluating items on a single year's financial statement. Another term for this type of analysis is common-sized statements. In addition, the raw account balances are displayed side by side with the corresponding percentages.

Which significant items are selected as base amounts? On the income statement the item chosen is usually Net Sales. Thus, Net Sales are assigned a value of 100, and all other amounts on the income statement are compared to Net Sales. On the balance sheet for assets, the base is usually the Total Assets balance, which is assigned a value of 100, and all other assets are compared to it. For liabilities and stockholders' equity the base chosen is usually Total Liabilities and Stockholders' Equity, which is assigned a value of 100, and each of their accounts are compared to this total.

To illustrate, the income statement and common-sized analysis for XYZ Company is displayed in Exhibit 13.3.

# Ratio Analysis

**Ratio analysis** is the relationship between one amount on a financial statement to another amount on the same or another statement. In other words, the two amounts can be from two different categories. For example, the accounts receivable turnover ratio computes Net Credit Sales divided by the Average Gross Accounts Receivable (if available). The point is, there must be a meaningful relationship for a ratio to be computed and used. Although there can be different classifications in practice, the following general classifications are discussed in this book:

- **Activity ratios** measure a company's efficiency in using its current assets and current liabilities.

**EXHIBIT 13.3**  XYZ Company Income Statement Vertical Analysis (in Thousands of Dollars) for the Years Ended December 31, 2010 and 2009

|  | 2010 | | 2009 | |
|---|---|---|---|---|
|  | Amount | Percentage | Amount | Percentage |
| Net Sales | $500.0 | 100.0 | $550.0 | 100.0 |
| Less: Cost of Goods Sold | 250.0 | 50.0 | 300.0 | 54.5 |
| Gross Margin | $150.0 | 30.0 | $250.0 | 45.5 |
| Operating Expenses |  |  |  |  |
| Selling Expenses | $55.0 | 11.0 | $75.0 | 13.6 |
| Administrative Expenses | 20.0 | 4.0 | 35.0 | 6.4 |
| Total Operating Expenses | $75.0 | 15.0 | $100.0 | 18.2 |
| Income from Operations | $75.0 | 15.0 | $150.0 | 27.3 |
| Add: Nonoperating Income | 15.0 | 3.0 | 0 | 0 |
| Income before Interest Expense and Taxes | $90.0 | 18.0 | $150.0 | 27.3 |
| Less: Interest Expense | 10.0 | 2.0 | 10.0 | 1.8 |
| Income before Taxes | $80.0 | 16.0 | $140.0 | 25.5 |
| Less: Income Taxes | 32.0 | 6.4 | 40.0 | 7.3 |
| Net Income | $48.0 | 9.6 | $100.0 | 18.2 |

- **Liquidity ratios** measure a company's ability to meet its short-term obligations (usually one year or less).
- **Solvency ratios** measure a company's ability to meet its long-term obligations as they become due.
- **Profitability ratios** measure the company's ability to earn a satisfactory profit and return on investment.
- **Market-based ratios** compare the company's current market price to its earnings and dividend yield.

Exhibits 13.4a through 13.4e present lists of common ratios under the headings shown previously. These lists are not exhaustive, but they show the most important ratios used in these categories.

## EXHIBIT 13.4a  Activity Ratio Analysis

| Title of Ratio | Formula | Application of Ratio |
|---|---|---|
| Accounts receivable turnover | Net Credit Sales/Average A/R[a] | Measures the company's effectiveness in collecting cash from its credit customers. The higher the value of the turnover, the more effective the company is in its collections. There is no rule of thumb here, as the ratio target will vary from industry to industry and from firm to firm. The accounts receivable ratio can be converted into days in the accounts receivable collection period by dividing 365 by the turnover. |
| Inventory turnover | Cost of Goods Sold/Avg. Inventory[a] | Measures the company's effectiveness in turning the inventory on hand into sales (i.e., how many times the company sold the average amount of inventory during the period). Obviously, the higher the ratio, the better. A lower ratio suggests a higher investment in inventory, slower-moving items due to poor quality or obsolescence, and other factors. The inventory ratio can be converted into days in the selling period (average age of inventory) by dividing 365 by the inventory turnover. |
| Accounts payable turnover | Cost of Goods Sold/Avg. Inventory[a] | Measures the company's effectiveness in paying its payables during the period. The higher the ratio, the better. Normally, a company receives discounts for early payment, so controls should be established to ensure that these discounts are taken. This ratio assumes that all or most of the payables are for purchase of inventory, and that little of the purchases is paid for with cash. The accounts payable ratio can be converted to days in the payment period by dividing 365 by the turnover. |

[a]Average means the beginning balance is added to the ending balance and divided by 2.

## EXHIBIT 13.4b  Liquidity Ratio Analysis

| Title of Ratio | Formula | Application of Ratio |
|---|---|---|
| Current ratio | Total Current Assets/Total Current Liabilities | Measures the company's ability to pay its short-term obligations. It indicates a margin of safety available to creditors. A higher ratio suggests that the company has sufficient liquidity to pay its current obligations on time when they are due and to take advantage of relevant discounts for early payment. The traditional rule of thumb for this ratio is 2/1, but it can vary from company to company. A company that has had trouble paying its short-term debts in the past will be held to a higher ratio. |

*(Continued)*

**EXHIBIT 13.4b** *(continued)* Liquidity Ratio Analysis

| Title of Ratio | Formula | Application of Ratio |
|---|---|---|
| Quick (acid test) ratio | Cash + ST Investments + AR/Total Current Liabilities | This is a more rigorous test of the company's liquidity available to pay short-term obligations than the current ratio. It excludes current assets that are not readily convertible to cash, such as prepaid items and inventory. It is often used in combination with the current ratio to evaluate liquidity. |
| Working capital | Current Assets – Current Liabilities | Similar to the current ratio, it measures the safety cushion available to creditors in raw dollars. |

**EXHIBIT 13.4c** Solvency Ratio Analysis

| Title of Ratio | Formula | Application of Ratio |
|---|---|---|
| Debt-to-equity ratio | Total Liabilities/ Total Shareholders' Equity | Suggests the proportionate claims of owners and outside debtors against the company's assets. Also measures a company's risk as an investment by measuring the extent it relies on debt rather than stockholder financing. Further, it measures the extent to which leverage is used to increase return on investment. The purpose and importance of this measure depends on the user: For creditors, it measures the cushion available for the company to pay its obligations and the cushion available in the event the firm goes into liquidation. For owners and prospective investors, it measures the extent to which the company uses outsiders' funds in order to increase their earnings per share through leverage. |
| Times interest earned (interest coverage ratio) | Income from Operations[a]/ Interest Expense | Suggests the number of times the interest obligation of the company is covered by the profits available to pay interest charges. As such, it is an indicator of the financial strength of the business. It also suggests how much of a decline in income a company can absorb before it has trouble paying its interest due. |
| Fixed assets to long-term liabilities ratio | Fixed Assets/ Long-Term Liabilities | Suggests the extent to which fixed assets are financed by long-term creditors. The lower the ratio, the higher the claim on fixed assets by long-term creditors. |

[a]Income from Operations = Income before Interest and Taxes. Thus, if net income is used, interest and taxes must be added back.

## EXHIBIT 13.4d  Profitability Ratio Analysis

| Title of Ratio | Formula | Application of Ratio |
|---|---|---|
| Gross margin ratio | Gross Margin[a]/ Net Sales | Measures the ratio of gross profitability to cover operating expenses, interest, taxes, and dividends after deducting cost of goods sold from net sales. Note that net sales means sales returns, and allowances are deducted from gross sales. It suggests the effectiveness of sales pricing policies and a manufacturing company's efficiency in producing products. Obviously, the higher the gross profit ratio, the better. |
| Return on common stockholders' equity | NI – Preferred Dividends/Avg. Common Stock-holders' Equity | Measures the amount of net income that was earned with the common stockholders' investment. Also, suggests how much income may be available for the payment of dividends. It is one of the best indicators of the overall efficiency of the firm to meet its profitability goals. It is useful for stockholders, prospective investors, and senior management of the company. |
| Return on assets (ROA) | Net Income + Inter-est/Avg. Total Assets[b] | This is considered by many to be the best measure of the overall profitability of the company. It is an indicator of how well management has used the investment in assets made by stockholders and creditors into the business. The higher the ROA, the more efficiently the company is employing contributed capital. |
| Earnings per share (EPS) | NI – Preferred Dividends/Wtg. Avg. No. Shares O/S[c] | Measures how much earnings per share for each share of common stock. EPS is a broad indicator of the operating performance of a company. |

[a]Gross Profit = Net Sales – Cost of Goods Sold.
[b]Average Total Assets = Beginning Assets + Ending Assets divided by 2. The assets are best measured at their replacement cost. If not, assets should be measured at gross value (i.e., accumulated depreciation is not deducted).
[c]Weighted average number of shares outstanding during year = Each stock issuance or redemption during year is assigned a weight using the number of shares involved. For example, if 1,000 shares of stock were issued twice during year and 2,000 were issued three times, the weighted average would be $(1,000 \times 2) + (2,000 \times 3)$ divided by 5 = 1,600 weighted average of shares issued.

In summary, ratio analysis can be very useful in evaluating the effectiveness and efficiency of a business. However, the ratio by itself is not very useful. Depending on the nature of the ratio, it should be compared to previous years, other items with the financial statements, or other companies within an industry. How does one establish a benchmark ratio for comparison outside of the business? Usually various ratio targets are well known within an industry through industry trade associations and other sources Often there is

## EXHIBIT 13.4e  Market-Based Ratio Analysis

| Title of Ratio | Formula | Application of Ratio |
|---|---|---|
| Price/earnings ratio | Common Market Price per Share/ Earnings per Share | Measures appreciation in value of a common stock in relation to its earnings; widely used as an indicator of whether to invest in common stock of company. |
| Dividend yield ratio | Dividends per Share/Current Market Price per Share | Measures the current payment of dividends on common stock in relation to its current market price per share. This is of primary concern to those investors who are very interested in dividend payout. A related measure is the ratio of dividends per share of common stock to its earning per share. |

## EXHIBIT 13.5a  NIKE, Inc. Balance Sheet May 31, 2006 and 2007

| | (in millions) | |
|---|---|---|
| | 2007 | 2006 |
| **Assets** | | |
| Current Assets | | |
| Cash and Cash Equivalents | $1,856.7 | $954.2 |
| Short-Term Investments | 990.3 | 1,348.8 |
| Net Receivables | 2,494.7 | 2,382.9 |
| Inventories | 2,121.9 | 2,076.7 |
| Deferred Income Taxes | 219.7 | 203.3 |
| Prepaid Expenses and Other | 393.2 | 380.1 |
| Total Current Assets | $8,076.5 | $7,346.0 |
| Plant, Property, and Equipment | $3,619.1 | $3,408.3 |
| Less: Accumulated Depreciation | 1,940.8 | 1,750.6 |
| Plant, Property, and Equipment, Net | $1,678.3 | $1,657.7 |
| Goodwill | 130.8 | 130.8 |
| Intangibles, net | 409.9 | 405.5 |
| Deferred Income Taxes and Other Assets | 392.8 | 300.4 |
| Other Long-Term Assets | –0– | 29.2 |
| Total Long-Term Assets | $2,611.8 | $2,523.6 |
| Total Assets | $10,688.3 | $9,869.6 |

*(Continued)*

**EXHIBIT 13.5a**  *(continued)* NIKE, Inc. Balance Sheet May 31, 2006 and 2007

| | (in millions) | |
| --- | --- | --- |
| | 2007 | 2006 |
| **Liabilities** | | |
| Current Liabilities | | |
|     Current Portion of Long–Term Debt | $30.5 | $255.3 |
|     Accounts Payable | 1,040.3 | 952.2 |
|     Notes Payable | 100.8 | 43.4 |
|     Accrued Expenses | 1,120.0 | 1,033.4 |
|     Income Taxes Payable | 109.0 | 85.5 |
|     Other Current Liabilities | 183.4 | 242.6 |
| **Total Current Liabilities** | $2,584.0 | $2,612.4 |
| Long–Term Debt | $409.9 | 410.7 |
| Deferred Income Taxes and Other | 668.7 | 561.0 |
| **Total Long–Term Debt** | $1,078.6 | $971.7 |
| **Stockholders' Equity** | | |
|     Common Stock | $2.8 | $2.8 |
|     Additional Paid–in Capital | 1,960.0 | 1,447.3 |
|     Preferred Stock | 0.3 | 0.3 |
|     Retained Earnings | 4,885.2 | 4,713.4 |
|     Comprehensive Income & Other | 177.4 | 121.7 |
| **Stockholders' Equity** | $7,025.4 | $6,285.5 |
| **Total Liabilities and Stockholders' Equity** (512,000,000 weighted shares outstanding) | $10,688.0 | $9,869.6 |

information available on best-practice companies that can be used for comparison. Also, financial statements for companies within an industry are public information. By obtaining these statements a company can easily compute the needed ratios of other companies for comparison.

## Extended Illustration Using Ratio Analysis

Exhibits 13.5a and 13.5b depict financial statements of NIKE, Inc., which will be used in the ratio analysis example.

**EXHIBIT 13.5b** NIKE, Inc. Income Statement (in Millions of Dollars) for the Year Ending May 31, 2007

| | |
|---|---|
| Net Sales | $16,325.9 |
| Less: Cost of Goods Sold | 9,165.4 |
| Gross Profit | $7,160.5 |
| Less: Operating Expenses | 5,028.7 |
| Income from Operations | $2,131.8 |
| Add: Nonoperating Income | 67.2 |
| Income before Interest and Taxes | $2,199.0 |
| Less: Interest Expense | 28.0 |
| Income before Taxes | $2,171.0 |
| Add: Net Gains and Unusual Items | 28.9 |
| Income before taxes | $2,199.9 |
| Less: Income Taxes | 708.40 |
| Net Income | $1,491.5 |

**EXHIBIT 13.6a** Activity Ratio Analysis

| Title of Ratio | Formula | Application of Ratio |
|---|---|---|
| Accounts receivable turnover | Net Credit Sales/Avg. A/R | $\frac{16,325}{2,439} = 6.69$<br><br>Accounts receivable turned over 6.69 times per year, or 365/6.69 = 54 days to collect receivables. (Assuming that all sales were on credit.) |
| Inventory turnover | Cost of Goods Sold/ Avg. Inventory | $\frac{9,165}{2,100} = 4.36$<br><br>Inventory turned over 4.36 times per year, or 365/4.36 = 83.7 days (average age of inventory). |
| Accounts payable turnover | Cost of Goods Sold/ Avg. A/P | $\frac{9,165}{996} = 9.2$<br><br>A/P turnover was 9.2 times per year, or 365/9.2 = 36.7 days required to pay payables. These ratio may signal a problem with taking discounts with vendors. (One assumes that all inventory was purchased on credit through accounts payable.) |

Using the NIKE, Inc. financial statements in Exhibits 13.6a through 13.6e, ratio analysis is performed. To evaluate these ratios, one needs to compare them to industry averages or to NIKE's competitors.

| **EXHIBIT 13.6b** Liquidity Ratio Analysis | | |
|---|---|---|
| **Title of Ratio** | **Formula** | **Application of Ratio** |
| Current ratio | Total Current Assets/Total Current Liabilities | $\dfrac{8,077}{2,584} = 3.1$<br><br>The 2007 current ratio of 3.1 times seems to be very good by any comparison. Compare to the industry average. |
| Quick (acid test) ratio | Cash + ST Investments + A/R/Total Current Liabilities | $\dfrac{5,342}{2,584} = 2.1$<br><br>After factoring out inventories and prepaid items, the 2007 quick ratio is 2.4. This seems good. |
| Working capital | Current Assets – Current Liabilities | Nike has $8,077 – 2,584 = $5,493 in working capital at the end of 2007. |

| **EXHIBIT 13.6c** Solvency Ratio Analysis | | |
|---|---|---|
| **Title of Ratio** | **Formula** | **Application of Ratio** |
| Debt-to-equity ratio | Total Liabilities/ Total Shareholders' Equity | $\dfrac{2,584}{7,025} = .37$<br><br>The ratio suggests that NIKE does not have excessive debt, but must be compared to industry average. |
| Times interest earned (interest coverage ratio) | Income from Operation/Interest Expense | $\dfrac{2,199}{28} = 78.5$<br><br>NIKE's income before interest covers interest expense 78.5 times, which is good by any standard. |
| Fixed assets to long-term liabilities ratio | Fixed Assets/Long-Term Liabilities (Fixed assets equals plant, property, and equipment only.) | $\dfrac{2,201.9}{1,078.6} = 2.04$<br><br>NIKE has a 2.04 ratio, which means its fixed assets covered long-term debt over 200%. |

**EXHIBIT 13.6d**  Profitability Ratio Analysis

| Title of Ratio | Formula | Application of Ratio |
|---|---|---|
| Gross margin ratio | Gross Margin/Net Sales | $\frac{7,161}{16,326} = .439$<br><br>This ratio shows that, on average, for every dollar of product NIKE sells, approximately 56.1% (1.0 − 0.439) is the cost of the item. |
| Return on common stockholders' equity | NI−Preferred Dividends/Avg. Common Stock-holders' Eqty. | Since NIKE has only $0.3 million of preferred stock, this ratio is irrelevant, since it is so small. |
| Return on total assets (ROA) | Net Income + Interest/ Avg. Total Assets | $\frac{1,492 + 28}{10,279} = .148$<br><br>NIKE has a 14.8% return on its investment in total assets. This seems to be a good return, but it should be compared to the industry average. |
| Earnings per share (EPS) | NI−Preferred Dividends/Wtg. Avg. No. Shares O/S | $\frac{1,492 - 3}{512} = 2.91$ |

**EXHIBIT 13.6e**  Market-Based Ratio Analysis

| Title of Ratio | Formula | Application of Ratio |
|---|---|---|
| Price/earnings ratio | Common Market Price per Share/Earnings per Share | $\frac{64}{2.91} = 22$<br><br>P/E ratio of 22 times earnings. |
| Dividend yield ratio | Dividends per Share/ Current Market Price per Share | $\frac{0.80}{64.00} = .0125$<br><br>NIKE has a dividend yield of only 1.25%, which would be low for those investors interested in dividend payments. |

# QUIZ

1. In horizontal analysis a comparison is made by expressing each item as a percentage of the:
   A. Stockholders' equity amount
   B. Current assets amount
   C. Net income amount
   D. Base year

2. In vertical analysis, the base amount for cost of goods sold would be:
   A. Gross margin
   B. Cost of goods sold
   C. Net sales
   D. Gross assets

3. Which of the following is an indicator of a company's ability to pay its current liabilities?
   A. Current ratio
   B. Acid-test ratio
   C. Amount of working capital
   D. All of the above
   E. None of the above

4. (True or false?) Solvency ratios measure the ability of a business to pay its long-term obligations.

5. The XYZ Company reported the following for the period 2008 through 2010:

|  | 2010 | 2009 | 2008 |
|---|---|---|---|
| Current Assets | $150,000 | $100,000 | $80,000 |
| Current Liabilities | $300,000 | $180,000 | $200,000 |

   Assuming the base year is 2008 and using horizontal analysis, compute the appropriate index numbers.

|  | 2010 | 2009 | 2008 |
|---|---|---|---|
| Current Assets |  |  |  |
| Current Liabilities |  |  |  |

6. Using the data in question 5, what is the current ratio for 2009?
   A. 55
   B. 1.8
   C. $80,000
   D. ($80,000)

7. The XYZ Company reported the following data:

|  | 2010 | 2009 |
| --- | --- | --- |
| Average accounts receivable | $300,000 | $280,000 |
| Net credit sales | $1,800,000 | $1,500,000 |

   What is the accounts receivable turnover for 2010?
   A. .167 times
   B. 6 times
   C. 5 times
   D. None of the above

8. Using the information in question 7, what would be the collection period?
   A. 60.8 days
   B. 73 days
   C. 50 days
   D. None of the above

9. An overall measure of profitability of a company is:
   A. Dividend yield
   B. Gross margin
   C. Asset turnover
   D. Return on total assets

10. A ratio that measures whether the company has excessive debt is:
   A. Times interest earned
   B. Return on equity
   C. Debt to equity
   D. Return on investment

11. A company has $500,000 in net income, $5,000 in preferred dividends, $6,000 in common dividends, 100,000 shares of stock outstanding (weighted), and a market price of stock $40. What are the earnings per share?
   A. $4.95
   B. $5.00
   C. $4.89
   D. None of the above

12. **Using the data in question 11, what is the price/earnings ratio?**
    A. 9.0
    B. 8.1
    C. 8.2
    D. None of the above

13. **A ratio that measures the company's ability to pay interest on its long-term obligations is:**
    A. Debt-to-equity ratio
    B. Acid-test ratio
    C. Dividend yield ratio
    D. Times interest earned ratio

14. **Vertical analysis is also called:**
    A. Ratio analysis
    B. Trend analysis
    C. Common-sized analysis
    D. Horizontal analysis

15. **An investor interested in stock price growth and dividends would probably look at which of the following:**
    A. Price/earnings ratio
    B. Dividend yield ratio
    C. Total earnings
    D. All of the above

# Final Exam

Chapter 1

1. **The two major components of stockholders' equity in the balance sheet are:**
   A. Assets and liabilities
   B. Revenues and expenses
   C. Income and common stock
   D. Contributed capital and retained earnings

2. **Which of the underlying concepts would support the immediate recognition of a loss?**
   A. Verifiability
   B. Consistency
   C. Understandability
   D. Conservatism

3. **Which statement would a decision maker review to answer the question, "How did my business perform this year?"**
   A. The balance sheet
   B. The Statement of Changes in Financial Position
   C. The income statement
   D. The funds flow statement
   E. None of the above

4. **Which of the following statements is most correct?**

    A. The principal role of the management accountant is to prepare the tax returns for submission to the IRS.

    B. The principal meaning of the concept of relevance in preparing the financial statements is as guidance in matching revenues with expenses.

    C. The Financial Accounting Standards Board is the group responsible for promulgating accounting standards for the preparation of financial statements.

    D. The income statement matches assets with liabilities.

5. **The two primary qualities that make accounting information useful are:**

    A. Verifiability and benefit achieved

    B. Cost effectiveness and feedback value

    C. Predictive value and the matching concept

    D. Relevance and reliability

6. **The Certified Management Accountant is "certified" by:**

    A. The Institute of Management Accountants

    B. The American Institute of Certified Public Accountants

    C. The Institute of Internal Auditors

    D. The Financial Executives Institute

7. **(True or false?) An interested party who needs information on investing activities would most likely consult the statement of changes in stockholders'equity.**

8. **(True or false?) The concept of neutrality means that accounting information is free from bias that is intended to attain a predetermined result or induce a particular mode of behavior.**

## Chapter 2

9. **An accountant receives a $5,000 retainer from a client to provide advice on financial matters. Assuming the client uses accrual accounting, which of the following is true?**

    A. The accountant should recognize the $5,000 when the cash is received.

    B. The accountant should not recognize the revenue until he provides the service.

    C. The accountant should recognize $1,000 when received and recognize $1,000 in each of the next four years.

    D. None of the above is true.

10. **(True or false?) The time period assumption means that business must report to users of financial statements periodically, usually at the end of a quarter or year.**

11. **The owner of a local furniture store tells the bookkeeper to write a check from the business's checking account for the repair of her home air conditioner. Which accounting assumption is she violating?**

    A. Period

    B. Monetary unit

    C. Going concern

    D. Accounting entity

12. **Which of the following statements is true concerning an accounting accrual?**

    A. Adjusting entries are usually made at the end of the period to record accruals.

    B. An accrual occurs when the revenue is earned and cash has not been received.

    C. An accrual occurs when the expense is incurred and cash has not been paid.

    D. All of the above are true.

    E. None of the above is true.

13. **A construction company has a long-term contract that lasts for several years to build a bridge. According to the accrual method of accounting, the company accountant should:**

    A. Accrue the amount of revenue earned on the contract at the end of each accounting period based on the percentage of completion of the contract.

    B. Compute the amount of total revenue earned on the contract when the bridge is completed.

    C. Compute the amount of revenue when cash payments are received.

    D. None of the above.

14. (True or false?) Similar to the dual entry concept, double-entry book-keeping systems require at least two entries to be made in the accounts.

15. Using the accounting equation, enter the missing amount in the following:

|   | ASSETS | LIABILITIES | STOCKHOLDERS' EQUITY |
|---|--------|-------------|----------------------|
| a. | $20,000 | $6,000 | _____ |
| b. | $80,000 | _____ | $70,000 |
| c. | _____ | $10,000 | $12,000 |

16. The matching principle is best described as:

A. Expenses are recognized in the same period as the related revenue based on the assumption that there is a cause-and-effect relationship.

B. Expenses are recognized when the related cash is received.

C. Revenue is recognized when related expense is incurred.

D. Revenue is recognized to balance the accounting equation.

## Chapter 3

17. A retail merchandising company will likely have which inventory accounts on the balance sheet?

A. Raw Materials

B. Merchandising Inventory

C. Work in Process

D. Merchandising Inventory and Work in Process

18. (True or false?) Sales less cost of goods sold is called "gross margin."

19. (More than one of the following answers may be correct.) The balance sheet account representing investments by owners in the company is:

A. Common Stock

B. Preferred Stock

C. Retained Earnings

D. Notes Payable

20. **The income statement reports revenues less expense:**

    A. For the end of the period
    B. For some time in the future
    C. For a specified period of time
    D. At the beginning of the fiscal year

21. **Which of the following is most true concerning a current asset?**

    A. The inventory was purchased during the current year.
    B. The value of the accounts is stated at Current Market Value.
    C. The cash on hand can only be used for current needs.
    D. The asset balance will be converted to cash during the coming year or the company's operating cycle.

22. **Which of the following is not a current liability?**

    A. Accounts payable
    B. Accrued interest payable
    C. Accrued taxes payable
    D. Bonds payable

23. **Classify the following accounts in the space provided with the following symbols: CL for current liabilities, LTL for long-term liabilities, and SE for stockholders' equity:**

    A. _____ Capital stock
    B. _____ Treasury stock
    C. _____ Mortgage payable
    D. _____ Accounts payable
    E. _____ Retained earnings
    F. _____ Wages payable

24. **In a manufacturing company, which of the following inventory accounts would be found on the balance sheet?**

    A. Work in Process
    B. Raw Materials
    C. Finished Goods
    D. All of the above
    E. None of the above

Chapter 4

25. **A sale of bonds and receiving cash would require a journal entry of:**

   A. A debit to Bonds Payable and a credit to Cash
   B. A debit to Cash and a credit to Bonds Payable
   C. A debit to cash and a credit to Bond Interest Payable
   D. None of the above

26. **Expenses paid in cash and recorded as a current asset before they are used are called:**

   A. Prepaid expenses
   B. Deferred expenses
   C. Unearned expenses
   D. None of the above

27. **The normal balance for an asset account is a:**

   A. Credit balance
   B. Debit balance
   C. Debit or credit balance
   D. None of the above

28. **The accumulated depreciation account is called a(n):**

   A. Asset account
   B. Expense account
   C. Asset-offset account
   D. Liability account

29. **Which of the following statements is false?**

   A. A dividend account is a permanent account.
   B. To post means to enter a transaction from the journal into an account.
   C. Each expense account is debited to increase its balance.
   D. Preferred stock is a stockholders' equity account.

30. **Which of the following statements is true?**

   A. Bonds Payable would be listed first in the liability section of the chart of accounts.
   B. A contra-asset account would be credited to decrease the balance.
   C. *Journalize* means to enter a transaction in the general ledger.
   D. An accounting cycle is normally one year.

31. For each account below, check in the appropriate column whether it has a normal debit or credit balance:

|  | Debit | Credit |
|---|---|---|
| A. Accumulated Depreciation | | |
| B. Prepaid Insurance | | |
| C. Dividends | | |
| D. Retained Earnings | | |
| E. Notes Payable | | |
| F. Office Equipment | | |

32. A company paid its electricity expense. Which accounts would be debited, and which would be credited?

A. Debit Electricity Expense, and credit Retained Earnings.

B. Debit Electricity Expense, and credit Cash.

C. Debit Occupancy Expense, and credit Accounts Payable.

D. None of the above

Chapter 5

33. Assume the 12/31 trial balance for machinery was $10,000. The machinery was acquired on January 1 of the same year, had a useful life of 10 years, and had an expected life salvage value of $1,000 at the end of its life. Assuming that the machinery will be depreciated evenly over its useful life, which of the following is the correct adjusting entry?

| A. 12/31 | Depreciation Expense | 900 | |
| | Accumulated Depreciation | | 900 |
| B. 12/31 | Accumulated Depreciation | 900 | |
| | Depreciation Expense | | 900 |
| C. 12/31 | Depreciation Expense | 1,000 | |
| | Accumulated Depreciation | | 1,000 |

D. None of the above

34. If expenses exceed revenues for the full accounting period, the income summary account:

A. Will have a debit balance before it is closed to Retained Earnings

B. Will have a credit balance before it is closed to Retained Earnings

C. Will have a debit balance after closing to Retained Earnings

D. None of the above

35. The reason that both expenses and dividends have a normal debit balance is that:

    A. They both are shown as assets on the balance sheet.
    B. Both expenses and dividend accounts have offsetting current liability balances in the liability section of the general ledger.
    C. Both expenses and dividends are offset against revenue in the income statement.
    D. Both expenses and dividends reduce stockholders' equity.

36. If the accountant fails to make a required adjusting entry for depreciation expense, the:

    A. Assets will be overstated and income will be overstated.
    B. Assets will be overstated and income understated.
    C. Assets will not be affected by income will be overstated.
    D. None of the above

37. Which of the following is not a step in the accounting cycle?

    A. Analyze each transaction.
    B. Make adjusting entries.
    C. Prepare a pre-adjusted trial balance.
    D. Provide interpretation of the financial statements to the company's management.

38. A rental company had a valid rental contract with a renter; however, it had not received $1,000 rent at the end of the period. What would the accountant do?

    A. Initiate legal proceedings against the renter.
    B. Debit Rent Receivable for $1,000, and credit Rental Income for the same amount.
    C. Debit Rental Income for $1,000, and credit Rent Receivable for the same amount.
    D. None of the above

39. Employees of a company were paid on December 20, and there were seven more workdays left in the month. The accountant computed the amount owing the employees for this period as being $22,000. What adjusting entry would be made on December 31?

    A. No entry is required, as the employees will be paid at the end of the first week in January.

B. Debit Wages Expense $22,000, and credit Income Summary for the same amount.

C. Debit Wages Expense $22,000, and credit Wages Payable for the same amount.

D. None of the above

40. The last step in the accounting process is:

A. Making closing entries.

B. Making adjusting entries.

C. Journalizing the closing entries.

D. Preparation of the post-closing trial balance.

41. On January 1 the company paid for two years of insurance in advance for $2,000. Assuming that proper entries were made at that time, what is the adjusting entry at the end of the year?

A. Debit Prepaid Insurance for $1,000, and credit Income Summary for the same amount.

B. Debit Insurance Expense for $1,000, and credit Prepaid Insurance for the same amount.

C. Debit Insurance Expense for $2,000, and credit Income Summary for the same amount.

D. None of the above

## Chapter 6

42. In preparing the balance sheet at the end of the period, which of the following would not be included in the Cash and Cash Equivalents balance?

A. Traveler's checks from customers

B. Money orders

C. The petty cash balance

D. Compensating cash balances with the bank

43. In preparing the bank reconciliation, how should interest earned on the cash in the company's bank account, per the bank statement, be handled?

A. Added to the book cash balance

B. Deducted from the bank balance

C. Deducted from the book balance

D. Added to both the bank and book balances

44. In the process of replenishing the petty cash fund, which of the following journal entries would most likely be made (more than one answer may be correct)?

A. A credit to Petty Cash Fund
B. A debit to Office Supplies Expense
C. A debit to the Cash account
D. A debit to Petty Cash Fund

45. Which of the following is a major step in managing cash?

A. Establishing cash internal controls
B. Preparing a cash budget
C. Establishing procedures to maximize cash flow
D. All of the above

46. Suppose a company owned the following trading securities at the end of the accounting period:

| Stock | Cost | Fair (Market) Value |
|---|---|---|
| Home Depot | $100,000 | $90,000 |
| Coca-Cola | $200,000 | $180,000 |
| Total | $300,000 | $270,000 |

What journal entry would be required at the end of the period?
A. A debit to Trading Securities for $30,000 and a credit to Unrealized Loss on Trading Securities for $30,000.
B. A debit to Comprehensive Income for $30,000 and a credit to Trading Securities for $30,000.
C. A debit to Loss on Trading Securities for $30,000 and a credit to Trading Securities.
D. None of the above

47. Which of the following is a not correct statement?

A. Held-to-maturity securities are valued at amortized cost plus accrued interest.
B. Trading securities are valued at fair value.
C. Available-for-sale securities are valued at fair value.
D. The equity method is required for a company holding greater than 50 percent of the common stock in another company.

48. XYZ Company purchased $100,000 of 10-year, 6 percent bonds at 105 with the intent of earning interest until the bonds matured. What would be the journal entry at the time of purchase?

    A. Debit Short-Term Investments for $105,000, and credit Cash for $105,000.
    B. Debit Investment in Bonds for $105,000, and credit Cash for $105,000.
    C. Debit Investment in Bonds for $100,000, debit Prepaid Interest for $5,000, and credit Cash for $105,000.
    D. None of the above

Chapter 7

49. LEB Industries uses the percentage-of-sales method for determining uncollectible accounts expense. During 2009, the company had $100,000 in total sales, 80 percent of which were on account. The balance in the Allowance for Uncollectible Accounts was $5,000. If the company assumes that 5 percent of credit sales will be uncollectible, the charge to Uncollectible Accounts Expense would be:

    A. Zero, since the Uncollectible Account already has $5,000
    B. $3,200
    C. $5,000
    D. $4,000

50. XYZ, Inc. uses the direct write-off method to handle uncollectible accounts. If the amount of uncollectible accounts is material, which accounting principle is XYZ violating?

    A. Realization
    B. Period
    C. Matching
    D. No principle is being violated

51. (True or false?) A company that has a warranty on the products it sells should charge the warrant expense at the time the product is returned for repair.

52. A company takes a 6 percent, 90-day promissory note for the sale of product worth $5,000 on December 1, 2xxx. At the end of the accounting period on December 31, what would be the interest income accrued?

    A. $25
    B. $75
    C. $300
    D. None of the above

53. Refer to question 52. What would be the total cash received at the end of 90 days?

   A. $5,050
   B. $5,075
   C. $5,025
   D. None of the above

54. Assume the following accounts receivable aging schedule and the estimated uncollectible percentages of accounts receivable.

| Age of Account | End of Accounting Period Balance of Accounts Receivable | Estimated Uncollectible Percentage | Amount Needed in Allowance Account at End of Period |
|---|---|---|---|
| 1–30 Days | $40,000 | 2 | $800 |
| 31–60 Days | 30,000 | 6 | 1,800 |
| 61–90 Days | 8,000 | 10 | 800 |
| Over 90 Days | 2,000 | 15 | 300 |
|  | $80,000 |  | $3,700 |

Further assume that the Allowance for Doubtful Accounts has a credit balance of $3,000 at June 30, the end of the accounting period. Using the accounts receivable aging method, what would be the journal entry at June 30?

   A. Debit Uncollectible Accounts Expense for $3,700, and credit Allowance for Doubtful Accounts for $3,700.
   B. Debit Uncollectible Accounts Expense for $700, and credit Allowance for Doubtful Accounts for $700.
   C. Debit Uncollectible Accounts Expense $6,700, and credit Accounts Receivable for $6,700.
   D. None of the above

## Chapter 8

*Problems 55 and 56 are based on the following data:*

| Item | Inventory Units | Unit Cost | Unit Replacement Cost | Total Cost | Total Replacement Cost | Lower-of-Cost-or-Market |
|---|---|---|---|---|---|---|
| A | 2,000 | $11.25 | $10.50 | $22,500 | $21,000 | $21,000 |
| B | 1,200 | $12.00 | $12.50 | 14,400 | 15,000 | 14,400 |
| C | 2,500 | $11.50 | $11.30 | 28,750 | 28,250 | 28,250 |
| Total |  |  |  | $65,650 | $64,250 | $63,650 |

55. Using the lower-of cost-or-market aggregate method, what would be the inventory adjustment?

    A. $600
    B. $0
    C. $2,000
    D. $1,400

56. Using the lower-of-cost-or-market item-by-item method, what would be the inventory adjustment?

    A. $600
    B. $0
    C. $2,000
    D. $2,400

*Use the following data for problems 57 through 59:*

| Date | No.of Units purchased | Unit Cost | Total Cost |
|---|---|---|---|
| January 1 (Beg. Inv.) | 2,000 | $9.00 | $18,000 |
| January 11 | 3,000 | $10.00 | 30,000 |
| February 15 | 2,000 | $11.50 | 23,000 |
| March 12 | 3,000 | $12.00 | 36,000 |
| Total purchases | 8,000 | | 99,000 |
| Total goods available for sale | 10,000 | | $117,000 |

SALES: Assume that that 2,500 units were sold on January 20, 1,500 units were sold on February 16, and 3,000 units were sold on March 15. Total sales = 7,000 units.

57. Using the FIFO periodic method, what is the value of the inventory at the end of the period?

    A. $36,000
    B. $28,000
    C. $35,100
    D. None of the above

58. Using the FIFO method, what is the cost of goods sold for the entire period?

    A. $89,000
    B. $81,000
    C. $81,900
    D. None of the above

59. Using the LIFO perpetual inventory system, what is the ending inventory on January 21?

    A. $36,000
    B. $24,000
    C. $23,000
    D. None of the above

60. Using the lower-of-cost-or-market rule, the lower limit (floor) price for inventory valuation is the selling price less:

    A. The replacement cost
    B. A normal profit margin
    C. Estimated costs of completion and disposal
    D. None of the above

## Chapter 9

61. A machine used in production was acquired for $100,000, plus $5,000 to set up the machine to get it operational and $3,000 to train personnel to operate it. The asset has a useful life of 10 years and a salvage value of $10,000. Using straight-line depreciation, what is the depreciation charge in the second year of use?

    A. $9,500
    B. $9,800
    C. $9,000
    D. $10,500

62. Refer to the facts in question number 61. Assume that the machine will produce 300,000 units of output over its useful life. Assume further that the machine produced 28,000 units during the first year of use. What would be the depreciation expense during that first year?

    A. $9,800
    B. $8,867
    C. $8,400
    D. None of the above

63. Refer to the facts in question 61. Assume that the company uses the sum-of-the-years' digits depreciation method. What would be the second year's depreciation expense?

    A. $17,273
    B. $16,364

C. $15,545

D. None of the above

64. XYZ Company purchased a computer system and paid the following costs:

| | |
|---|---:|
| Purchase price | $30,000 |
| Sales tax | 2,100 |
| Installation | 3,000 |
| Training of personnel | 10,000 |
| Total costs | $45,000 |

What should be recorded as the cost of the computer system?

A. $45,100

B. $35,100

C. $32,100

D. None of the above

65. XYZ Company incurred $300,000 in research and development costs to develop a patent on a new product. XYZ was immediately sued for patent infringement. One month later the case was settled in XYZ's favor, but the company spent $50,000 in legal costs to defend the patent. The Patent account would contain which of the following amounts after the successful defense?

A. $350,000

B. $300,000

C. $250,000

D. $50,000

66. XYZ Company traded in (exchanged) an old lathe for a new one. The old lathe cost $30,000 and had accumulated depreciation of $25,000. The old machine had a fair value of $10,000, because of its excellent condition. XYZ paid $20,000 in cash—plus the trade-in of the old machine—for the new machine. What should be the cost recorded in the accounting records for the new machine?

A. $30,000

B. $25,000

C. $35,000

D. None of the above

67. Capitalized land costs would include all of the following except:

    A. Local assessment for paving
    B. Legal costs in closing
    C. Any assumption of liens and mortgages
    D. All of the above

68. Which of the following is not a trait of plant, property, and equipment?

    A. They are to be used in the company operations.
    B. They are tangible in nature.
    C. They are assumed to be subject to depreciation.
    D. All of the above

Chapter 10

69. A debenture bond is a(n):

    A. Term bond
    B. Convertible bond
    C. Unsecured bond
    D. Callable bond

70. A bond will sell at a premium when the:

    A. Stated rate is higher than the effective (market) rate
    B. Effective (market) rate is higher than the stated rate
    C. Stated rate is higher than the nominal rate
    D. None of the above

71. A two-year, $5,000 note is signed in return for the purchase of a piece of equipment. The interest rate on the note is 5 percent, but the market rate of interest is 6 percent. How much interest will be paid to the holder of the note at the end of the first year?

    A. $300
    B. $250
    C. $50
    D. None of the above

72. The carrying value of a bond under the effective interest method is:

    A. Face value minus any interest paid
    B. Face value minus actual interest expense
    C. Face value
    D. Face value less any discount or plus any premium amortized

73. On January 1, 2010, the XYZ Company issued bonds maturing in 10 years with a face value of $100,000 and a stated rate of 10 percent. XYZ received $96,000 in cash proceeds from the sale. How much cash will the XYZ Company pay bondholders on the first semiannual payment?

    A. $4,800
    B. $4,900
    C. $5,000
    D. None of the above

74. Employers do not make deductions from employees' paychecks for:

    A. Social security taxes
    B. Federal income taxes
    C. Employees' union dues
    D. Federal unemployment taxes

75. A liability is current if it is due within one year or the company's operating cycle, whichever is:

    A. Longer
    B. Shorter
    C. Comes due first
    D. Probable

76. Assume that on January 1, 2010 a company issues $20,000 of bonds due in five years with a stated rate of interest of 7 percent when the market (effective) rate of interest is 6 percent. Also assume that that interest is payable semiannually. If the present value interest factor of a lump sum ($n = 10$, $i = 6$ percent) is 0.744 and the present value interest factor of an annuity ($n = 10$, $i = 6$ percent) is 8.530, what are the total proceeds from the sale of the bonds?

    A. $20,000
    B. $20,851
    C. $19,149
    D. None of the above

## Chapter 11

77. (True or false?) A feature of common stock is the right to participate in the management of the corporation.

78. Which of the following is not a major advantage of a corporation?

    A. Subject to governmental regulations
    B. Indefinite life
    C. Ownership is easily transferred
    D. Separate legal existence from the stockholder

79. A company that held 10,000 shares of treasury stock that cost $12 per share reissued the shares for $15 each. Which of the following is incorrect?

    A. Debit Cash for $150,000.
    B. Credit to Treasury Stock for $120,000.
    C. Credit Common Stock for $150,000.
    D. Credit Additional Paid-in Capital for $30,000.

80. A company declared a three-for-two stock split. Which of the follow is correct?

    A. Common Stock would be credited for the number of shares issued times the market price at the date of payment.
    B. Retained Earnings is reduced by the number of shares issued times the par value.
    C. No journal entry would be made in the books.
    D. None of the above

81. A company issued 20,000 shares of preferred stock with a par value of $100 for $105. Which of the following entries would not be made?

    A. Credit Preferred Stock for $2,000,000.
    B. Credit Additional Paid-in Capital—Preferred Stock for $100,000.
    C. Debit Cash for $2,100,000.
    D. Credit Preferred Stock for $2,100,000.

82. (True or false?) Subscribed stock means that a stock has been sold with a down payment, is unissued, and the remainder is due to be paid later.

83. A company issued shares it owned in a subsidiary as a regular property dividend. Which of the following is not true?

    A. Retained Earnings would be decreased by the fair value of the asset.
    B. Property Dividends Payable would be credited at the declaration date.
    C. Retained Earnings would be decreased by the cost of the asset.
    D. The shares of the subsidiary company would be issued on the payment date.

84. **The two major components of shareholders' equity are:**

    A. Contributed capital and additional paid-in capital.
    B. Preferred stock and common stock.
    C. Contributed capital and retained earnings.
    D. Common stock and treasury stock.

Chapter 12

85. **In defining cash and cash equivalents, which of the following is not considered a cash equivalent?**

    A. A NIKE bond
    B. Treasury bills
    C. Money market fund
    D. Commercial paper

86. **(True or false?) Payment of dividends is classified as a financing activity.**

    *Use the following information for problems 87 to 89:*

    | | |
    |---|---:|
    | Purchase of insurance | $10,000 |
    | Cash proceeds from loan | 14,000 |
    | Cash paid on interest | 800 |
    | Cash collected from sales | 53,000 |
    | Bonds issued | 50,000 |
    | Salaries paid to employees | 9,200 |
    | Purchase of equipment | 40,000 |

87. **How much net cash came from operating activities?**

    A. $33,800
    B. $33,000
    C. $(7,000)
    D. $53,000

88. **How much net cash came from investing activities?**

    A. $64,000
    B. $50,000
    C. $(50,000)
    D. $(40,000)

89. **How much net cash came from financing activities?**

    A. $63,200
    B. $50,000
    C. $64,000
    D. $14,000

90. **(True or false?) The amount of net cash flow under operating activities will be the same under both the direct method and the indirect method.**

91. **Which of the following transactions would increase the net cash flow from operating activities?**

    A. The collection of a short-term notes payable from a customer
    B. The issuance of a bond at a premium
    C. The sale of equipment at a gain
    D. The purchase of a lathe for cash

92. **Which of the following would not be reported on the statement of cash flows?**

    A. Dividends paid in cash
    B. A two-for-one stock split
    C. A sale of bonds at a discount
    D. Increase in taxes payable

Chapter 13
93. **Which of the following is a solvency ratio?**

    A. Total liabilities to total stockholders' equity
    B. Price/earnings ratio
    C. Inventory turnover
    D. Accounts receivable turnover

94. **The most extreme measure of liquidity is:**

    A. Current ratio
    B. Accounts receivable turnover
    C. Working capital
    D. Acid-test ratio

95. The Berry Company reported the following data:

| | 2010 | 2009 |
|---|---|---|
| Average accounts receivable | $600,000 | $560,000 |
| Net credit sales | 3,600,000 | $3,000,000 |

What is the accounts receivable turnover for 2010?
A. .167 times
B. 6 times
C. 5 times
D. None of the above

96. Using the information in question 95, what would be the average collection period?
A. 60.8 days
B. 73 days
C. 50 days
D. None of the above

*The following information is used in questions 97–98.*

| Liabilities and Stockholders' Equity | |
|---|---|
| Current Liabilities | $200,000 |
| Long–Term Liabilities | 150,000 |
| Total Liabilities | $350,000 |
| Stockholders' Equity | 150,000 |
| Total Liabilities and Stockholders' Equity | $500,000 |
| **Income Statement (Partial)** | |
| Net Sales | $750,000 |
| Interest Expense | $8,000 |
| Net Income | $45,000 |

97. **What is Berry Company's debt/equity ratio?**

    A. 1.0
    B. 2.33
    C. 7.0
    D. None of the above

98. **What is Berry Company's times interest earned ratio?**

    A. 93.8
    B. 18.8
    C. 5.6
    D. 6.625

99. **In vertical analysis, the base amount for comparison on each income statement item is:**

    A. Net sales
    B. Sales
    C. Gross profit
    D. Net income

100. **A measure of the company's ability to pay its current liabilities is:**

    A. Current ratio
    B. Acid-test ratio
    C. Both of the above
    D. None of the above

# Answers to Quizzes and Final Exam

Chapter 1

1. False (A state authority in the state where the CPA will practice is responsible for such certification.)

2. False (The partners in the business entity are personally responsible for all debts and financial obligations of the partnership entity.)

3. True

4. True

5. False (The Financial Accounting Standards Board now sets generally accepted accounting principles; however, other accounting organizations may influence their setting.)

6. False (While it may be useful for a person to be certified as a CPA, there is no legal requirement for such certification in a business organization. However, some businesses (such as a large corporation) may make certification as a CPA or Certified Management Accountant a qualifying requirement for employment in some positions. Legally, certification as a CPA is only required for persons in private practice who attest to the accuracy of financial statements.)

7. A, C, D, and F

8. E

9. B

10. D

11. C

12. **B** (The Internal Revenue Service is guided by federal tax law, not by generally accepted accounting principles.)

13. **A**

14. **C**

15. **E**

## Chapter 2

1. True (The development of an accounting standard requires solicitation of input from all accounting stakeholders, extensive research, exposure of potential standards to all interested parties soliciting more input, and five FASB members voting for its approval. This process helps assure the general acceptance of the standard.)

2. False (While auditors in the performance of their responsibilities may use the Conceptual Framework, it is not the foundation for developing *auditing* standards. It is the foundation for developing *accounting* standards.)

3. True

4. False (Assets are recorded at cost and are not revalued as their price changes.)

5. True

6. **A**

7. **C**

8. **D**

9. **C**

10. **A**

11. **A** (I), **B** (D), **C** (NE—an asset account is increased and another asset is decreased), **D** (I)

12. **A** (A), **B** (A), **C** (L), **D** (SE), **E** (L), **F** (SE)

13. **A** ($4,000), **B** ($10,000), **C** ($20,000)

14. **B**

15. **C**

## Chapter 3

1. False (The balance sheet presents the ending balances of all assets, liabilities, and stockholders' equity at a stated point in time—that is, a snapshot of the financial condition of the company.)

2. True

3. False (Net book value refers to the carrying amount (cost) of an asset less accumulated depreciation.)

4. True

5. False (The diluted EPS is reported at the end of the income statement.)

6. A. BS, B. IS, C. IS, D. BS, E. N, F. IS, G. BS, H. BS

7. B

8. D

9. A

10. D

11. C

12. C

13. B

14. A

15. D

## Chapter 4

1. True

2. False (The general journal or a specialized journal is the point of original entry into the accounting system.)

3. False (Unearned Fees, a liability account, would be credited, since the fees have not been earned.)

4. True

5. False (The Accumulated Depreciation account would have a credit balance, and it is an offset, or contra, account to an asset account.)

6. C

7. B

8. D

9. D

10. A

11. A

12. B

13. D

14. C

15. C

## Chapter 5

1. True
2. False (Dollar signs are never entered into journals or ledgers.)
3. False (The first step is to analyze the transaction.)
4. True
5. False (A deferred account would most likely require an adjustment.)
6. C
7. B
8. A
9. D
10. A $\left( \$10,000 \times \dfrac{4}{12} \times .06 = \$200 \right)$
11. C
12. B
13. B
14. D
15. A

## Chapter 6

1. D
2. C (The petty cash fund would be reimbursed for $980.)
3. C
4. B
5. False (The petty cash fund can have any amount up to a predefined maximum.)
6. D (No entry to books is made until after a reimbursement form is submitted by the custodian.)
7. A (Banking relations may be an important step, but it isn't a major one in managing cash.)
8. C
9. D
10. A
11. B
12. C
13. A
14. A ($100,000 \times 25\% = \$25,000$)
15. B

## Chapter 7

1. **C**
2. **A**
3. True
4. **B** $(80,000 \times .80 \times .04 = 2,560)$
5. False (Net realizable value = $80,000 - 2,560 = $77,440)
6. **B**
7. **D**
8. True
9. True
10. **A**
11. **D** $\left( 20,000 \times .06 \times \dfrac{30}{360} = 100 \right)$
12. **C**
13. **B** ($1,240 = 2,240 - $1,000)
14. True
15. **D**

## Chapter 8

1. **C** (The replacement cost cannot be lower than the floor value, so the $10.50 is compared to the cost of $9.50; thus, $9.50 is used.)
2. False (Title would change upon the customer's receipt of the goods.)
3. **A**
4. **B**
5. **D** (The older, lower costs would be charged to cost of goods sold. Thus, lower cost of goods sold results in higher net income.)
6. **A**
7. **D** (If gross profit percentage is 60 percent, then $100 - 60\% \times $100,000 = $40,000.)
8. **B** (If cost of goods available less ending inventory equals cost of goods sold, the ending inventory is: $60,000 - Ending Inventory = $40,000. Ending Inventory = $20,000.)
9. **C** ($54,150 - $53,750 = $400)
10. **A** ($54,150 - $53,150 = $1,000)
11. **D**
12. **B** (1,000 units @ $11 + 1,000 units @ $10 = $21,000)

13. **A** (9,000 units purchased less 7,000 units sold equals 2,000 units on hand. This results in the following computation.)

| Cost of Goods Available for Sale: | $102,000 |
| --- | --- |
| Less: Ending Inventory: 2,000 × $12 = | 24,000 |
| Cost of Goods Sold: | $78,000 |

14. **C** $\left( \dfrac{\$43,000}{4,000} = \$10.75;\ 2,000 \times \$10.75\ = \$21,500 \right)$

15. **D**

Chapter 9

1. **A** ($10,000,000 − 8,000,000 = $2,000,000)
2. **D**
3. **C**
4. **B** $\left( \left( \dfrac{\$20,000 + 1,000 - 1,000}{10} \right) = \$2,000 \right)$

5. **D** $\left( \left( \dfrac{\$20,000 + 1,000 - 1,000}{200,000} \right) = \$.10 \text{ per unit. } \$.10 \times 18,000\ = \$1,800 \right)$

6. **A** (10 + 9 + 8 + 7 + 6 + 5 + 4 + 3 + 2 + 1 = 55. Depreciable base = $20,000 + 1,000 − $1,000 = $20,000. $20,000 × $\dfrac{9}{55}$ = 3,273 rounded.)
7. **B**
8. **C**
9. True
10. **D**
11. **E**
12. **A** [$50,000 − (200,000 − 130,000) = $20,000]
13. **D**
14. False (R&D costs are expensed in the period in which they occur.)
15. True

Chapter 10

1. **C**
2. **B**
3. **A**
4. **D** ($800,000 $\times$ .10 $\times \dfrac{6}{12}$ = $40,000)
5. **D** [$3,000 + (3,000 $\times$ .062) + (3,000 $\times$ .0145)] = $3,229.50. The employer match for Social Security is 6.2 percent, and for Medicare, 1.45 percent.)
6. **A**
7. **A** ($200,000 $\times \dfrac{6}{12} \times$ .06 = $6,000 cash interest)

$$\text{Amortization of discount}: \quad \frac{\$200,000 \times .02}{(10 \times 2)} = \$200$$

$$[\$6,000 + \$200] = \$6,200 = \text{Interest expense}$$

8. **B** ($10,000 $\times$ .05 = $500. The interest payment is based on the stated rate.)
9. **C** ($5,000 $\times$ .06 = $300)
10. **D** ((Payment – Interest Paid) = ($1,871 – 300 = $1,571))
11. **A** [PV of bonds at maturity: $10,000 $\times$ 0.744) + (PV of interest payments: $10,000 $\times$ .07 $\times \dfrac{6}{12}$ = $350; $350 $\times$ 8.530) = ($7,440 + $2,986) = $10,426.]
12. **B** (Principal of Bond at Maturity – Proceeds of the Sale of the Bonds = $10,000 – 10,426 = $426.)
13. **A** (Carrying Value $\times$ Effective Rate of Interest = $10,426 $\times$ .06 $\times \dfrac{6}{12}$ = $313)
14. **C** $\left(\text{Interest paid – Interest Expense} = \left(\$10,000 \times .07 \times \dfrac{6}{12}\right) - \$313 = \$37\right)$
15. **B** (Previous Carrying Value – Premium Amortized = $10,426 – $37 = $10,389)

Chapter 11

1. **A**
2. **D**
3. **B** (Stock in a subsidiary would be an investment and shown as an asset.)
4. **C**
5. **C** (A small dividend results in the market price being used to debit Retained Earnings with offsetting credits to Common Stock and Paid-in Capital in Excess of Par.)

6. A

7. B

8. B

9. D (Common Stock Subscribed would be credited for $10,000. Common Stock would be credited, and Common Stock Subscribed would be debited later when the balance is paid and the stock is issued.)

10. C

11. A

12. A

13. D

14. True

15. D

## Chapter 12

1. A (I), B (O), C (F), D (F), E (O)

2. A

3. C

4. D

5. A: increase; B: decrease; C: increase; D: decrease; E: decrease

6. C

7. B

8. D ($10,000 – $50,000 = $40,000)

9. True

10. B ($200,000 + 20,000 – 10,000 = $210,000)

11. A ($20,000 + 30,000 + x = $25,000; x = –$25,000)

12. False

13. B

14. D

15. E

## Chapter 13

1. D

2. C

3. D

4. True

5. (see below)

|  | **2010** | **2009** | **2008** |
|---|---|---|---|
| Current Assets | 187.5 | 125 | 100 |
| Current Liabilities | 150 | 90 | 100 |

6. A $\left(\dfrac{80,000}{180,000} = .555\right)$

7. B $\left(\dfrac{1,800,000}{300,000} = 6\ Times\right)$

8. A $\left(\dfrac{365}{6} = 60.8\ Days\right)$

9. D

10. C

11. A $\left(\dfrac{\$200,000 - 5,000}{\$100,000} = \$4.95\right)$

12. B $\left(\dfrac{40}{4.95} = 8.1\right)$

13. D

14. C

15. D

Final Exam

1. D

2. D

3. C

4. C

5. D

6. A

7. False (The Statement of Cash Flows would be consulted.)

8. True

9. B

10. True

11. D (The owner's personal assets should be separate from that of the business.)

12. **D**

13. **A**

14. True

15. **A** ($14,000), **B** ($10,000), **C** ($22,000)

16. **A**

17. **B**

18. True

19. **A** and **B**

20. **C**

21. **D**

22. **D**

23. **A.** SE, **B.** SE, **C.** LTL, **D.** CL, **E.** SE, **F.** CL

24. **D**

25. **B**

26. **A**

27. **B**

28. **C**

29. **A**

30. **D**

31.

|  | Debit | Credit |
|---|---|---|
| a. Accumulated Depreciation |  | x |
| b. Prepaid Insurance | x |  |
| c. Dividends | x |  |
| d. Retained Earnings |  | x |
| e. Notes Payable |  | x |
| f. Office Equipment | x |  |

32. **B**

33. **A** $\left( \left( \dfrac{10,000 - 1,000}{10} \right) = \$900 \text{ for one year's depreciation} \right)$

34. **A**

35. **D**

36. **A**

37. **D**

38. B
39. C
40. D
41. B (($2,000/2 years) = $1,000)
42. D
43. A
44. B and D
45. D
46. C
47. D (The equity method is required when the company owns 20 percent but not greater than 50 percent of another company's stock.)
48. B
49. D ($100,000 × .8 × .05 = $4,000)
50. C
51. False (Based on the matching principle, the company should estimate the liability in the period in which the sale occurs and charge Warrant Expense for that amount.)
52. A ($5,000 × .06 × $\dfrac{30}{360}$ = $25)
53. B (The total interest due, plus the principal: $5,000 × .06 × $\dfrac{90}{360}$ = $75, plus $5,000 = $5,075)
54. B ($3,700 − $3,000 = $700)
55. D ($65,650 − $64,250 = $1,400)
56. C ($65,650 − $63,650 = $2,000)
57. A (3,000 × $12 = $36,000)
58. B

| | |
|---|---|
| Cost of goods available | $117,000 |
| Deduct: Ending inventory | 36,000 |
| Cost of goods sold | $81,000 |

59. C ((2,000 × $9) + (500 × $10) = $18,000 + 5,000 = $23,000.)
60. B
61. A $\left(\left(\dfrac{\$100,000 + 5,000 - 10,000}{10}\right) = \$9,500.\right.$ Training is charged to current period expense.$\Big)$

62. **B** $(28,000 \times \$.31667 = \$8,867)$

63. **C** $(10 + 9 + 8 + 7 + 6 + 5 + 4 + 3 + 2 + 1 = 55.$ Depreciable base = $\$100,000 + 5,000 - 10,000 = \$95,000.$ Depreciation expense $\$95,000 \times \dfrac{9}{55}$ = $\$15,545$ rounded.)

64. **B** (Training costs are expensed in the period in which incurred.)

65. **D** (R&D costs are charged as an expense during the period in which they are incurred.)

66. **A** (The new asset should be recorded as its fair value. However, in absence of that figure it must be assumed that the cash paid of $20,000 and the fair value of the old traded-in machine of $10,000 would equal the fair value of the new machine.)

67. **D**

68. **D**

69. **C**

70. **A**

71. **B**

72. **D**

73. **C** $\left(\$100,000 \times .10 \times \dfrac{6}{12} = \$5,000\right)$

74. **D** (The employer must pay unemployment taxes.)

75. **A**

76. **B** ((PV of Bonds at maturity: $20,000 \times 0.744$) + (PV of interest payments: $\$20,000 \times .07 \times \dfrac{6}{12} = \$700;$   $\$700 \times 8.530) = (\$14,880 + \$5,971) = \$20,851$)

77. False

78. **A**

79. **C**

80. **C**

81. **D**

82. True

83. **C**

84. **C** (Contributed capital and "earned capital" are the two major components of the SE Section.)

85. **A**

86. True
87. **B** ($53,000 − 9,200 − 800 − 10,000 = $33,000)
88. **D**
89. **C** ($14,000 + 50,000 = $64,000)
90. True
91. **A**
92. **B**
93. **A**
94. **D**
95. **B** $\left( \dfrac{3,600,000}{600,000} = 6 \ times \right)$
96. **A** $\left( \dfrac{365}{6} = 60.8 \ Days \right)$
97. **B** $\left( \dfrac{350,000}{150,000} = 2.33 \right)$
98. **D** $\left( \dfrac{45,000 + 8,000}{8,000} = 6.625 \ times \right)$
99. **A**
100. **C**

# *Glossary*

**Accounting adjustments** include the financial impact of changes in accounting principle, accounting methods, or estimates on the reported net income.

**Accounting cycle** is a series of steps that an accountant goes through from the point that a business transaction occurs until all the financial statements are prepared.

**Accounting entity assumption** is when an accounting entity sets the boundaries for which accounting records must be maintained and financial reporting must be completed. The accounting entity for record keeping is normally a business or economic entity (corporation, partnership, or sole proprietorship); nevertheless, governmental groups and nonprofit organizations can also be accounting entities.

**Accounting equation** is the foundation of the double-entry bookkeeping system. It is based on the fact that assets are acquired by using either borrowed money (liabilities) or contributed capital (stockholders' equity). Thus, the following algebraic equation holds: Assets = Liabilities + Stockholders' Equity.

**Accounts receivable aging method** estimates the amount of uncollectible accounts in an ending balance of accounts receivable by setting up an aging schedule and then making an estimate of how much of each age's balance will not be collectible.

**Accrual basis of accounting** means that revenues are recognized when they are *earned* using the realization assumption and expenses are recognized when they are *incurred* using the matching assumption.

**Accumulated depreciation** is an asset-offset account or contra-asset account that reflects the accumulated depreciation expense over the life of an asset. It is deducted from the historical cost of the asset on the balance sheet to get a net book value.

**Activity ratios** measure a company's efficiency in using its current assets and current liabilities.

**Adjusting entries** are made at the end of the accounting period in order to allocate revenue and expenses to the proper accounting period using the revenue realization and matching principles.

**Administrative expenses** are all general expenses to operate the company, such as executive salaries, office salaries, supplies, depreciation, bad debt expense, and insurance.

**Allowance method** is a process for determining the amount of uncollectible accounts for a period. An estimate is made of bad debts at the end of each accounting period in order to match the bad debt expense with the related sales.

**Amortization** is the process of prorating the value of an asset (usually an intangible) and charging it to Expenses over its useful or legal life.

**Articles of incorporation** for a corporation state such things as the purpose of the corporation and how it will be governed.

**Authorized shares of stock** are the maximum of shares of stock that can be issued as established in the corporation's charter.

**Available-for-sale security** is a debt or equity security that is not classified as either a held-to-maturity security or a trading security and is reported at fair value. It is held for an indefinite period of time with no intention of selling for profit.

**Balance sheet,** or statement of financial position, is a statement that describes the financial situation of a business enterprise at a specific point in time, such as the end of the year. It is divided into assets, liabilities, and stockholders' equity.

**Board of directors** is a body of elected or appointed individuals who oversee the governance of a corporation (or other organizations) as defined in the corporation's bylaws.

**Bond** is a formal interest-bearing contract known as a bond indenture that is issued by large organizations for the purpose of raising capital to carry out organizational strategies.

**Callable bonds** give the company the option of buying back bonds at a specified price before the bonds' maturity date.

**Callable preferred stock** means that the preferred-stock holders can be forced to sell their stock back to the company at the "call price" in the stock contract.

**Capital lease** is when the lessee assumes some of the risks of ownership and enjoys some of the benefits. Thus, the lease is capitalized as an asset (present value of the lease payments) on the balance sheet with an offsetting liability on the balance sheet.

**Cash** is the most liquid asset and is generally defined as those unrestricted items that are acceptable to a bank for deposit.

**Cash basis of accounting** means *revenues* are recognized and recorded when cash is *received*, and *expenses* are recognized and recorded when cash is *expended*.

**Cash equivalents** are generally defined as liquid assets that are readily convertible into cash and that will mature in a relatively short period of time not to exceed 90 days. Cash equivalents should have a low risk of lost of value. Examples would be money market funds, marketable securities, and commercial paper.

**Cash flow statement** shows the amount of all cash flows coming into the business enterprise and the amount of cash flows that have gone out of that business enterprise during a specific period of time (usually the fiscal year). The statement is divided into operating activities, investing activities, and financing activities.

**Certified Fraud Examiner** is a designation awarded by the Association of Certified Fraud Examiners. This specialty in accounting is concerned with the detection, investigation, and prevention of fraud. The individuals practicing in this field are identified as forensic accountants or fraud auditors. Many of these accountants are employed by federal agencies such as the Central Intelligence Agency, the Federal Bureau of Investigation, and the Drug Enforcement Agency.

**Certified Internal Auditor (CIA)** is a designation awarded to auditors who have met the educational requirements and passed a rigorous exam established by the Institute of Internal Auditors (IIA). CIAs are employed by businesses or governmental organizations and are responsible for assuring the integrity of the accounting system and for reviewing management and financial practices and making recommendations for improvements.

**Certified Management Accountant (CMA)** is a designation given to accountants who have met the educational requirements and the professional competence in management accounting established by the Institute of Management Accountants (IMA). The IMA issues a CMA certificate to those who qualify. Unlike the Certified Public Accountant (see below), the CMA is not certified by a state authority.

**Certified Public Accountant (CPA)** is a designation given to accountants who have met certain educational requirements, passed a rigorous qualifying examination, and possess qualifying public accounting experience requirements established by a state licensing authority (normally called a State Board of Accountancy). They are then licensed by a state authority to attest to the accuracy of organizational financial statements issued to external parties by a business or nonprofit entity.

**Common stock** is a form of equity ownership in a corporation and defines the holder's voting rights in the corporation and entitles the holder to a share of the company's profits through dividends or capital appreciation of the stock.

**Common stockholders** are owners of a corporation with specified rights and responsible for electing a board of directors and voting on corporate policy. In the event of liquidation, common shareholders have rights to a company's assets only after bondholders, preferred shareholders, and other debt holders have been paid in full.

**Comparability** is an underlying concept or assumption that involves the quality of accounting information that enables users to identify similarities and differences between two sets of economic data. This requires accountants to measure and report accounting information in a similar manner among different business entities.

**Conservatism** is an underlying concept or assumption that states that when faced with two alternative measurements of valuation—both of which have reasonable support—the one that understates rather than overstates the business entity's net income or financial position must be selected.

**Consigned goods** are items that are possessed by one party (agent) but owned by another.

**Consistency** is an underlying concept or assumption that holds that the same accounting policies and procedures must be used from period to period so that proper evaluation can be made of the business entity's progress over time. Business entities are allowed to change accounting methods, if they can show that the newly adopted accounting method is "preferable" to the old one.

**Contributed capital** is stock purchased by stockholders at par or stated value, plus capital in excess of par, donated stock, and the resale of treasury stock.

**Convertible bonds** are bonds that can be exchanged by the holder for a specified number of shares of corporate stock.

**Convertible preferred stock** means that the preferred-stock holders can convert preferred shares to common stock at a ratio stipulated in the stock contract.

**Copyright** is a federally granted legal protection to authors, musicians, painters, sculptors, and other creations and expressions.

**Corporation** is a business entity that is financially and legally separated from its owners and is chartered by an individual state. Its owners are not legally liable for the corporation's debts and liabilities. A corporation can be a profit or nonprofit enterprise. Ownership in a profit enterprise is divided into units called *common stock*.

**Cost of Goods Sold** represents, for a merchandising (retailing) company, the amount of inventory sold to customers during a period. For a manufacturing company, it represents the cost of goods manufactured that have been sold during the period. The latter would include cost of raw materials, labor, and overhead consumed in the manufacturing process to manufacture the finish product.

**Coupon (bearer) bonds** have detachable coupons and are cashed in on a specific dates. They are easily transferred on the open market.

**Cumulative preferred stock** means that when the company does not pay the preferred-stock holders an annual dividend, those dividends are then cumulated and must be paid before any dividends are paid to common-stock holders.

**Current assets** are those assets that are expected to be sold or used up within the next year or an operating cycle.

**Current liabilities** are debts and obligations of the business that are to be settled by expending cash or another current asset within the next year or operating cycle, whichever period is longer.

**Debenture bond** is an unsecured bond.

**Depreciation** is the spreading of the cost of a fixed asset against income over its useful life due to wear and tear from use and passage of time.

**Direct method** for preparing the statement of cash flows (also called the income statement method) reports cash receipts (inflows) and cash disbursements (outflows) from operating activities in detail.

**Direct write-off method** for accounting for uncollectible accounts is when the account is written off in the period in which it is determined that it is uncollectible.

**Discontinued operation** refers to gains or losses resulting from the selling, abandoning, or otherwise disposing of part of a company's operations.

**Discounting** means to compute the present value of future cash flows.

**Double declining balance method** is an accelerated depreciation method based on the declining book value of the asset.

**Dual entity concept** posits that an accounting transaction affects (i.e., increases or decreases) at least two accounts. It is the basis for the double-entry book-keeping system.

**Earnings per share** is a metric computed by dividing the net income by the number of common stock shares outstanding.

**Equity method** of accounting for investments means that the investor records the initial investment at cost and the investor reports its proportional share of the investee's income on its income statement each period.

**Extraordinary item** refers to a gain or loss from an event that is unusual in nature and infrequent in occurrence.

**Financial Accounting Standards Board (FASB)** is an independent body made up of businesspeople, practicing accountants, and accounting academicians. It sets accounting standards that are commonly known as **generally accepted accounting principles (GAAP)** that govern the preparation of financial statements issued outside the business entity.

**First-in, first out (FIFO)** method assumes that the first items purchased in an inventory are the first items sold.

**FOB** means "free on board."

**FOB destination** means that the title passes when the purchaser receives the goods, and the seller is responsible for the cost of freight.

**FOB shipping point** means that title passes at the point of shipment, and the purchaser is responsible for the cost of the freight.

**Full disclosure principle** states that a fundamental purpose of financial reporting is to provide information necessary for users of the financial statements to make informed decisions. Thus, if there is information other than that provided on the financial statements themselves, then this information should be reported.

**Future value of an annuity** computes the future value of a series of payments or receipts made at specific time periods at a given interest rate.

**General journal** is often referred to as the book of original entry into the accounting system. That is, it is the point at which all business transactions are entered into the accounting records. The term "general" is used because it is not a specialized journal, such as a sales journal. All transactions that are not entered into special journals are entered into the general journal.

**General ledger** is a collection of accounts that form the major accounting records of a business that uses the double-entry accounting system.

**Generally accepted accounting principles (GAAP)** govern the preparation of financial statements issued outside the business entity. GAAP is a set of standards, principles, conventions, rules, guidelines, and procedures that have evolved over time by various professional bodies; since 1972 they have been set by the FASB. GAAP evolve and change as business conditions change.

**Going concern assumption** means that unless there is information to the contrary, it is assumed that a business entity will operate indefinitely.

**Goodwill** is the excess of cost over the market value of net assets of a purchased company.

**Gross profit method** means that the company's historical gross profit percentage (gross profit as a percentage of sales) is used to estimate the amount of gross profit and cost of goods sold. From these computations the ending inventory is estimated.

**Held-to-maturity securities** are debt securities that the company has the positive intent and ability to hold to maturity. These securities are generally purchased for the purpose of earning interest or selling for a profit in the future.

**Historical cost principle** holds that assets and liabilities should be recorded at cost, which is the amount given or received in an exchange transaction.

**Horizontal analysis** compares each item on a financial statement with that same item on statements from previous periods.

**Income statement,** or the profit and loss statement, summarizes all of the revenues (sales) that a business has earned during a specific period of time (usually one year) less all of the expenses (resources) consumed in generating that revenue. The resulting figure is called "net income" and is an indication of the performance of the enterprise during the specified period of time (usually the fiscal year).

**Indirect method** for preparing the statement of cash flows starts with net income reported on the income statement and adjusts this figure for items that did not affect cash.

**Intangible assets** are long-lived, nonmonetary assets that cannot be seen, touched, or physically measured. Examples are goodwill, copyrights, trademarks, and franchise fees.

**Issued shares** are the number of authorized shares of stock that have been sold by the corporation.

**Last-in, last out (LIFO)** method assumes that the most recent (last) purchases were the first sold during the period.

**Liquidity ratios** measure a company's ability to meet its short-term obligations (usually one year).

**Long-term liabilities** are obligations that are due beyond a year or an operating cycle and require the payment of cash, goods, or services to settle. Since it is long term, it is usually a financing arrangement that requires a periodic payment of principal and interest.

**Lower-of-cost-or-market** rule states that inventory should be carried at the lower of its cost or market value (replacement cost) on the date of the balance sheet.

**Management accounting** is the process of preparing detailed and timely financial and cost information for managerial decision makers for use in their planning, managing, and control roles in a profit or nonprofit enterprise.

**Manufacturing company** purchases raw materials, adds labor, and overhead, and manufactures a finished product for sale. Its inventories include raw materials, work in process, and finished goods.

**Marketable securities** are those short-term investments from extra cash that can be converted back to cash at a readily marketable price.

**Market-based ratios** compare the company's current market price to its earnings and dividend yield.

**Mark-to-market** means that the company assigns a value to an asset (in this case, a security) based on its fair market value.

**Materiality** is an underlying concept or assumption that holds that the magnitude of an omission or misstatement of accounting, in light of surrounding circumstances, makes it probable that the judgment of a reasonable person relying on the information would have to have been changed or influenced by the omission. Simply said, it means that an item or transaction is material if it is large enough to influence an investor's decision.

**Merchandising company** purchases ready-to-sell merchandise for resale; its inventory would consist of unsold items on hand at the end of an accounting period.

**Monetary unit assumption** holds that a business unit should include only quantifiable transactions. In the United States the dollar is the most quantifiable common unit of measurement.

**Net book value** refers to the carrying value of an asset less accumulated depreciation.

**Noncumulative preferred stock** means that annual dividends that are not paid to preferred-stock holders are lost.

**Operating lease** is when the lessor (owner) transfers only the right to use the property to the lessee, who does not assume any risk of ownership.

**Opportunity costs** are the costs associated with giving up the next best opportunity in an investment decision.

**Outstanding shares** are the number of shares of stock actually owned by stockholders, which equals issued shares less shares of treasury stock.

**Par value** is the nominal value of a stock that is assigned by the corporation upon its issuance. Par value is unrelated to its market value.

**Partnership** is a business owned by two or more persons. Similar to the sole proprietorship, it acquires assets and services, adds value to and may convert these assets into products, and sells the output to consumers. Partners are personally responsible for the business's debts and liabilities. Partners normally draw up a legal document called a *partnership agreement* that specifies the partnership relationships, for example, how the profits will be divided and how work will be divided.

**Periodic inventory system** requires that the inventory records be updated periodically, usually at the end of the accounting period.

**Perpetual inventory system** requires that the real-time updating of the inventory records occurs each time there is a purchase, a sale, or return.

**Preemptive right** is the stockholder's right to maintain fractional ownership in the corporation by purchasing a proportional share of future shares issued by the corporation.

**Preferred stock** is owned by preferred-stock holders. They are not true owners of the company but have certain preferences over common-stock holders. Namely, they are paid dividends before common-stock holders and take precedence over common-stock holders in the liquidation of company assets.

**Present value of an annuity** computes the present value of a series of payments or receipts made periodically over equally spaced periods of time, usually at the end of such periods.

**Profitability ratios** measure the company's ability to earn a satisfactory profit and return on investment.

**Property dividends** are payments to stockholders other than in cash.

**Purchase discount** is a reduction in the purchase price by the seller for prompt payment of a receivable.

**Ratio analysis** is the relationship between one amount on a financial statement to another amount on the same or another statement. In other words, the two amounts can be from two different categories, as required.

**Registered bonds** are issued in the name of the owner and require the surrender of the bond certificate at time of maturity.

**Relative fair market value method** is used to allocate the costs of a basket of assets purchased with one price. For example, a building, the land on which it sits, and equipment in the building are purchased for one price.

**Relevance** is an underlying concept or assumption that holds that financial accounting information must be related to and significant to the decision being considered. As such, it must make a difference in a decision by helping users to form predictions about the outcomes of past, present, and future events or to confirm or correct prior expectations. In short, this information must be timely, have predictive value, and have feedback value.

**Reliability** is an underlying concept or assumption that requires accounting information to be faithfully represented, capable of being verified, and reasonably free of error and bias. To be useful, financial information must be reliable as well as relevant.

**Retained earnings** is the amount of income earned since the company's inception less any net losses and less any dividends paid to stockholders.

**Selling expenses** are all expenses incurred by the company in generating sales, such as sales commissions, advertising, and promotions.

**Serial bonds** are issued to mature at dates spread over time. This bond is often used to avoid having to establish a sinking fund.

**Sinking fund** is a type of escrow account in which monies are periodically transferred to pay off bonds at maturity.

**Sole proprietorship** is a business owned by one person. It acquires assets and services, adds value to and may convert these assets into products, and sells the output to consumers. The sole proprietorship is not separate from its owner in terms of financial responsibility and liability. Thus, the owner is personally responsible for the business's debts and liabilities.

**Solvency ratios** measure a company's ability to meet its long-term obligations as they become due.

**Specific identification method** keeps track of each item in the inventory and each item sold. That is, it specifically identifies each item sold and assigns the actual cost paid when the item was purchased.

**Statement of cash flows** shows the amount of cash inflows and cash outflows for a business enterprise during a specific period of time. The cash flows are broken down into operating activities, investing activities, and financing activities.

**Statement of changes in stockholders' equity** shows the changes in stockholders' equity of the business entity during the same period of time as the income statement. Basically, it is used to bridge the gap between the amount of stockholders' equity of a business at the beginning of the accounting period and the amount of equity at the end of the period. This statement takes into consideration such things as the increase in equity from issuance of stock and net income, and decreases in equity from dividends and a net loss.

**Stock dividend** is an issuance of additional shares of stock to existing stockholders on a pro rata basis without receiving any payment for them.

**Stockholder** (also called *shareholder*) is an individual who owns or another company that owns one or more shares of stock in a corporation.

**Stock split** is the issuance of a significant number of shares of stock by simply reducing its par value and issuing a proportionate number of shares.

**Straight-line depreciation** is the simplest of the depreciation methods in that it is determined by dividing the depreciable base by the expected useful life measured in time.

**Subscribed stock** shares are shares of stock that have been sold with a down payment given but the remaining amount owed has been deferred. Subscribed shares are not issued until payment has been received.

**Timeliness** is an underlying concept or assumption that requires the providing of accounting information to decision makers before it loses its capacity to influence their decisions.

**Time period assumption.** Because of the going concern assumption, it is assumed that businesses will last for a long period of time. Yet interested parties need periodic accounting information to make decisions about the business. Thus, artificial time periods are established for reporting financial information to users. Normally, businesses report quarterly and annually.

**Trademark** is a distinctive sign or symbol, word, or phrase used by an individual business, or other legal entity that distinguishes the company's product or service from another.

**Trading security** is a debit or equity security that is bought and held principally for the purpose of selling it in the near term.

**Treasury stock** means that the company has repurchased its own stock and elects not to retire it.

**Trial balance** is a listing of the current balances of all accounts in the general ledger. All debit accounts must equal credit accounts.

**Understandability** is an underlying concept or assumption that states: the quality of accounting information needs to be such that users perceive its significance in terms of how it is communicated and the use of clear and appropriate terminology.

**Units-of-output method** depreciation assumes that the depreciation of an asset is a function of its use or production instead of the passage of time.

**Unrealized gain** means that a security has a gain in market value but the security has not yet been sold.

**Unrealized loss** means that a security has a loss in market value but the security has not yet been sold.

**Verifiability.** An underlying concept or assumption, which holds that two or more accountants must get the same or very similar results (or a consensus) when using the same measurement methods.

**Vertical analysis** is a technique whereby a significant item on a financial statement is selected as a base value and all other items are expressed as a percentage of that amount. The analysis involves items on a single year's financial statement.

**Weighted average method** determines the units and cost of the goods available for sale and uses that to compute an average cost per unit, which is then used to value both cost of goods sold and the ending inventory.

**Worksheet** is a tool used by accountants to assemble all of the accounts in the general ledger in one place in order to make any adjustments to the accounts prior to preparing the financial statements.

# *Index*

# *The simple way to ace your management accounting class!*

## Contents

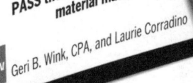

# *Making complex accounting principles as easy as 1-2-3!*

## Contents

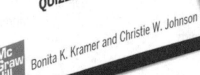

# *All there is to know about financial statements— without the headache!*

## Contents

# business math

## DeMYSTiFieD

### A SELF-TEACHING GUIDE

- 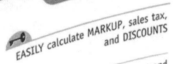 EASILY calculate MARKUP, sales tax, and DISCOUNTS

- UNDERSTAND DEPRECIATION, inventory, and financial STATEMENTS for income tax purposes

- MASTER a SCIENTIFIC CALCULATOR to do lengthy COMPUTATIONS

- LEARN the MATHEMATICS of borrowing, SAVING, and INVESTING money

**Allan G. Bluman**

McGraw Hill

# Learn the ins and outs of business math— the fast and easy way!

## Contents

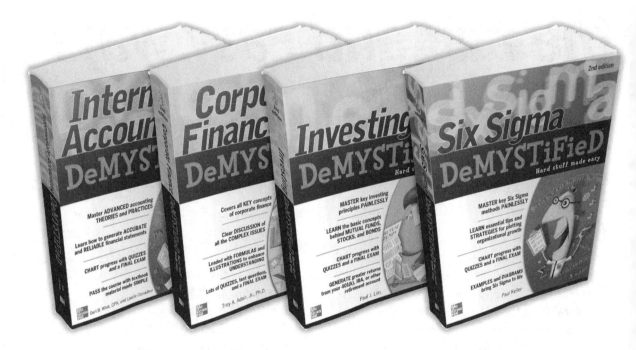